Coexistence in the Aftermath of Mass Violence

Coexistence in the Aftermath of Mass Violence demonstrates how imagination, empathy, and resilience contribute to the processes of social repair after ethnic and political violence. Adding to the literature on transitional justice, peacebuilding, and the anthropology of violence and social repair, the authors show how these conceptual pathways—imagination, empathy and resilience—enhance recovery, coexistence, and sustainable peace. Coexistence (or reconciliation) is the underlying goal or condition desired after mass violence, enabling survivors to move forward with their lives. Imagination allows these survivors (victims, perpetrators, bystanders) to draw guidance and inspiration from their social and cultural imaginaries, to develop empathy, and to envision a future of peace and coexistence. Resilience emerges through periods of violence and its aftermaths through acts of survival, compassion, modes of rebuilding social worlds, and the establishment of a peaceful society.

Focusing on society at the grass roots level, the authors discuss the myriad and little understood processes of social repair that allow ruptured societies and communities to move toward a peaceful and stable future. The volume also illustrates some of the ways in which imagination, empathy, and resilience may contribute to the prevention of future violence and the authors conclude with a number of practical and policy recommendations. The cases include Cambodia, Rwanda, Sierra Leone, Somaliland, Colombia, the Southern Cone, Iraq, and Bosnia.

Eve Monique Zucker is a Lecturer in the Departments of Anthropology at Columbia University and Yale University.

Laura McGrew is a practitioner and researcher who completed her PhD in peace studies at Coventry University.

Coexistence in the Aftermath of Mass Violence

Imagination, Empathy, and Resilience

Edited by
Eve Monique Zucker
and Laura McGrew

UNIVERSITY OF MICHIGAN PRESS

Ann Arbor

Copyright © 2020 by Eve Monique Zucker and Laura McGrew
All rights reserved

For questions or permissions, please contact um.press.perms@umich.edu

Published in the United States of America by the
University of Michigan Press
Manufactured in the United States of America
Printed on acid-free paper
First published November 2020

A CIP catalog record for this book is available from the British Library.

Library of Congress Cataloging-in-Publication Data

Names: Zucker, Eve Monique, editor. | McGrew, Laura, editor.
Title: Coexistence in the aftermath of mass violence : imagination, empathy, and resilience /
    edited by Eve Monique Zucker and Laura McGrew.
Description: Ann Arbor : University of Michigan Press, 2020. | Includes bibliographical
    references and index. |
Identifiers: LCCN 2020028760 (print) | LCCN 2020028761 (ebook) | ISBN 9780472074655
    (hardcover) | ISBN 9780472054657 (paperback) |
    ISBN 9780472127191 (ebook)
Subjects: LCSH: Reconciliation—Cross-cultural studies. | Coexistence—Cross-cultural
    studies. | Ethnic conflict—Cross-cultural studies. | Transitional justice—Cross-cultural
    justice.
Classification: LCC JZ5597 .C64   2020 (print) | LCC JZ5597 (ebook) | DDC 303.6/9—dc23
LC record available at https://lccn.loc.gov/2020028760
LC ebook record available at https://lccn.loc.gov/2020028761

Cover: Photograph © Rudy Lu, 2010. Courtesy rudyluphotos.com

*This book is dedicated to all those who have survived
the pain and violence of wars, genocides, and atrocities,
and to the memory of those who have perished.*

Acknowledgments

We would first like to thank Alex Hinton and Nela Navarro from Rutgers Center for the Study of Genocide and Human Rights (CGHR) for their invaluable advice and for their support of the first iteration of this project, a symposium held at Rutgers University, Newark, in November of 2015. In addition, the volume greatly benefited from the insights and intellectual contributions of Kosal Path, who was involved in the original creation and first phase of the project. Also, we thank Dennis Klein, a participant in the first symposium, for hosting an all-day manuscript workshop at Kean University with support through Kean's Master of Arts in Holocaust and Genocide Studies Program. Joining us at the workshop was David Simon, from the Yale Genocide Studies Program, who generously shared his thoughts and advice on each of the papers and the volume as a whole.

We would also like to express our appreciation to this volume's contributors for sharing their knowledge, insights, creativity, and their patience, and also to those who were involved in earlier iterations of this project, in particular Roy Licklider and Martha Stroud, who gave helpful perspectives along the way. Sadly, Benny Widyono, one of the original participants in the Rutgers symposium, passed· away in early 2019. The paper he presented at the symposium presented a comparison between the aftermaths of the Khmer Rouge in Cambodia and the 1965–1966 massacres in Indonesia. Well known for his kind heart, intelligence, humor, and wit, he is missed by many.

The support and advice provided by Elizabeth Demers and Danielle Coty at the University of Michigan Press throughout the publishing process is enormously appreciated. We also thank the anonymous reviewers who gave us helpful advice, Mark Scott for his copyediting talents, and Kevin Rennells for guiding the volume to press. We would also like to thank our families and friends for their support and patience through this long process, especially Karl Malone, Saoirse Zucker-Malone and Sebastian Zucker-Malone, and Chris, Jeff, and Lynn McGrew.

Finally, our gratitude goes out to the many people whose experiences are the subject of this volume. We are honored that they have shared stories of their difficult pasts with us, as well as their thoughts, hopes, and dreams. We are humbled in the face of their courage and resilience. We are grateful as they have helped us move a step forward toward making sense of how people cope with mass atrocities and rebuild their lives.

A Word about the Project. This volume began as a project in 2014: *Reflections in the Aftermath of War and Genocide* by the two coeditors and Kosal Path. Since then a consortium has been established under the same name to continue to bring scholars and practitioners together to enhance our understanding of recovery and healing in the aftermath of mass violence and work toward preventing such events in the future. Other consortium projects include: the symposiums *Societies Emerging from Conflict: The Aftermath of Atrocity* in 2016 (the result of which was a book edited by Dennis Klein), *Memorialization Unmoored: The Virtualization of Material Mediums of Social Memory* in 2018 (organized by Eve Zucker and David Simon at Yale University), and *Sites of Reckoning: Memorials, Museums & Fractured Truth(s) in the Aftermaths of Mass Violence* to be held in 2020 (organized by Jennie Burnet and others at Georgia State University, New York University, and Rutgers University).

Contents

List of Illustrations xi
List of Abbreviations xiii

1 | Introduction 1

Part 1: Imagination

2 | In the Realms of Ritual and Enchantment: Imagination and
Recovery in the Aftermath of the Khmer Rouge 29
Eve Monique Zucker

3 | "And to This New Life We Are Striving":
The Role of Imagination in Post-Conflict Sierra Leone 53
Friederike Mieth

4 | Imagining Alternatives:
Cambodia, Accountability, and Compassion 71
Toni Shapiro-Phim

Part 2: Empathy

5 | "You Can't Bake Bread without the Flour":
Empathy and Coexistence in Cambodia 97
Laura McGrew

6 | Cultivating Empathy and Coexistence:
Testimony about Rescue in the Rwandan Genocide 125
Jennie E. Burnet

7 | The Rescuers:
The Role of Testimony as a Peacebuilding Tool
to Create Empathy 149
Leora Kahn

Part 3: Resilience

8 | Women's Survival and Memory Narratives in the
Southern Cone: Resilience and Gender Justice   171
Bernardita Llanos

9 | Toward Resilient Cultural Initiatives of Memory
and Reconciliation among Rural Displaced Populations
in Transitional Colombia   194
Ricardo A. Velasco

10 | The Politics of Resilience in Somaliland:
The Contribution of Political Community and Autonomy
to Post-Conflict Stabilization and Coexistence   218
Matthew Gordon

11 | Conclusion   244

Contributors   255

Index   259

Digital materials related to this title can be found on the Fulcrum platform via the following citable URL: https://doi.org/10.3998/mpub.11302800

Illustrations

2.1. The Enchanted Wedding Chest "The Stone Box" 41
4.1. *The Lives of Giants*, Sophiline Arts Ensemble,
Bryn Mawr College 80
5.1. A religious ceremony with the NGO Kdei Karuna as
part of a dialogue and healing project 116
7.1. Josephine Dusabimana 151
7.2. Borivoje and Ljubinka Lelek 153
7.3. Sarajevo, Bosnia, outdoor exhibit 156
7.4. Augustin Kagmaore 159
7.5. Aliya Khalaf Salih and Ameera 164
9.1. Gardens in canoes, or "Jardines en Balsa," to promote
food autonomy among rural coastal communities 211
9.2. Narrative workshop with displaced indigenous youth
in the village of Jaqué 213

Abbreviations

APD—Academy for Peace and Development [Somaliland]
BBC—British Broadcasting Corporation
CNMH—National Center of Historical Memory [Colombia]
CNRR—National Commission for Reparation and Reconciliation
    [Colombia]
ECCC—Extraordinary Chambers in the Courts of Cambodia
ESMA—Mechanical Navy School [Southern Cone]
FARC—Revolutionary Armed Forces of Colombia
HIJOS—Children for Identity and Justice Against Forgetting and Silence
    [Southern Cone]
ISIS—Islamic State of Iraq and Syria
IV—Interview
MH—Sub-commission of Historical Memory [Colombia]
MIR—Movement of the Revolutionary Left [Southern Cone]
NGO—Nongovernmental Organization
PTSD—Post-traumatic Stress Disorder
RPF—Rwandan Patriotic Front
SCPD—Somaliland Centre for Peace and Development
SNM—Somali National Movement
SOC—Sense of Coherence
UN—United Nations
UNDP—United Nations Development Programme
UNOSOM—UN Mission in Somalia
UNTAC—United Nations Transitional Authority in Cambodia
US—United States
USAID—US Agency for International Development
WHO—World Health Organization

1 | Introduction

Eve Monique Zucker and Laura McGrew

When wars and genocides come to an end, what happens afterwards is as important as what brought them about in the first place. In the chaos, rubble, and depravity that characterizes many postwar and post-genocide environments, opposing groups must come to live with one another again. The enormity of this challenge may be further complicated by the lack of clear categories among survivors. Victims, perpetrators, bystanders, collaborators, and rescuers are not necessarily discrete categories but are often fluid and overlapping.[1] Moreover, in aftermaths of conflicts such as civil war the different sides occupied by former combatants are also not always straightforward, as soldiers may have defected to the other side or families may have—through choice or circumstances—had members on opposite sides.[2] These "splits" within families are often arbitrary given forced conscription or cases where a family attempts to manage their losses by sending one son to fight on one side and another to fight on the other side. For victims, perpetrators, collaborators, and others, the excruciating prospect of living together once again in the aftermath of genocide (often because there is no choice due to lack of land or economic opportunity) is riddled with difficulties, not least of which is that each is a reminder to the other of what has passed. This volume asks, how do people under such circumstances come to live with one another again? How do they do so in a manner that creates a durable peace so that societies and individuals can live and prosper? How do they remake their worlds (Das et al. 2001) under these circumstances? These questions concern the concept of coexistence. We define coexistence as the state whereby individuals or groups can live together peacefully, with tolerance, respect, and stated or unstated agreement to resolve conflicts without violence.

The processes leading from mass violence toward social repair are nonlinear, precarious, and unpredictable. They also vary from context to context and culture to culture. Broadly, these processes may include some form of dialogue and the fashioning of narratives that provide a story of conflict that different sides can live with. They additionally require locating and utilizing what resources are available—material, cultural, legal, or otherwise—to address the countless ruptures wrought by the violence while being wary of not reproducing structural conditions that contributed to the violence in the first place and taking steps to safeguard the society from further violence and social disintegration. This volume examines these processes to better understand how communities and societies are rebuilt; how victims, perpetrators, bystanders, and formerly warring factions are able to live with one another again in a productive and meaningful fashion; and how peace can be established in a manner that works toward preventing mass violence in the future. Our inquiries rely upon three exploratory themes: imagination, empathy, and resilience.

The urgency of improved understandings of these aftermaths is critical as wars continue to be waged (as this is going to press) in Afghanistan, Yemen, Nigeria, Syria, and in Central Africa; genocides continue to occur (against the Yazidi, Uighurs, and Rohingya) and others are possible; and terror attacks continue globally. Through the years we have each worked on aftermaths of atrocity; imagination, empathy, and resilience emerged as significant and meaningful conceptual and practical sites and processes to recovery and coexistence. These sites and modes of recovery, underexamined in the literature on social repair in the case of imagination, and unexamined in combination with one another, offer new understandings and more nuanced, and ultimately more effective, interventions, in cases where such interventions are taking place. We also consider these sites and modes of recovery where there is no outside intervention, but rather where they emerge through the actions of individuals, groups, and communities who draw on their own cultural resources at the local level to contend with the rupture of the past. Imagination, empathy, and resilience augment or complement each other as approaches of social mending through local and transnational institutions and processes. These sites of mending include religious institutions and practices, local customs and beliefs, schools, economic development programs, dialogue interventions, memorialization efforts, or other local and peacebuilding or transitional justice practices. Together they offer new approaches to understanding the complexities of recovery, suggest avenues into the promotion of a culture of peace, and instigate insight into local peace practices that can pave the way toward coexistence.

The Aftermath: Temporal and Practical Considerations

It is said that after a war ends, for those who survive, a new form of war begins. Poverty, starvation, homelessness, uncertainty, loss, finding the will to move on, and learning to live with one another again present significant challenges. The duration of this second battle is uncertain, and tentative steps toward rebuilding can easily be undone as new factors complicate healing and violence may re-erupt. Living with one another again in the aftermath of a treacherous past is laden with uncertainty, and the historical, cultural, political, and economic circumstances and resources available differ substantially from case to case. Time is a significant factor in the recovery from war and genocide as the types of challenges and available resources for solving them change over the years.

Immediately after a conflict or genocide, recovery efforts are needed (attending the wounded, burying the dead, locating displaced persons, providing food and shelter, etc.). In addition, civil order must be established and maintained and perpetrators identified and prevented from committing further acts of violence.[3] In this early period in the aftermath, survivors of mass atrocity often express a desire to get on with their lives and are "more ready to forget than recall the traumatic memories of the past" (Suarez-Orozco and Robben 2000, 16). During and beyond the initial triage period are the challenges of pervasive distrust of the state and of others in the community, the erosion or lack of working institutions, and the rise in criminality that demobilization combined with a weak legal system and a lack of law enforcement brings. Moreover, the possibility of a renewed conflict may cast doubt on efforts to build a future. Given that in the early 21st century 90 percent of armed conflicts were in places that had already experienced civil war (Walter 2010), faith in the future is understandably tenuous at best. After the myriad injustices produced during mass violence, societies must construct moral and structural boundaries and ways to cope with cycles of revenge that may occur (Jockusch, Kraft, and Wunschmann 2016). In addition to all of this, individuals and communities are tasked with contending with a range of new realities, ideologies, and practices that may be brought in with transitional justice and development agencies: a changed economy (for example from socialism to capitalism or from local to global), new religions, new forms of government, exposure to global viruses, a human rights ideology, an influx of foreigners, and others. Rapid transformation brings its own dangers, including new forms of violence and corruption, in some cases sorcery accusations, domestic violence, and disease.

With the passage of time come the difficult steps toward understanding the violence that occurred, learning new truths, creating new narratives, educating the young about the violence, and finding ways to memorialize. As numerous studies have shown, the struggles that survivors endure often persist for decades and the trauma of the event is passed on to later generations in myriad ways (Dashorst et al. 2019; Kanavou and Path 2017; Robben and Suarez-Orozco 2000, 44). Moreover, it is not only the victims of violence that suffer but the effects of trauma on perpetrators can also be long lasting and impact their families for years to come (Kanavou and Path 2017). More than three decades after the Khmer Rouge ended, for example, among former Khmer Rouge prison guards "the predominance of emotional responses such as fear and uncertainty that were initially generated . . . are still in effect, as well as a lack of empathy toward the prisoners" (Kanavou and Path 2017, 88). Thus the effects of violence are lingering on individuals, communities, and societies at large. Therefore when individuals and groups from opposing sides in a conflict or occupying different positions in a genocide come to live with one another again, the memories and social and psychological scars of violence further strain already tense social relationships. Communities are haunted by a treacherous past that they may wish to forget (McGrew 2017; Robben and Suarez-Orozco 2000, part 1; Zucker 2013). This is the challenge of coexistence.

Coexistence

The need for coexistence, both as a desired goal and a long but necessary process in recovery from mass violence, is an underlying assumption of this volume. Refugees returning after mass violence often have no choice but to return to their homes—victims next door to perpetrators and bystanders. By utilizing various resources available and through the processes of empathy, imagination, and resilience, individuals and societies manage, to the degree this is possible, their recovery and the rebuilding of their shattered worlds. Coexistence is the minimum requirement for the peace needed for people to survive and thrive. While reconciliation may be the ideal end-state, coexistence is attained more quickly and with less difficulty, and is more practical. Coexistence and reconciliation travel along a continuum: from an anarchic state of war to a theoretical utopian state with perfect harmony, from zero to total peace, and from simple coexistence to forgiveness and consensual reciprocity. But the process of achieving coexistence or reconciliation is not linear and these stages or degrees may not always occur in a progressive sequence. Interim stages of coexistence can be described in terms of "passive coexistence," meaning negative peace (absence of violence), or as "active coexistence," meaning positive peace (capacity to deal with conflict nonviolently and creatively) (Galtung 2001, 3). Coexistence may also be described as a cold peace.[4] The "amount" of coexistence or reconciliation can also be described by its "depth" and can be referred to as thin or thick (Crocker 2002, 528). Coexistence does not necessarily include the difficult components of apology and forgiveness that are more commonly expected in deep reconciliation. Coexistence is less personal or emotional than reconciliation and comprises a condition where individuals, communities, or nations can live together, trade, develop, resolve conflicts peacefully, and share a future, but where full relationships are not yet built or developed. On the other hand, reconciliation is a more advanced state than coexistence and is characterized by relationships with mutual trust and understanding (McGrew 2018; Staub and Pearlman 2001, 206–7).[5]

Fundamental to coexistence are relationships between individuals and groups. How, when, where, and to what extent have relationships been impacted, and between whom? As relationships mend, where do these bonds take place, and how can the relationships be sustained in the future? In John Paul Lederach's work on peacebuilding *The Moral Imagination* (2005), he has suggested that it is through the imagining of new "webs of relationships," a process requiring creative and constructive change, that transcendence from violence can be achieved. This volume examines these relationships as they are imagined and enacted in different social, geographical, historical, and cultural contexts. Coexistence (and reconciliation) are studied in a variety of fields, including anthropology, international relations, genocide studies, law, peace studies, political science, psychology, and sociology (Pouligny, Chesterman, and Schnabel 2007, 2–3). The diverse contributors to this volume, through an assortment of case studies, demonstrate pathways to peaceful coexistence through the lenses of imagination, empathy, and resilience.

Imagination, Empathy, and Resilience

Imagination

Broadly, imagination encompasses all that is not fully present to our senses: places where we are not now, worlds where we have not yet been, realms we cannot see, and all that is not presently before us. Imagination is also the ability to create, which includes the crafting of stories, visions, and all manner of innovation. Imagination is what makes us human, and as some have suggested it was a key development in evolution that made humans different from all other species (Bloch 2008). Our ability to tell stories and create fiction not only makes us human (Harari 2015) but allows us to produce nations and identities, enable belonging, and provide transcendence of individuals and societies that surpass an individual's mortal existence (Anderson 1983; Bloch 2008; Taussig 1997). The power of the imagination makes it an essential component in rebuilding individual lives, communities, and societies in the wake of violence and provides the means through which to narrate the past and envision the future.

Until now, imagination is virtually absent in the literature on post-conflict recovery, whether it be in peace studies, transitional justice, or in anthropology. The one notable exception is Lederach (2005), who argues that moral imagination,[6] accompanied by a set of ideas (people are in "webs of relationships" that include their enemies, acceptance of risk, creativity, and "paradoxical curiosity"—embrace of complexity), is essential to recovery from mass atrocity. Defining moral imagination as "the capacity to imagine something rooted in the challenges of the real world yet capable of giving birth to that which does not yet exist" (ix), he places emphasis on the creativity necessary to imagine new ways of living together. Imagination emerges in several of the chapters taking a number of forms, including as a means by which possible futures are envisioned, enchanted and spiritual worlds are revivified, social and moral worlds are made anew, notions of belonging are constructed, and empathetic connections to others are established.

Empathy

The term empathy is pervasive in contemporary discourse, frequently referenced in daily life, politics, education, health care, and even neuroscience—yet it nonetheless remains difficult to measure. Empathy is defined as the ability of one person to move beyond sympathy or feeling sorry for "the other," to step into their shoes and imagine what the other person is experiencing and feeling, and then to communicate acknowledgment. This volume explores various aspects of empathy, including its importance at the heart of fostering better intergroup relations (Bruneau and Saxe 2012; Halpern and Weinstein 2004; Huyse 2003) and how victims and perpetrators' shared narratives through empathy can promote coexistence (Bruneau and Saxe 2012). Empathy is sometimes described as occurring only in the later stages of reconciliation (Huyse 2003, 19–21) and feelings of empathy may wax and wane. The expression of empathy, through for example the process of empathic listening, can be done through words, affect and expression, gestures, and actions: Decety (2011) differentiates between a large range of affective, cognitive, and behavioral components of empathy (35). Empathy can create resilience during periods of violence, contribute to the potential of peace, and is also a distinguishing characteristic of those courageous people who risk their lives to save others (rescuers).

Resilience

Resilience can be a trait, a process, or an outcome (Southwick et al. 2014). In this volume we see resilience as all three. As a trait it emerges in the flexibility and the ability to adapt to changing circumstances (for example through new interpretations of traditional concepts or adoption of new ideas, ideologies, and practices), and it can also be present in durable values, traditions, and practices that transcend the war and violence and thus can provide moral guidance and pathways to healing and repair. As a process, resilience may include a multitude of acts such as modeling rescuer behavior raising social and political awareness, the strengthening of human rights, and restoring and adapting traditions. As an outcome, it is survival itself, the recovery of social and cultural traditions and relations, and durable peace. We recognize that resilience is not intrinsically positive, that is, negative attitudes, prejudices, and stereotypes can also be resilient and work to obstruct peaceful relations and even fuel further violence. In this volume, however, the concept is developed as it emerges as a positive trait in the efforts of rebuilding lives, worlds, and social relations and working toward creating an enduring (and yes, resilient) peace.

Resilience, often considered as the ability to bounce back (Zolli and Healy 2013), has become a conceptual focal point to address and respond to a wide range of issues from trauma, natural disasters, and economic recessions. The idea of "bouncing back" however does not map well onto situations of recovery from mass violence. Individuals and societies may harbor traits of resiliency, but they do not "bounce back" fully into who, what, or where they were before the violence (see for example Ajdukovic, Kimhi, and Lahad 2015). In other words, resilient individuals or societies that have experienced trauma do not return to the state they were in before the violence, but rather their resilience takes expression in their ability to rebuild, adapt, and move forward (2015, vi–vii). In circumstances of aftermaths of mass atrocity, resilience takes on new definitions and meanings among "individuals, families, organizations, societies, and cultures" (Southwick et al. 2014).

A triad of forms of resilience appears in the chapters of this volume: durability, adaptation, and fortification. Durability is found in cultural practices, beliefs, structures, and mechanisms that weathered the violence, reemerging in its wake and providing a resource for recovery. The second form is adaptation, emanating from the adoption or utilization of new tools or ideas such as human rights discourses or development practices, or a shift in attitude or belief such as the acceptance of change or a more tolerant perspective, self-reliance, or serendipitous geopolitical and socio-structural conditions. Third is the idea of fortification, that is, in the wake of the violence how victims find the means to strengthen their position within society through solidarity and activism; for example, acts that reduce the the likelihood of future victimhood and promote a sustainable coexistence. In both the second and third forms, resilience is then a process.

Linkages

Coexistence, imagination, empathy, and resilience are inextricably connected yet distinct from one another. Chayes and Minow (2003), in their work on Rwanda and Bosnia, recognized that the ability to imagine a new future is essential to achieving successful coexistence or reconciliation. We broaden their observation, extending the role of imagination in social repair to include its interconnectivity with empathy and resilience. Empathy, which incorporates imagining being in another's shoes, is integral to the processes of coexistence and social repair. Empathy also can be a component of resilience in that higher levels of empathy reduce the likelihood of future violence. This is an argument posited by Steven Pinker (2011), who sees the relative decrease in violence through the course of human existence as in part a result of our expanding circles of empathy[7] derived from technological advances, increased literacy, and strong governments. Through these processes, Pinker argues that our expanding circles from family, to community, to nation has allowed us to imagine and treat other peoples' interests as comparable to our own, thereby dovetailing with Benedict Anderson's (1983) ideas concerning notions of belonging that traverse beyond our immediate interactions to constitute communities and nations. Therefore empathy is not only linked with imagination but, from Pinker's argument, creates a barrier or fortification (i.e., provides resilience) against the propensity for violence. It accomplishes this by making the consideration for the welfare of others part and parcel of consideration of one's own interests. Recognizing oneself in others therefore reduces the desire to subjugate the "other" to conditions we would not ourselves wish to endure.

Resilience is also connected to imagination and empathy through our value systems. An illustration of this is Robert Wright's observation that the Golden Rule—"Do unto others as you would have them do unto you"—is present in one form or another in most cultures and religions (2009). The resilience of this moral tenet is found among rescuers in situations of genocide and also provides a foundation for remaking societies. The capacity to achieve sustainable coexistence requires the resilience of values, the ability to recognize and imagine others' interests (a component of empathy), and then to act socially in a manner that reflects these values.

Imagining a future of peaceful coexistence, creating a more empathetic community, and fortifying resilience against stresses that may lead to violence are all ways in which these concepts and approaches serve as a preventative to future atrocities. Focusing on these three sets of ideas and practices allows for more robust understandings and approaches toward strengthening and fortifying the social and moral fabric that are the bedrock for achieving a level of peace where individuals can live meaningful and purposeful lives without fear of repeated mass violence.

How to Live Together Again—Moral Considerations

The imagination of "alternative paths" to peace (or at least to coexistence) is one of the intellectual and practical terrains explored in this volume. Fundamental moral tenets or ideas about how people ought to live together or coexist may be a starting point for imagining a peaceful future. The process of return to civilization in the aftermath of mass violence implies a set of moral frameworks. By "civilization" we appeal to Vattana Pholsena's (2013) definition that in its "fundamental sense" civilization is "a state of affairs counterposed to the violence and savagery that residents experienced during the war . . . as well as its aftermath" (182). It is a morally laden concept that includes notions of right and wrong in how to behave and how society ought to be. Blueprints for these notions may be drawn from different sources that may include a current regime's political and religious orientations, traditional beliefs and institutions, or external sources such as those emanating from the domains of international human rights or development work. These varying sets of beliefs and practices shape understandings of mass violence and inform collective memory. In this volume this moral notion of the good in a philosophical sense pervades and informs the memories, discourses, visions, and actions of the survivors of wars and genocides as they set about the difficult task of rebuilding lives and communities. This notion of the good, however, should not be considered static or uncontested. As anthropologist James Fernandez (2002) noted, it "is the unsettlement and uncertainty of any moral order that is the constant challenge to the moral imagination" (38). In circumstances of radical social change in the aftermaths of war and genocide; moral order is precarious at best, as new (and more complex) notions of right and wrong or good and bad must replace the categorization of these moral categories as they operated during a genocide or war. This process of moral interpretation is subject to myriad influences including but not limited to international human rights, development, economic forces, traditional sources within a society such as religious institutions, and other local belief systems.

Approaches to Recovery after Mass Violence

Peacebuilding, Transitional Justice, and Responsibility to Protect

In the past three decades a growing industry has developed to bring justice, as well as political, social, and economic reconstruction, to countries and societies ravaged by war and genocide. These processes constitute "peacebuilding," a term coined by Johan Galtung in the 1970s that became more recognized internationally with United Nations Secretary General Boutros-Boutros Ghali's 1992 "Agenda for Peace" that defined peacebuilding as "action to solidify peace and avoid a relapse into conflict" (United Nations Secretary General 2001). International assistance for peacebuilding and reconstruction has gradually increased over time, its rise due in part to the failure of the international community to prevent mass atrocities such as those in Cambodia (1975–79), the Balkans (1990s), and Rwanda (1994). With this has come a mounting interest in hybrid peacebuilding models bringing local actors into the process, as recommended in the Secretary-General's Policy Committee 2007 statement emphasizing the importance of national ownership.[8]

Transitional justice, born in the aftermath of World War II, aims to bring about the repair of wrongdoings of the past, prevent such acts or events from happening again, and to establish human rights (Shaw, Waldorf, and Hazan 2010, 3). Various combinations of "pillars" of transitional justice have been delineated: prosecutions, truth-telling mechanisms, institutional reform, lustration, reparations, reconciliation, dialogue, and national consultations.[9] Transitional justice, despite its lofty goals, has proven inherently problematic given its narrow focus on its "pillars" and its top-down, imposed-from-outside, prescriptive approach—problems shared by other similar approaches. For example, scholars such as Monk and Mundy (2014) have signaled the perils of a "new international technocracy of peacebuilding" whereby the international community may not address root causes of conflicts and may even exacerbate the existing structural violence, prioritizing their own interests (2, 5).[10] Too often transitional justice discourse and practices seeking to help local communities and societies to "come to terms" with the past fail to "grapple with the messiness" (Hinton 2010, 1) of these interactions, as their efforts to help may overlook the interests and worldviews of locals, be exclusionary, and disrupt local processes of healing already taking place (Kent 2011; Lottholz 2017). Cognizant of these shortcomings, this volume shifts the beliefs, approaches, and ideologies about recovery clearly onto the locals affected by the violence. How do they narrate and frame the past, take steps toward reestablishing communal norms and practices, and what resources do they use? Victim-centered approaches are of utmost importance in these processes, within the context of bottom-up recovery, in order to ensure sustainability, healing, coexistence, and perhaps reconciliation several decades later.

Bottom-Up: "The Local Turn"

Charbonneau and Parent (2012) have argued that the peacebuilding and transitional justice literature has been relatively lacking in bottom-up approaches, particularly in relation to social repair at the community level. However, in the past decade there has been a surge in local peacebuilding and bottom-up scholarship (for example, Firchow and Mac Ginty 2016; Millar 2014; Nettelfield and Wagner 2014). Autesserre (2014, 2017), a strong advocate of local approaches, zeroes in on lessons learned from (relative) *successes* (rather than on failures) of local peacebuilding initiatives such as in Somaliland, Congo, and Colombia. She also unpacks the often-misguided assumptions that inform too many interventions led by international institutions and agencies. And as Shaw, Waldorf, and Hazan (2010) have observed, the local has also become a focal point for transitional justice literature while noting there has also been a return to Nuremberg norms against impunity, as well as a UN prohibition against amnesties for war crimes. In anthropology, where the participant-observation method dictates a bottom-up approach, there have been a number of studies of aftermaths of mass atrocity from the perspective of local actors and communities (for example, Abramowitz 2014; Burnet 2012; Jing 1996; Theidon 2014), however few enter the mainstream literature on post-conflict recovery.

This volume joins the growing corpus of studies on peacebuilding and post-conflict recovery taking a bottom-up approach, sometimes called the "local turn."[11] Its chapters discuss a range of local approaches and practices, providing new insights into hybrid approaches to peacebuilding and local ways of interpreting and taking actions to bring about coexistence and establish a future of peace. As other studies have recognized, Anna Tsing's concept of "friction" (Tsing 2005) is helpful when thinking about the contact zone where international peace and justice agencies and organizations, events and processes, global institutions, and local communities and cultures come together (Arthur and Yakinthou 2018; Hinton 2010). The notion of friction encapsulates the "the awkward, unequal, unstable, and creative qualities of interconnection across difference" (Tsing 2005, 4). This "friction" between recovery initiatives instigated by local communities, which rub up against top-down nationally mandated peacebuilding or transitional justice processes, has the potential to assemble new, innovative, and culturally appropriate responses that may speed recovery.

There are two forms of local approaches that appear in these chapters, sometimes separately but also sometimes together. The first examines local processes of social repair that occur without outside intervention. That is, there are no agencies or outside entities organizing or facilitating social repair processes but rather these processes are occurring within the culture and communities themselves. In these cases, the local communities find pathways to social recovery though traditional and cultural resources or through imported resources that they have selected for inspiration. The second type of local approach refers to transitional justice and peacebuilding programs that focus on local communities. These two forms of local approach can (and often do) operate simultaneously in the same locality.

In Toni Shapiro-Phim's chapter, classical Khmer dance performances are rewritten by innovative local writers and choreographers to recognize the violence and suffering of the past and suggest alternatives to the cycle of violence that has marred Cambodian history. Laura McGrew shows how Cambodian victims and perpetrators living side by side improve their relationships (with the help of NGO community dialogue projects) through developing empathy. Jennie Burnet discusses the intersections between local and international actors' efforts toward peace in her study of rescuer testimonies in Rwanda—testimonies that had previously been subsumed in the national rhetoric of victim innocence and perpetrator guilt and which may lead to new pathways to coexistence. Matthew Gordon's analysis of the Somaliland case shows how local traditional leaders, using principles of traditional conflict resolution, have managed to hold the country together in a state of coexistence in the face of international pressure to join a failed international peace process in Somalia. The local is also a key construct in Ricardo Velasco's analysis of memory and reconciliation processes with displaced populations in Colombia. He argues that in remote and marginalized areas the grassroots approaches are more effective than top-down edicts from the national level, given their sustainability and their capacity to promote civic engagement and strengthening social ties. Leora Kahn's chapter shows how narratives of courageous rescuers can change local community relations and promote empathy between opposing groups—this is demonstrated through her work documenting, archiving, and exhibiting rescuer testimonies worldwide in several different conflict settings. Friederike Mieth discusses how Sierra Leoneans choose to coexist with one another not because they particularly yearn for reconciliation but rather that they imagine this will help them achieve the socioeconomic development that will enable them to build a better future. In Bernardita Llanos's chapter, women who survived violence in the Southern Cone have in several cases banded together to fight for women's rights as a barrier against future gendered atrocities, calling for social justice to address both the past and the future. Finally, Eve Zucker illustrates the role of local stories, rituals, and myths in rebuilding social relations in the aftermath of the Khmer Rouge.

About the Volume

Multiple Perspectives

While there has been a surge of interest in transitional justice, social repair, and peacebuilding over the past two decades, when compared to the copious collection of texts on genocide and mass violence more broadly, there are remarkably few studies available that offer a cross-disciplinary, multiregional perspective. Literature on the topic of recovery in the aftermath of mass violence that fulfills that description illuminates various aspects of recovery, providing perspectives on social healing, national-level political reconciliation, local and transitional justice processes, and design of specific projects in fields such as education and religion (Charbonneau and Parent 2012; Chayes and Minow 2003; Das et al. 2001; Klein 2017; Muna 2006; Pouligny, Chesterman, and Schnabel 2007; and Shaw, Waldorf, and Hazan 2010). In addition to the multiregional edited volumes there have also been a number of ethnographic monographs on social repair. These include Sharon Abramowitz (2014) on the humanitarian efforts to promote recovery and peace through treatment of psychosocial and mental health issues in the aftermath of civil war in Liberia; Jun Jing (1996) on the role of commemoration and religion to address the violence of the past and rebuild community in post-Maoist China; Kimberly Theidon (2014) on social repair in the aftermath of Peru's civil war; and also the work of contributors from this volume, Jennie Burnet (2012) on gender and recovery in Rwanda and Eve Zucker (2013) on social memory and morality in the aftermath of mass violence in Cambodia. This volume contributes to this growing body of literature on recovery in the aftermath of mass violence, offering a unique and previously unstudied window into social repair through the concepts and practices of imagination, empathy, and resilience. These three concepts are considered in the chapters that follow as they emerged within the different cultural and historical contexts studied. The multiple perspectives brought to this volume derive not only from the range of contexts and circumstances discussed within the chapters but also from the varying professional and disciplinary backgrounds of its contributors, including peace studies, sociocultural anthropology, the arts, social justice, development, diplomacy, language and literature, peace and conflict studies, and documentary filmmaking.

Gender

Violence and recovery are experienced differently by men, women, and other gendered persons. In memorialization efforts by states and international institutions, gender representation is often not equal, and some voices are not heard (Elander 2017). The chapters in this volume highlight the experiences of men and women; however, in some chapters special attention is given to the gendered experiences of violence and recovery. Llanos's chapter focuses exclusively on women's experiences and responses in South America's Southern Cone, and women are the main subjects in

Shapiro-Phim's chapter. Stories of women, and stories told by women, appear throughout much of the volume, such as in the accounts of Rwandan women rescuers in Burnet's chapter and in Bosnia and Iraq in Kahn's. We also see women taking leadership positions as new opportunities became available to them in Somaliland (Gordon). The integral role of women achieving and maintaining coexistence cannot be overstated.

Methodologies

The methodologies employed by the contributors include participant-observation in local communities and structured and/or unstructured interviews among survivors (including victims, perpetrators, and bystanders) of mass violence. Each author has had a long and intimate experience with their case study, having studied the country presented for years, if not decades. The various cases presented reveal local understandings of what imagination, empathy, resilience, and coexistence mean in these differing social, historical, cultural, and political contexts as they are expressed through individual and communal narratives, political activism, social and religious practices, performative arts, storytelling, and other social practices. The different cases illustrate places where the conceptual themes are expressed through local responses to mass violence and as acts of mending. We aim to situate these findings within broader understandings found within the theoretical domain of scholarly literature as well as the practical domain of humanitarian practices and policies. By including both senior, experienced experts and newer voices, the volume benefits from the wisdom of experience and fresh insights. Moreover, the contributors have been in dialogue with each other for over two years, writing in concert with one another, making the book more a symphony of ideas rather than a series of soloist pieces. Another feature of the volume is the inclusion of social justice activism and the roles of culture and the arts in the processes of recovery. These varying forms demonstrate a variety of ways of interpreting the trauma of the past and open up new possibilities for recovery.

The Structure of the Book

The book is divided into the three main themes: imagination, empathy, and resilience. While each of the chapters takes a grassroots perspective, some cases integrate wider transitional justice, peacebuilding, development, and human rights into their discussion (Mieth, McGrew, Burnet, Llanos, Velasco, and Gordon—chapters 3, 5, 6, 8, 9, and 10), whereas others focus only on local processes and ideas and do not include transitional justice or other outside agencies or programs (Zucker chapter 2 and Shapiro-Phim chapter 4). Three of the chapters focus on social justice activism—two through video testimony (Kahn chapter 7 and Velasco chapter 9) and one through the performative arts (Shapiro-Phim chapter 4).

Part 1—Imagination

The first section of the book focuses on social repair in the aftermath of mass violence through the concept and practices of the imagination, a conceptual theme that is relatively new to literature on social repair after mass atrocity. The contributors here highlight through detailed ethnographic analysis the ways in which imagination emerges as a medium and resource for contending with the violent past and building a future. Alternative worldviews of society and social relationships are explored in these chapters through the mediums of the performative arts, rituals, myths and stories, development, and changing social and political circumstances.

The role of the imagination in Zucker's chapter 2, "In the Realms of Ritual and Enchantment: Imagination and Recovery in the Aftermath of the Khmer Rouge," is situated in a former Khmer Rouge area of Cambodia. At the time of the research there were no transitional justice programs operating in this area and villagers drew from their own culture and traditions to take steps toward contending with the Khmer Rouge past and rebuilding their community. Zucker shows how a moral template for building a more harmonious future is drawn from local rituals, stories, and myths that present an idealized imagined past. Everyday social realities of inequality and a residue of distrust left over from the Khmer Rouge period, however, challenge the empathetic aspects that are necessary to achieve the vision. Zucker illustrates the ways in which social and moral imagination was activated in the remaking of present relations, connecting with the ancestral past, and considering the future of the community—thereby creating a sense of continuity in the wake of rupture. She suggests that the generative and transcendental qualities of the imagination make it a uniquely potent site for recovery in the aftermath of atrocities.

In Mieth's chapter 3, "'And to This New Life We Are Striving': The Role of Imagination in Post-Conflict Sierra Leone," Sierra Leoneans shun the idea of looking at the past to navigate how one ought to live and instead find virtue in the idea and practices of "development." Due to their need to secure the basic essentials of food, water, and shelter, Sierra Leoneans place their hopes in the magic of development to solve their immediate problems, so they can "move on" to a more prosperous and peaceful future together. There is no expressed interest amongst Mieth's informants in dwelling on the violence of the past where they see no solutions for improving their circumstances. Mieth suggests that by trying to understand how Sierra Leoneans imagine the future, we can also better understand their relations to the past and the present.

Whereas Mieth's interlocutors imagine possibilities in the future through the concept of development, Shapiro-Phim's are beckoned to imagine alternative historical trajectories other than the genocidal Pol Pot past and to consider different ways of being in the world. Through the imaginary realm of the theater, Shapiro-Phim's chapter 4, "Imagining Alternatives: Cambodia, Accountability, and Compassion," shows how the theater can provide audiences with an opportunity to imagine different scenarios of the past and present political violence in Cambodia, arguing that aesthetic and expressive cultural production offers a unique and powerful voice and vision. Through the work of the choreographer and Khmer Rouge survivor Sophiline Cheam Shapiro, we see how audiences are invited to imagine the possibility for accountability on the pathway to peaceful coexistence.

Part 2—Empathy

Part 2 of this volume explores empathy between victims and perpetrators, as well as the NGO staff that work with them, in a variety of settings, including Cambodia, Rwanda, Bosnia, and Iraq. In chapter 5, "'You Can't Bake Bread without the Flour': Empathy and Coexistence in Cambodia," McGrew examines the definitions of empathy provided by a small 2017 sample of Cambodians working in the fields of dialogue, transitional justice, and/or recovery from mass violence. Most of these definitions are compatible with the literature and emphasize the need to take some kind of action in order to show empathic behavior. More extensive research conducted between 2000 and 2013 with victims, bystanders, and accused perpetrators reveals that some victims have both privately and publicly and sincerely forgiven the direct or indirect perpetrators of crimes during the Khmer Rouge period, showing empathy toward them. On the other hand, some victims remain profoundly angry and vengeful, several of whom also live with the daily effects of their trauma such as anger, sadness, and depression. Very few perpetrators and former Khmer Rouge have shown empathy toward their former victims, more often focusing on their own suffering during and after the regime—these dismissive responses of perpetrators toward the violent past often cause great distress amongst victims. The ways different individuals and communities develop empathy for the other (or do not) are important to consider when designing interventions in the aftermath of mass violence to promote healing, coexistence, and reconciliation.

In research on the roles of Rwandan women in reconciliation, Burnet in chapter 6, "Cultivating Empathy and Coexistence: Testimony about Rescue in the Rwandan Genocide," found that grassroots women's organizations that used structured encounters of empathetic listening between genocide widows and women whose husbands were imprisoned for genocide crimes succeeded in facilitating the women to work together and reduce conflict in their communities. Burnet relies upon a growing body of interdisciplinary literature on coexistence in the aftermath of mass atrocities that places empathy at the heart of fostering better intergroup relations. Burnet's chapter discusses the potential for testimony about rescuers—who have taken great risks as they empathize with the dire situations of others—to promote peaceful coexistence in Rwanda, as well as the implications of national-level discourses. These narratives model empathy for Rwandans of all ethnicities, and they offer opportunities for (Tutsi) genocide survivors to see the good, or potential good, in their fellow Rwandans whether Hutu, Tutsi, or Twa.

Kahn in chapter 7, "The Rescuers: The Role of Testimony as a Peacebuilding Tool to Create Empathy," similarly to Burnet, writes about the importance of documenting rescuer testimony in order to promote empathy and coexistence. Having collected numerous testimonies of rescuers in Rwanda, Iraq, and Bosnia, she examines the characteristics of rescuers and their behavior in the face of violence. Her project on rescuer testimonies further includes the showcasing of rescuers' testimonies in exhibits in the countries where the violence occurred. These exhibits honor those who bravely risked their lives to help others and allow their stories to serve as models for today's youth of how one can act morally and maintain empathy for others even in the most treacherous times.

Part 3—Resilience

Part 3 of the book focuses on resilience through case studies in the Southern Cone, Colombia, and Somaliland. Llanos's chapter 8, "Women's Survival and Memory Narratives in the Southern Cone: Resilience and Gender Justice," compares memory narratives as a form of resilience and gender justice in Argentina, Chile, and Uruguay; testimonies given by courageous women in front of truth commissions, and in other venues (court testimony, TV programs, etc.), show the healing power of storytelling. Llanos's extensive experience in the region provides the reader with poignant and searing narratives from individual women survivors, as well as additional testimonial evidence from films and books. She argues that as women use narratives to revisit the past, they create a more democratic and just society when their voices are finally heard—now many years after the abuses. Through shared suffering and experiences of violence the women develop empathy between themselves, and as a result become more resilient in the present. Acknowledging the difficulties of coexistence, the women request democratic, judicial, and gender-sensitive institutional reforms as part and parcel of social repair.

Velasco's chapter 9, "Toward Resilient Cultural Initiatives of Memory and Reconciliation among Rural Displaced Populations in Transitional Colombia," suggests that rural communities and individuals demonstrate and create resilience through testimonials contesting dominant state narratives of past violence in Colombia, and through cultural processes that foster civic engagement and the recovery of practices that help displaced families face their concrete material needs. These grassroots movements, he argues, provide marginalized communities with a voice and a medium for solidarity allowing them to participate in the processes of post-conflict nation-building and coexistence now dominated by state institutions. Yet he cautions that if historical structural inequalities are reproduced by centralized reforms, peace and coexistence may not be sustainable. Velasco's chapter (as well as Llanos's) call for new formulations in the postviolence context to bring the subaltern sectors of society that suffered to the forefront of participation, thereby enhancing solidarity and resilience that may serve as a preventative for future violence and enable a more peaceful and inclusive society.

In chapter 10, "The Politics of Resilience in Somaliland: The Contribution of Political Community and Autonomy to Post-Conflict Stabilization and Coexistence," Gordon examines the extraordinary collective resilience demonstrated in little-studied Somaliland. The resilience is evident in the twenty-five years of peace and stability despite enormous internal and external challenges—notably an ongoing conflict in neighboring Somalia and international efforts to integrate Somaliland into Somalia's (failed) peace process. Gordon, focusing on the political, argues that two factors account for this collective resilience: first, the existence of a shared *political community* to bind society together, and second, the absence of external constraints on Somaliland society's *political freedom to act* (autonomy). He calls for a conducive environment for experimentation, adaptation, and growth to address potentially destabilizing issues such as conflict, power-sharing, justice, and national identity formation. Liberated from externally imposed timelines or state-building blueprints and drawn together by powerful traditional structures of dispute resolution and reconciliation, actors within Somaliland society had the incentive and opportunity to overcome intercommunal mistrust, weather political storms, and engage in the slow-moving dialogue that was required to complete lengthy processes of peacebuilding and state-building.

Conclusion

Through the concepts and practices of imagination, empathy, and resilience, the authors in this volume have highlighted different dimensions of, and pathways to, coexistence and recovery in the aftermath of war and genocide. Certain understandings inform the text. First is the understanding that the categories of victim, perpetrator, bystander, and rescuer are fluid and overlapping and based on individual experiences and local context. Second, the inclusion of social justice activism through the arts— such as dance, music, narrative, and film—is essential to address the issues faced by victims and perpetrators in the aftermath of violence. Third, we consider it imperative to include studies of mass violence events from different contexts and parts of the world for the purpose of comparative analysis. While the book is a bit weighted toward Cambodia (three of the nine chapters, not counting this introductory chapter), it is arguably one of the largest cases of mass violence since the Holocaust and has had the benefit of time that allows us to study different healing and reconciliation processes to take effect. Given the early and extensive UN peacebuilding presence in Cambodia, it has been a "test case" for a great variety of local and international social repair processes—including the trials of the Khmer Rouge leaders, other international human rights and development interventions, and local religious and community efforts and processes— making it a good comparison for the other cases. And fourth and finally, we believe it is crucial for scholars from a variety of disciplines to engage with practitioners in peacebuilding and post-conflict interventions work. The aim of this volume is to expand understandings of recovery in the aftermath of war and genocide, demonstrate new pathways to peace and coexistence, and open up possibilities for policy and local practices that benefit from the insights on the roles of imagination, empathy, and resilience.

NOTES

1. See for example Ea and Sim (2001) and Levi [(1986) 2017]. Ea and Sim show how forced recruitment of rural Cambodian youth to be guards (perpetrators) at Tuol Sleng Prison illustrates the overlap of victim/perpetrator categories. In Levi's work, the Jewish concentration camp prisoners, the *sonderkommandos*, occupied what he calls the "gray zone" as they worked for the Nazis against their fellow prisoners.

2. See Kwon (2013) and Zucker (2013).

3. See Ian Buruma (2013) *Year Zero: A History of 1945* for a detailed account of the challenges and complexities of this process (in this case in post) in the immediate aftermath of war. While his book examines the cases of World War II Germany and Japan, the logistical, humanitarian, judicial, moral, and political circumstances are applicable to other situations in the immediate aftermath of wars and genocides.

4. Another similar term, nonlethal coexistence, was coined by Kriesberg (1998, 183).

5. See David Bloomfield (2006, 16) in *On Good Terms: Clarifying Reconciliation* for further examination of the relationship between coexistence and reconciliation: "But as positive peace is the presence of social or structural justice and of positive relationships so positive coexistence would be the presence of something more dynamic: shared values, positive relationships, interaction and interdependence, respect, trust and cooperation. Coexistence as end-state simply means an accommodation, a much more achievable goal than reconciliation as an end-state."

6. The concept of moral imagination is usually credited to Edmund Burke (1783–1785), an Anglo-Irish statesman and philosopher. The idea was taken up by a number of conservative thinkers. A core tenet of the philosophy is the notion of consideration and awareness of numerous possibilities.

7. Pinker is drawing on Peter Singer's (2011) *The Expanding Circle: Ethics, Evolution, and Moral Progress*.

8. See United Nations Peacebuilding Fund (2017) Definitions and Policy Development. Available at http://www.unpbf.org/application-guidelines/what-is-peacebuilding/#fnref-1937-3

9. See for example United Nations Secretary General (2010). Guidance Note of the Secretary-General: United Nations Approach to Transitional Justice, March 2010. Available at https://www.un.org/ruleoflaw/files/TJ_Guidance_Note_March_2010FINAL.pdf and https://www.ictj.org/about/transitional-justice

10. See also De Coning (2016).

11. See Lottholz (2017).

REFERENCES

Abramowitz, Sharon. 2014. *Searching for Normal in the Wake of the Liberian War*. Philadelphia: University of Pennsylvania Press.

Ajdukovic, Dean, Shaul Kimhi, and Mooli Lahad. 2015. *Resiliency: Enhancing Coping with Crisis and Terrorism (NATO Science for Peace and Security Series E: Human and Social Dynamics)*. Amsterdam: IOS Press.

Anderson, Benedict. 1983. *Imagined Communities: Reflections on the Origin and the Spread of Nationalism*. London: Verso.

Arthur, Paige, and Christalla Yakinthou, eds. 2018. *Transitional Justice, International Assistance, and Civil Society: Missed Connections*. Cambridge: Cambridge University Press.

Autesserre, Severine. 2014. *Peaceland: Conflict Resolution and the Everyday Politics of International Intervention*. New York: Cambridge University Press.

Autesserre, Severine. 2017. "International Peacebuilding and Local Success: Assumptions and Effectiveness." *International Studies Review* 19 (2017): 114–32.

Bloch, Maurice. 2008. "Why Religion Is Nothing Special but Is Central." *Philosophical Transactions of the Royal Society B* 363 (June 12): 2055–61. https://doi.org/10.1098/rstb.2008.0007

Bloomfield, David. 2006. *On Good Terms: Clarifying Reconciliation. No 14, 1-42* [online]. Berlin: Berghof Research Center for Constructive Conflict Management. Available at http://www.berghof-conflictresearch.org/en/publications/berghof-reports/

Bruneau, Emile, and Rebecca Saxe. 2012. "The Power of Being Heard: The Benefits of 'Perspective-giving' in the Context of Intergroup Conflict." *Journal of Experimental Social Psychology* 48, no. 4 (July): 855–66.

Burnet, Jennie. 2012. *Genocide Lives in Us: Women, Memory, and Silence in Rwanda*. Madison: University of Wisconsin Press.

Buruma, Ian. 2013. *Year Zero: A History of 1945*. New York: Penguin Books.

Charbonneau, Bruno, and Genevieve Parent, eds. 2012. *Peacebuilding, Memory and Reconciliation: Bridging Top-Down and Bottom-Up Approaches*. New York: Routledge.

Chayes, Antonia, and Martha Minow, eds. 2003. *Imagine Coexistence: Restoring Humanity after Violent Ethnic Conflict*. San Francisco: Jossey-Bass.

Crocker, David A. 2002. "Punishment, Reconciliation, and Democratic Deliberation." *Buffalo Criminal Law Review* 5: 509–49.

Das, Veena, Arthur Kleinman, Mamphela Ramphele, and Pamela Reynolds, eds. 2001. *Remaking a World: Violence, Social Suffering, and Recovery*. Berkeley: University of California Press.

Dashorst, Patricia, Trudy M. Mooren, Rolf J. Kleber, Peter J. de Jong, and Rafaele J. C. Huntjens. 2019. "Intergenerational Consequences of the Holocaust on Offspring Mental Health: A Systematic Review of Associated Factors and Mechanisms." *European Journal of Psychotraumatology* 10, no. 1. https://doi.org/10.1080/20008198.2019.1654065

De Coning, Cedric. 2016. "From Peacebuilding to Sustaining Peace: Implications of Complexity for Resilience and Sustainability." *Resilience* 4, no. 3: 166–81.

Decety, Jean. 2011. "The Neuroevolution of Empathy." *Annals of the New York Academy of Sciences*. Special Issue: Social Neuroscience: Gene, Environment, Brain, Body 1231 (2011): 35–45.

Ea, Meng-Try, and Sorya Sim. 2001. *Victims and Perpetrators? Testimony of Young Khmer Rouge Comrades*. Phnom Penh, Cambodia: Documentation Center of Cambodia.

Elander, Maria. 2017. "In Spite: Testifying to Sexual and Gender-based Violence During the Khmer Rouge Period." In *Queering International Law: Possibilities, Alliances, Complicities, Risks*, edited by Dianne Otto. London: Routledge.

Fernandez, James. 2002. "Rhetoric and the Moral Order: A Critique of Topological Approaches to Culture." In *Rhetoric and Culture Conference*. Mainz: Institut für Ethnologie, Johannes Gutenberg University. Available at http://home.uchicago.edu/~jwf1/jwfwork.htm

Galtung, Johan. 2001. "After Violence, Reconstruction, Reconciliation, and Resolution: Coping with Visible and Invisible Effects of War and Violence." In *Reconciliation, Justice, and Coexistence*, edited by Mohamed Abu-Nimer, 3–24. Lanham: Lexington Books.

Halpern, Sylvie, and Harvey M. Weinstein. 2004. "Rehumanizing the Other: Empathy and Reconciliation." *Human Rights Quarterly* 26: 561–83.

Harari, Yuval. 2015. *Sapiens: A Brief History of Humankind*. New York: Harper.

Hinton, Alexander Laban. 2010. "Introduction: Toward an Anthropology of Transitional Justice." In *Transitional Justice: Global Mechanisms and Local Realities after Genocide and Mass Violence,* edited by Alexander L. Hinton, 1–22. New Brunswick: Rutgers University Press.

Huyse, Lucien. 2003. "The Process of Reconciliation." In *Reconciliation after Violent Conflict: A Handbook,* edited by David B. Bloomfield, Theresa Barnes, and Lucien Huyse, 19–39 [online]. Stockholm: International Institute for Democracy and Electoral Assistance. Available at http://www.idea.int/publications/reconciliation/upload/reconciliation_chap02.pdf

Jing, Jun. 1996. *The Temple of Memories: History, Power, and Morality in a Chinese Village*. Stanford: Stanford University Press.

Jockusch, Laura, Andreas Kraft, and Kim Wünschmann, eds. 2016. *Revenge, Retribution, Reconciliation: Justice and Emotions between Conflict and Mediation*. Jerusalem: The Hebrew University Magnes Press.

Kanavou, Andrea Angeliki, and Kosal Path. 2017. "The Lingering Effects of Thought Reform: The Khmer Rouge S-21 Prison Personnel." *Journal of Asian Studies* 76, no. 1: 87–105.

Kent, Lia. 2011. "Local Memory Practices in East Timor: Disrupting Transitional Justice Narratives." *International Journal of Transitional Justice* 5, no. 3: 434–55. https://doi.org/10.1093/ijtj/ijr016

Klein, Dennis, ed. 2017. *Societies Emerging from Conflict: The Aftermath of Atrocity*. Newcastle on Tyne: Cambridge Scholars Press.

Kriesberg, Louis. 1998. "Coexistence and the Reconciliation of Communal Conflicts." In *The Handbook of Interethnic Coexistence*, edited by Eugene Weiner, 182–98. New York: Continuum.

Kwon, Heonik. 2013. "Cold War in a Vietnamese Community." In *Four Decades On: Vietnam, the United States, and the Legacies of the Second Indochina War*, edited by Scott Laderman and Edwin A. Martini, 84–102. Durham: Duke University Press. Available at https://doi.org/10.1215/9780822378822-005

Lederach, John Paul. 2005. *The Moral Imagination: The Art and Soul of Building Peace*. Oxford: Oxford University Press.

Levi, Primo. 2017 (1986). "The Gray Zone." In *The Drowned and the Saved*. New York: Simon and Schuster.

Lottholz, Philipp. 2017. "Critiquing Anthropological Imagination in Peace and Conflict Studies: From Empiricist Positivism to a Dialogical Approach in Ethnographic Peace Research." *International Peacekeeping* 25, no. 5: 695–720.

Mac Ginty, Roger. 2010. "Hybrid Peace: The Interaction Between Top-Down and Bottom-Up Peace." *Security Dialogue* 41 (2010): 391.

McGrew, Laura. 2017. "Changing Narratives of Victims and Perpetrators in Cambodia: Community Responses to Dialogue Interventions in the Presence of the Extraordinary Chambers in the Courts of Cambodia (ECCC)." In *Societies Emerging from Conflict: The Aftermath of Atrocity*, edited by Dennis Klein. Newcastle upon Tyne: Cambridge Scholars Publishing.

McGrew, Laura. 2018. "Victims and Perpetrators in Cambodia: Communities Moving towards Reconciliation on a Rocky Road." In *Reconciliation in the Asia-Pacific: Practices and Insight*, edited by Bert Jenkins, D. B. Subedi, and Kathy Jenkins. Singapore: Springer.

Millar, Gearoid. 2014. *An Ethnographic Approach to Peacebuilding: Understanding Local Experiences in Transitional States*. New York: Routledge.

Monk, Daniel B., and Jacob Mundy. 2014. "Introduction." In *The Post-Conflict Environment: Investigation and Critique*, edited by Daniel B. Monk and Jacob Mundy. Ann Arbor: University of Michigan Press.

Nettelfield, Lara J., and Sarah E. Wagner. 2014. *Srebrenica in the Aftermath of Genocide*. New York: Cambridge University Press.

Pholsena, Vatthana. 2013. "A Social Reading of a Post-Conflict Landscape: Route 9 in Southern Laos." In *Interactions with a Violent Past. Reading Post-Conflict Landscapes in Cambodia, Laos and Vietnam*, coedited with Oliver Tappe, 157–85. Singapore: NUS Press.

Pinker, Steven. 2011. *The Better Angels of Our Nature: Why Violence Has Declined*. New York: Viking Books.

Pouligny, Beatrice, Simon Chesterman, and Albrecht Schnabel, eds. 2007. *After Mass Crime: Rebuilding States and Communities*. New York: United Nations Press.

Robben, Antonius C. G. M., and Marcelo M. Suárez-Orozco. 2000. *Cultures under Siege: Collective Violence and Trauma*, Part 1. Cambridge: Cambridge University Press.

Shaw, Rosalind, Lars Waldorf, and Pierre Hazan, eds. 2010. *Localizing Transitional Justice: Interventions and Priorities after Mass Violence*. Palo Alto: Stanford University Press.

Singer, Peter. 2011. *The Expanding Circle: Ethics, Evolution, and Moral Progress*. Princeton: Princeton University Press.

Southwick, Steven M., George A. Bonanno, Ann S. Masten, Catherine Panter-Brick, and Rachel Yehuda. 2014. "Resilience Definitions, Theory, and Challenges: Interdisciplinary Perspectives." *European Journal of Psychotraumatology* 5. https://doi.org/10.3402/ejpt.v5.25338

Staub, Ernest, and Laurie A. Pearlman. 2001. "Healing, Reconciliation, and Forgiving after Genocide and Other Collective Violence." In *Forgiveness and Reconciliation: Religion, Public Policy and Conflict Transformation*, edited by R. G. Helmick and R. L. Peterson, 205–27. Philadelphia: Templeton Foundation Press.

Suárez-Orozco, Marcelo M., and Antonius C. G. M. Robben. 2000. "Interdisciplinary Perspectives on Violence and Trauma." In *Cultures under Siege: Collective Violence and Trauma*, edited by Antonius C. G. M. Robben and Marcelo M. Suárez-Orozco, 1–41. Cambridge: Cambridge University Press.

Taussig, Michael T. 1997. *The Magic of the State*. New York: Routledge.

Theidon, Kimberly. 2014. *Intimate Enemies: Violence and Reconciliation in Peru*. Philadelphia: University of Pennsylvania Press.

Tsing, Anna. 2005. *Friction: An Ethnography of Global Connection*. Princeton: Princeton University Press.

United Nations Secretary General. 1992. *An Agenda for Peace*. A/47/277, June 17. New York: United Nations. Available at http://www.un-documents.net/a47-277.htm

United Nations Secretary General. 2010. *Guidance Note of the Secretary-General: United Nations Approach to Transitional Justice*. March. New York: United Nations. Available at https://www.un.org/ruleoflaw/files/TJ_Guidance_Note_March_2010FINAL.pdf

Walter, Barbara F. 2010. "Conflict Relapse and The Sustainability of Post-Conflict Peace." September 13, 2010, World Bank Development Report 2011, Background Paper. Available at http://web.worldbank.org/archive/website01306/web/pdf/wdr%20background%20paper_walter_0.pdf

Wright, Robert. 2009. *The Evolution of Compassion*. TEDSalon 2009 Compassion. https://www.ted.com/talks/robert_wright_the_evolution_of_compassion

Zolli, Andrew, and Ann Marie Healy. 2013. *Resilience: Why Things Bounce Back*. New York: Simon & Schuster, reprint edition.

Zucker, Eve Monique. 2013. *Forest of Struggle: Moralities of Remembrance in Upland Cambodia*. Honolulu: University of Hawaiʻi Press.

Part I | Imagination

2 | In the Realms of Ritual and Enchantment

Imagination and Recovery in the
Aftermath of the Khmer Rouge

Eve Monique Zucker

In early 1970 the Khmer Rouge, a communist guerrilla group, entered a cluster of upland village hamlets in southwestern Cambodia and staked out a base for themselves in the hills above the settlements. These settlements were home to upland people who made their living through swidden agriculture, wet and dry rice cultivation, and trade in forest goods. Their world was one inhabited by a panoply of tutelary and ancestral spirits, Hindu deities, ghosts, magical forest hermits, and potent places and objects. This enchanted realm, normally invisible, was part of people's social and moral world.

Along with the Khmer Rouge came other forces to the region—the communist Vietnamese, Cambodian government troops, and a small group known as the White Khmer.[1] These groups engaged in a bloody civil war that ended in 1975 with a victory for the Khmer Rouge, whose genocidal reign of terror under which two million Cambodians perished lasted until the Vietnamese defeated them in early 1979. A return to civil war for two decades followed, thus making the region a Khmer Rouge base and battlefield for nearly thirty years. During the first civil war in the early 1970s, the villagers in the area were forced to choose sides. Some joined the Khmer Rouge and others the government forces. The choice of which side to join was often arbitrary, dictated by circumstance and the need to survive. When the Khmer Rouge took full control of the region in 1973 (two years before they conquered the whole of the country) they targeted those they considered traitors and enemies for execution. These executions took place in an atmosphere where accusations were rife and circumstances of starvation, fear, and grave uncertainty prevailed. Among the villagers, some of whom had reported on others by choice or duress, the categories of victim and perpetrator were often blurred and indistinct, reminiscent of Primo Levi's "Gray Zone" (1986 [2017]). The damage to village relations and the tensions that were present thirty years after their return to the villages were products of the painful memories of betrayals, distrust, and cataclysmic damage to the moral and social foundation of these village societies wrought by the Khmer Rouge.

Pondering how Cambodians recover from such devastation, historian David Chandler (1996) asks "when a society, like Cambodia's in the 1830s, 1840s, and 1970s, appears to have come to an end, where does one look for explanations?" (99). That is, in the aftermath of historical devastation, how have Cambodians made sense of these periods, allowing them to carry on? Chandler finds these answers in Cambodian religious writings and traditional tales. These sources provide moral explanations and provide guidance on how the world, including its social relations, ought to be, and that tell about how sometimes things go wrong and terrible things happen. Anne Hansen (2008), a scholar of Cambodian Buddhism, has similarly located Cambodian understandings and responses to the trauma and anxiety of mass violence in Cambodian Buddhist writings. In accordance with Chandler and Hansen, this chapter views myths, religious writings, rituals, and stories as templates for responding to such circumstances and for considering how to live with one another. Looking to the imaginative, or what I call the enchanted or spiritual realm of the Cambodian social world, it shows how local stories and rituals can be a source for recovery and the establishment of peaceful coexistence. These events, places, and the stories associated with them offer access to other worlds that can provide meaning, stability, and potentiality after the destruction and chaos wrought by the treachery of the Khmer Rouge regime. I argue that the durability and stability of the imaginary realm provides a source of resilience in the face of radical social change and a template for learning to live with one another again and building a future. Using a variety of examples (a harvest ritual festival, moral tales, imaginary spirits, and features of modernity), this chapter demonstrates how imagination emerges in post-violence settings and contributes to repairing the rupture to the enduring set of social relationships that constitute village society. Repair here is understood broadly to mean the repair of the moral and social structure itself that includes the set of relationships between the living, dead, and future generations of the village community, as well as the rural and urban or village and state relations. It involves rebuilding trust and the necessary linkages to remake and maintain social moral community that transcends the rupture of the Khmer Rouge past.

The chapter sits on the margins of scholarly discourse on transitional justice and peacebuilding literature because it is an attempt to understand social repair entirely through local practices that are not specifically created for this purpose. The processes and components I suggest here are subtle and emerge through the acts of storytelling and the making of a ritual festival. While the pieces may feel disparate at times, I weave them together toward the end and in the conclusion to demonstrate how they speak to peaceful coexistence and social repair more broadly.

There are two underlying ideas that undergird this chapter. One is that sources of healing and recovery from mass trauma are found *within* Cambodian culture itself. In other words, there are processes, mechanisms, and sources that provide the means to understand, absorb, and manage the rupture of mass violence that are not dependent on foreign transitional justice or peacebuilding tools, methods, or processes. These may include religious practices, myths and stories, communal events, and understandings of previous traumatic historical episodes in Cambodian history. This idea that social repair may draw on traditional moral sources is also present in the chapters by Gordon, Kahn, and Shapiro-Phim (this volume); however, in this chapter only the local social and cultural practices are included.[2]

The second idea forming the basis of this chapter is that relationships underpin Cambodian concepts of moral order and society, as is evident in the numerous traditional stories, moral tales, and myths.[3] Here I consider certain kinds of social relationships expressed in the ritual context and in the enchanted world. In particular, I focus on the distinction between what anthropologist Maurice Bloch (2008) has called the transactional social and transcendental social. The transactional social comprises our immediate interactions that are visible, such as face to face interactions. Transcendental interactions, on the other hand, include ancestors, nonliving descendants, spirits, deities, larger kinship groups, nations, religious groups, and other social groups. An integral feature of the transcendental social is that it is imaginary, that is, it is unconstrained by temporal, geographical, or physical constraints. Thus, "what the transcendental social requires is the ability to live very largely in imagination" (Bloch 2008, 10). That is, imagination is a requirement for relationships between individuals' and communities' relations with their ancestors, descendants, fellow citizens, and the supernatural. These types of relationships provide stability that counters the flux of transactional social relations because they are unconstrained by time and space. Put differently, an individual's sense of connection to those that came before him or her and those that came after offers a sense of meaning and longevity. This imagined continuum thus counters the rupture and upheaval of war and genocide: there was a before and there will be an after. The Khmer Rouge, proclaiming their victory as year zero, precisely sought to annul this imaginary of a pre-Khmer Rouge past, and the future they envisioned was disconnected from the memory that came before it.

The Merriam Webster dictionary defines imagination as "the act or power of forming a mental image of something not present to the senses or never before wholly perceived in reality."[4] Imagination is the possible, and the realm just beyond the possible. And imagination is creative, allowing us to invent, construct, and innovate. It may also be the very basis for sociality;[5] as Bloch (2008) posits, "the capacity to imagine other worlds . . . is the very foundation of the sociality of modern human society." Given its transformative power, embrace of potentiality, generative qualities and capacities, and ventures into the impossible, imagination arguably plays an integral role in any effort toward, or actualization of, peaceful coexistence. This is not to suggest however that imagination necessarily produces positive acts, ideas, or perspectives. It can just as easily be a source of fear that may lead to "othering" and violence, or prevent individuals and groups coming together.[6] However, in this chapter it is the positive employment of imagination toward managing the violent past, rebuilding social relationships, and envisioning a more peaceful future that I focus on.

The word for imagination in Khmer, the Cambodian language, is *kar srumeul sramei*. While *sramei* means "to imagine," the word also contains "*meul*," which means to look or to see. "To see" carries moral implications and is a conduit between the transcendental and transactional worlds (Zucker 2013, 67–68); it also suggests the recognition of another's humanity as discussed further along. Some of these concepts and idioms were inverted and twisted by the Khmer Rouge under whose gaze ordinary citizens were deprived of humanity (Um 2015, 29).

The Khmer Rouge targeted the realm of transactional relations in their efforts to reset Cambodian society by emptying the cities and moving people to different parts of the countryside, separating families, and dismantling communal institutions. They also sought to eradicate several of the preexisting transcendental relations between humans and the spirit world. Statues of tutelary spirits, Hindu deities, and Buddha; ancestral mortuary towers; sacred drums; and religious temples were all destroyed and religious practices and ancestral traditions were banished. This eradication of all vestiges of the previous order was fundamental to the Khmer Rouge blueprint, which dictated that the nation must be purified of contaminating beliefs and practices to allow its communist utopian vision to be realized.

Given this, the restoration of relations with the ancestral spirits and the enchanted and spiritual realm more broadly is a step toward recovery, and the remaking of communal ties may reinstate some sense of stability after the upheaval. The imagining of other worlds makes new and old relationships possible, relationships that offer alternative identities to those imposed by the Khmer Rouge. In the chaos of the aftermath of mass violence and genocide, as people set about remaking their worlds (Das et al. 2001), normally submerged elements of the moral order tend to rise to the surface as individuals and communities consider how to rebuild and how to live. The ideas and ideals of the past may be supported, contested, developed, or disregarded perhaps for new ideas available through the introduction of new institutions and ideologies (see Mieth this volume). In this chapter the ideal is considered through a village ritual, through the ancestral past (also in Gordon, this volume), and through the problems and aspirations of modern-day living.[7]

Background

The ethnographic research in this chapter derives from my fieldwork among residents of a cluster of villages in a forested mountainous region in southwestern Cambodia between 2002 and 2003, again in 2010, and briefly in 2019. I lived in the village during the 2002 to 2003 period, observing and participating in the everyday life of the communities in the area. During this time, I conducted numerous interviews on specific traditions and practices and concerning local histories, and engaged in countless conversations with villagers and their neighbors. Later in 2010, I made several visits to the village area and conducted interviews following up on the previous research.

The village where I based myself, which I call O'Thmaa,[8] is located in a region that was known during the Khmer Rouge occupation of this area from early 1970 to late 1998 as "The Forest of the Struggle" (*Prei Brâyut*), meaning the area where the revolutionary struggle emanated from. Most villagers practiced Theravada Buddhism, and a few Christianity. High illiteracy rates, a history of continuous forced displacement from the 1970s to the late 1990s, a shortage of arable land, and an overall lack of resources placed the village and its surrounds among the lowest ranks of Cambodia's socioeconomic ladder. Economic disparity among villagers arising out of the market economy, the effects of the war and the Khmer Rouge regime, varying levels of education, and the politics over land and resource extraction had left some families worse off than others. The wealth gap between these families was not radical but enough to create new tensions among residents who before the civil war of the early 1970s lived a relatively egalitarian existence according to villagers.

The region has a history of guerrilla warfare and was a battle-zone given its strategic location and topographical characteristics.[9] When the Khmer Rouge established a base in the nearby mountains in 1970, they recruited many of the villagers who were fleeing the fighting. Recalling this time, a villager explained: "Many of us willingly joined the Khmer Rouge. Lon Nol [the government] did not trust us. We were very scared! If we didn't join the Khmer Rouge, they might accuse us anyway, they wouldn't have believed us. So, we had to run. . . . We trusted the Khmer Rouge. That's why we went with them."[10]

Hardship and starvation prevailed on the mountain, but the Khmer Rouge were sufficiently successful in their efforts to ward off their enemies. Another villager explained:

> They had two different factions. The one (based) inside [closer to the capital] was Lon Nol, the one (based) here was Khmer Rouge. . . . There was a lot of turmoil (*vukvor*). In 1970 we were torn apart, some joining the Khmer Rouge and others joining Lon Nol. There was fighting then. . . . There was no food to eat, we had to eat the leaves and the roots from the trees. Some died of starvation. . . . We had to go with them (the Khmer Rouge). We were forced to. We could not stay in the village.[11]

By 1973 the Khmer Rouge were in control and forcibly relocated the local population into a cooperative where they ate and labored together. It was during these years that some villagers accused others of traitorous activities—accusations that led to the executions of many of the men in the village. As a villager who served under both the Khmer Rouge and the government said, "Some of the people here did a lot of things—killed everyone."[12] Another man who had been a government soldier exclaimed: "Everyone in the village was killing each other!"[13] Based on numerous interviews it appears that what might be meant by "to kill" is to make an accusation guaranteed to lead to the execution of someone; however, it remains not entirely clear. Regardless, the memory of the accusations and the killings were to become a source of distrust and tense relations thirty years later. As one villager put it: "Here they are friendly, but I do not know what they think in their hearts—because in the past, the old people (the generation of elders) died because of their own people. They had said derogatory and inflammatory things and a lot of them died."[14]

From 1970 to the mid-1990s, most men and many women were conscripted by the Khmer Rouge, the government, or both. Some had remained Khmer Rouge after 1979, staying with the Khmer Rouge along the Thai border where they fled after Vietnam invaded, whereas others had joined the government. A few joined the Khmer Rouge after 1979. Most of the Khmer Rouge defected from 1996 onward, the last surrendering in 1999. Through the permutations of power over the years the villagers were forcibly relocated numerous times for purposes of security or as required by policy. It was only in the late 1990s when villagers were able to return home that they began the difficult process of rebuilding their lives and communities after nearly thirty years of absence.

From the early 1970s, the Khmer Rouge had endeavored to erase the social and moral order of the past, replacing it with a utopian vision that formed and enabled their own "imagined community" (Anderson 1991) called "Democratic Kampuchea." However, the transcendental world that existed prior was not erased but temporarily submerged. Villagers noted that during and immediately after the time of the Khmer Rouge, the spirit world was left relatively unattended, which they articulated as a decline in belief. As a result, the spirits were said to be less potent and visible than before. However, over time, in a demonstration of the resilience of the Cambodian imaginary, the spirit world reemerged initially tentatively and later with greater force,[15] as the examples in the following sections of an annual harvest ritual and two stories in the enchanted realm of the Cambodian imaginary illustrate.

Imagining the Bon Dalien Harvest Ritual Festival

February 2003 marked the third celebration of the Bon Dalien annual ritual harvest festival in O'Thmaa since the late 1960s. Each year the village festival is part of a succession of such celebrations in villages across the region. It is traditionally celebrated annually as the rice harvest is completed in January or February. Because of the two civil wars and the Pol Pot years, the festival had not been celebrated in the village of O'Thmaa since 1969, when it was revived in 2000 after residents of the villages in the area were able to return to their homes after the second civil war ended.

This annual ritual festival is a demonstration of village pride and community as young and old work together to create this seasonal celebration. It is the largest festival of its type, involving the whole village and neighboring communities. The Dalien festival differs from other Khmer religious holidays in that it is a local event organized entirely by the villagers and takes place within the village rather than at the temple. Invitations are issued to the temple's monks and to the neighboring villages, and those villages in turn reciprocate. Representation of the village through Bon Dalien and through a collective offering at other villages' festivals showcases village identity and pride and brings communities together.

The ritual celebration of the Bon Dalien includes offerings of prayers and food to the ancestral guardian spirits for the harvest; a request for sufficient rain and a plentiful harvest in the coming year; homage to the ancestors; and the transference of the tradition to the next generation. As a Buddhist layman from the village posited: "We have done Dalien in the past and our children will continue to hold this ceremony into the future."[16] Villagers work together to create the festival, preserving the traditions of their common ancestors, and recognizing that doing so is an expression of community. As one villager put it: "The bon is a village affair. The work is divided equally among the villagers."[17] As such the ritual festival is a moment that contains possibilities for the demonstration and reinforcement of cultural and communal resilience and is a wellspring of imagination of communal identity and belonging. These potentialities are not only found in the celebration of the festival itself but also in the anticipation and production that begins before the celebration. Nevertheless, as some villagers noted, the festival on the year I was there did not have full participation among the village residents: "It is difficult, people in the village don't have solidarity with each other . . . some people do not involve themselves." "They are different than the old people (earlier generations) before."[18]

The challenges of recreating a sense of community and belonging in the aftermath of the devastation of the Khmer Rouge cannot be overstated. After the internal violence from the early years of the Khmer Rouge terror, social relations were often strained and exacerbated by extreme poverty, rampant illness (including malaria and HIV/AIDS), and rapid social, economic, and political change. Families generally refrained from socializing much with their neighbors as they worked to rebuild their lives and scratch out a living. Some villagers would reminisce about a time before the wars and the Khmer Rouge when people were said to have lived in harmony and peace and when no one had much more than the other—an ideal summed up in the phrase "the old people loved one another" that was repeatedly articulated in conversations about the pre-Khmer Rouge past during my time in the village.

Despite villagers' attempts to rebuild their lives and their community and bury the memory of the early civil war and the Pol Pot era, it continued to haunt their everyday lives. Mutual trust and concern that form the base of social interactions had been tarnished by the treacherous past. It thus came as some surprise to me to learn of the village event, Bon Dalien, given the austerity in communal relations that I observed in the early months of my fieldwork.

The first mention of the event occurred early on in my fieldwork. In a conversation with the village development chief, he shared that in a couple of months there would be an amazing event held in the village. "Just wait and you will see. . . . When everyone finishes the harvest all the villagers will come together and hold a great party. . . . People will come from all over, from as far as Phnom Penh! We will clear an area for the guests to park their cars."[19]

A few weeks later, when talking to the chief in the neighboring village, I was told the same story and they proudly showed me the road they had built, neatly lined with white stones, that traveled up to their festival site. The construction of parking lots and roadways for special events may not seem unusual; however, in this region that was quite remote at the time, cars were an anomaly. It left me to wonder who were these visitors who would travel by car to this poverty-stricken ex-Khmer Rouge region on the wilderness frontier to celebrate their local harvest festival?

Later, on the night of the festival, I observed that no cars arrived apart from the trucks delivering a music system and supplies. And yet, I heard no one remark on this absence. The apparent lack of attention or concern over the missing urbanites and their cars, and the vagueness over their identity, gave me pause to think about why the villagers might have been making such grandiose claims: the build-up in anticipating the festival was obviously not a component of people's actual expectations. This and other observations led me to understand that the festival itself was presented to me and spoken about more broadly in its idealized, if not actual manifestation.[20] The vision of how it ought to be is a vital part of pulling the villagers together and motivating them to produce the festival. In a somewhat Geertzian sense,[21] the creation of an imagined exemplary form of the ritual festival can be seen as an end in itself. But there may also be other reasons as I explain further along.

Returning to the days leading up to the festival, the village's third in three decades, joy and camaraderie were apparent as in the joking question "do you dance?" (*che roam, at?*) that villagers would ask one another with a smirk or a giggle. In considering the question, a couple of the older women,[22] after having imbibed on a couple of cups of rice wine, put on an impromptu performance for onlookers featuring a traditional dance as well as a comedic version of the so-called modern dance moves. Meanwhile, some villagers worked to clear a portion of forest for the festival, add colorful flags, and build a row of long tables for the communal meal. Day-Glo posters of Buddha were suspended from the newly constructed monk's shelter along with garlands of forest leaves, coconut fronds, and smaller flags said to pay homage to forest spirits and the spirits of the village and farmland.

On the festival day, a group of women and girls prepared the communal stew, as a group of men sat nearby engaged in friendly banter over beer and local rice whiskey. Among them was a former Khmer Rouge commander from another region who had recently settled in the area to set up a sawmill to profit from illegal logging. Next to him were two other former Khmer Rouge soldiers from the area, and the village development chief who had fought for the government in the second civil war and whose father had been one of those executed based on accusations in the first. Finally, there was the police chief, who was stationed in the village but was from another part of the province.

The mood was buoyant and festive. By afternoon the trucks arrived with food and beverages and a mobile sound and dance system that was soon blasting Khmer pop across the normally sedate wilderness. A group of men erected shrines to the Hindu deities (*teveda*) and the village tutelary spirit, *Ta Pia Srok*, and placed offerings for the ancestors. A Buddhist layman from the village explained: "Ta Pia Srok is the biggest spirit. It is for this spirit that we do the Dalien Ceremony for. He is the spirit who looks after the village and its people."[23] Rice is given as an offering to the guardian spirit in exchange for the health and fertility of the villagers and agricultural land, and when the festival closes it is sent to the temple for the monks. These ritual preparations for the tutelary spirits and *teveda* (Hindu deities) are accompanied by additional offerings to the ancestral spirits.

By evening the ritual festival activities had commenced with the reciting of prayers and blessings by the monks and Buddhist laymen and a short speech by the village chief. More families arrived from the village and its neighbors. A notable exception was the village elder who several villagers claimed had reported their family members to the Khmer Rouge in the early days of the revolution.[24] Also joining the group was a new resident in the village, a former Khmer Rouge who villagers generally avoided.

The meal was served at the long tables while the boys and girls mingled as they awaited the dance music. Finally, the center dance pole lit up and an eruption of Khmer pop music brought the youths and then the elders to the dance circle. The music switched to traditional Khmer music, and the dancers formed a moving circle, their hands, arms, and feet undulating to the music. The dance of the ancestors and that of the villagers became a continuum that flowed forth to the future with each child's graceful step. This reconnection between the past of the ancestors and the present appeared to overcome, if only momentarily, the rupture of the terrible past. And yet it was a small step toward building and fortifying a connection between a pre-Khmer Rouge past, the present, and the future.

The next morning the monks returned and the ancestral spirits were sent off with prayers, food, tobacco, and water. A miniature carved elephant and oxcart were provided for their voyage back to the enchanted wilderness from whence they came. The Bon Dalien closed with the monks' prayers and the completion of their meal.

With its "time out of time" quality, the festival had allowed the imagination of a different world. During the course of the event everyday codes of social interaction and behavior were exchanged for those of the ritual festival—rather than eating at home with their families, the villagers had cooked and eaten together; instead of returning home after work, they had stayed up all night and danced; and boys and girls usually shy with one another had openly flirted. These ritual norms present an antithesis to everyday social behavior, forming what Victor Turner has called communitas,[25] that is, the stage of ritual where sentiments of camaraderie and egalitarianism are established between participants, and that a portion of such sentiments will be carried back into society at the ritual's close, thereby reinforcing and strengthening it.[26] While Bon Dalien did not have the full strengthening of solidarity as suggested by Turner, it nonetheless arguably provided a sense of community or connectedness among villagers and with their ancestral past and the world of the spirits. It delivered an exemplary spectacle, hosting visions of an ideal social and moral world, and encapsulated people's hopes and aspirations into a vision of peace, community, continuity, and an openness to possibility. The ritual festival became a site where these visions were reproduced through the inclusion of traditional and modern elements and through the participation of much of the community. Although not all the villagers participated, old and young alike had gathered together to plan and prepare for the celebration, and during the festival itself communal ties to each other and the ancestral, guardian, and other spirits of the Cambodian imaginary were revivified and strengthened. A villager later reflecting on the festival observed: "That is why we live. If we live, we have to look after each other whether we are relatives of each other or not. We must join together and be happy together."[27]

In the Bon Dalien celebration, the relationships with the guardian spirits, ancestors, and other entities in the Cambodian imaginary were reaffirmed, creating a continuum with the past and therefore providing some level of mending to the massive devastation wrought by the Khmer Rouge in this village community and in the Cambodian nation as a whole. Specifically, the observance of the ritual festival establishes a social durability (or resilience) and transcendence that overcomes the mortality of its participants and endures despite the massive devastation to Cambodian society and culture through the destruction wrought by the Khmer Rouge wars and genocide. This continuum also stretches into the future as young people participate and create their own relationships both transactionally with each other and transcendentally through the invisible relations being formed and acknowledged with ancestors and the spirit world. The ritual is thus an imaginative process through which the past, present, and future are created and recreated. There are yet other dimensions of Bon Dalien that will be addressed below, but first it is necessary to lay out a bit more about the Khmer imaginary.

Moral Inspiration and Resilience in the Cambodian Imaginary: Enchanted Weddings and Forest Hermits

While Bon Dalien invoked the Cambodian imaginary through the connection to the ancestral past and spirit world, the following stories further illustrate how Cambodian imaginary provides a source for moral inspiration for living peacefully together and how its enduring existence triumphs over the violence of the Khmer Rouge. These stories recalled by villagers and repeated over generations provide notions of the ideal, but they are also cautionary tales reminding people about the value of virtue and how possibilities diminish when individuals are dishonest and untrustworthy. Villagers told these stories in the aftermath of the war and genocide when I stayed in the village and continue to tell them today.

The first story features a peculiar shaped boulder named "The Stone

Fig. 2.1. The Enchanted Wedding Chest "The Stone Box"

Box" (*Thmâ Brâaþ*) that sits just outside the village on the side of a mountain. The Stone Box represents an ancestral past where people were said to be honest with one another and with the spirit world and when magic and enchantment prevailed. It is also considered to be one of the local features of the landscape that ties the residents of this area together as a people from a shared place and history.[28] With its multiplicity of meanings and connection to ideas of morality and community it provides, like the story that follows it, a poetic representation or blueprint for peaceful coexistence reminiscent of John Paul Lederach's (2005) work on poetic or metaphorical models and pathways for coexistence.

Villagers say that the boulder is actually a box or chest that contains all the accoutrements necessary for a wedding ceremony, and that the box is presided over by the ancestral guardian spirit of the mountain and a magical forest hermit (*neak sachchan*). Long ago when villagers were to hold a wedding, they were given access to the chest providing that proper prayers were offered and with the promise that the items would be returned after the conclusion of the wedding ceremony. For years the ancestors remained loyal to their promise. However, with the passing of time their honesty diminished, and sometimes they failed to return the items. With this decline in moral virtue came the disenchantment of the box as it began to harden over time, becoming eventually the boulder that it is today. It is said that people became increasingly greedy and dishonest and no longer accorded the guardian spirit the respect they once did. Thus, as their virtue declined, so did their access to the enchanted world and the treasures they drew from it. This story like other Khmer folktales contends with the issue of the way things ought to be and what sometimes happens.[29] As in David Chandler's influential essay, "Songs from the Edge of the Forest" (1996), the telling of the tale restores the past in its telling, offers a model of how people ought to live together, and cautions against unvirtuous behavior.[30]

Despite the boulder's present hardened surface, there remains a residue of enchantment within that may be revealed under certain circumstances. I describe this in more detail elsewhere (2013, ch. 3); however, as a brief example, I was told that the boulder would not appear in photographs since it belonged to the enchanted ancestral world and not the world of the present. Its appearance in a photo (as shown here) is only a result of the magical intervention of its spiritual guardian, from whom permission was asked to photograph it. This idea that there is a hidden enchanted world that may on occasion become visible is not unique to Cambodia. Leah Zani recounts that in postwar Laos she was told a story about how the virtuous ancestors revealed an enchanted realm to a pair of American pilots during the Second Indochina War, allowing them to see for an instant a vision of an ideal peaceful Laos in the midst of the war (Zani, Leah 2019, 3–8). Zani notes that the revealing of the peaceful virtuous world both signals the immorality in wartime Laos and offers a vision of an alternative (5).[31] Zani's interpretation of the existence of parallel realms and the story she tells resembles aspects of the Cambodian enchanted realm and the stories attached to it.

As anthropologist Michael Lambek (2000)[32] writes: "religion works by *realizing* the imagined, rendering it even more real than appearance and, indeed, even inverting the ordinary relationship between representations and their objects such that the imagined may serve as the basis against which appearance is judged." Thus, the boulder (see fig. 2.1) is a representation of what it really is—a wedding chest. Exemplifying this, villagers told me that the sapling growing in its crevice (fig. 2.1) is the key to the wedding chest. While Lambek is addressing religion more broadly, the set of supernatural beliefs and powers he is referring to work similarly to the enchanted imaginary of the spirit world discussed here. Moreover, we see through this story of virtue and honesty that the largely invisible enchanted world offers a moral template on how people ought to live together. That it is connected to weddings, which in Cambodia are at the root of creating social relationships (and ultimately society itself), is not coincidental as we will see again below.

The many spirits that inhabit the enchanted world—ancestral, magical, and divine—are considered by Cambodians to have the power to influence individuals' and communities' well-being. If people accord the spirits proper respect and behave morally then they will reap the benefits of the spirits' protection. As such the spirits provide moral inspiration, security, and a means of healing by helping individuals and communities live well and prosper through their blessings. In the aftermath of the violence, we see that the powers of the spirits and enchanted world emerged from the destruction with resiliency and potency, despite the Khmer Rouge's attempts to destroy them. In fact, their reemergence is entirely due to people's belief that in this context is inseparable from the acts of telling stories about them and respecting them through ritual offerings. And, because the enchanted world prevails (although perhaps less visibly than in the ancestral past), it offers a creative template for interpreting the memory of the violence (as I discuss elsewhere)[33] and envisioning a moral future as will be become clear in the following passages.

It is said that long ago some of the elder members in the community "knew how to see everything," meaning they maintained the necessary virtue and were able see the otherwise invisible enchanted realm. This ability of "knowing how to see" is illustrated in a story about a pair of village ancestors, a man and a woman, who with the help of a magical forest hermit gained entrance to the normally hidden enchanted realm. In the tale, the forest hermit invites them to a mythical wedding, where they see a bride and groom astride elephants with colored tusks and also a number of traditional wedding items such as betel nut. The betel nut and its accompaniments are substances considered to be conducive to the making of social relations in Cambodia (see Zucker 2013, ch. 6). However in the enchanted world of these story, these items take on enormous proportions, appearing much larger than usual thereby suggesting enchanted context. The storyteller explained that the wedding was only revealed to the couple because of their honesty:

> Our ancestors were very good people—incredibly honest and that is why they could see all of this. If they had not been good people, they wouldn't have been able to see them. At that time people were

very honest—if they were going fishing and planned to catch three fish, then they would only catch three and no more. It is because of this honesty that it was possible for them to see the people on the elephants.

Honesty is linked to predictability and an implicit trust. Those who are honest do precisely what they say they will do, no more and no less. Their intentions and actions are transparent. This level of predictability allows them to be trusted by the enchanted forest hermit, who himself manifests these traits (*neak sachchang*, meaning literally a person who tells the truth). The predictability inherent in this notion of honesty and truthfulness contrasts the uncertainties and unpredictability of life and social change, including radical upheaval such as that wrought by mass violence. Predictability as described is a virtue that is depicted and drawn from the imagined enchanted world where the ideal vision of how people ought to live can be located.

In the story of the wedding we find the connection to the ancestors and the making of kin and community all told through the medium of marriage between clans. In the aftermath of the mass destruction to Cambodian society, these stories provide a generative site for social and moral renewal. The enchanted world, that is, the Cambodian imaginary, is laden with potentiality in remaking social relationships in the aftermath of the Khmer Rouge. The stories like the stone chest and the enchanted wedding are sites where social change is negotiated as individuals and communities draw on their moral tales and pass them down to their children. As part of the transcendental imaginary they also present an alternative to the precariousness of existence. That is, the imaginary with its myths, stories, and enchanted beings provides durable resilience that transcends the rupture wrought by the violence of war and genocide.

Seeing and Not Seeing: Other Challenges, Other Imaginations

Thus far the discussion in this section has focused on the visible and invisible realms of the Cambodian imaginary and its relationship to social repair by being a site capable of negotiating social change. The stories shared above discussed how the metaphorical trope of seeing (or not seeing) is connected to the moral and social value of honesty, reliability, and trust. In this section I discuss a further dimension of this notion of seeing and not seeing as it emerged in the post-violence context in the village—a context where the community is not only contending with the trauma of the past but also with new challenges and hardships that accompany rapid social and economic change. The challenging economic circumstances in the village revealed another dimension of seeing and not seeing—one associated with the concept of empathy. As discussed in McGrew's chapter (this volume), there is no specific word for empathy in the Cambodian language. While empathy is often expressed in terms of understanding or knowing another's heart, it may also be articulated through the metaphor of seeing.

As stated earlier, this region is predominantly poor, however a variety of factors including unequal land distribution, the rise of the market economy, the loss of family members, and widespread illness has resulted in some residents having a bit more than others. In already difficult circumstances, these emergent inequalities created further strain on social relations in addition to those incurred from the Khmer Rouge period. For example, it was asserted by some of the poorest members of the community that their wealthier neighbors "do not see" those with less. In the words of a villager:

> They do not have relations with the poor. They are afraid that if they have relations with poor people, the next day their wealth will be gone. This is because the wealthy *don't see poor people*. They only see those people of equal (or greater) wealth. These days they want to see only rich people.[34]

The circumstances described by the villager are reminiscent of those described by anthropologist David Graeber (2006), which he referred to as the dead zone of the imagination—the area where those with more do not identify or empathize with those with less. They are unwilling to do what he called the "interpretive labor" that is the imaginative identification with the "other." In unequal social and economic arrangements, the interpretive labor is lopsided. Those with less do the interpretive labor to empathize with those with more, while those on the higher end do nothing. This seeing and not seeing fits the circumstances described by the villager and demonstrates that the challenges of building community and peace may be further complicated by varying economic circumstances that hamper the empathy necessary for building social relations.

Returning now to the story of Bon Dalien, prior to the festival itself, the village leaders spoke about the festival as a spectacular event that would draw visitors potentially from as far as the nation's capital. Why was it important to present this vision of the festival? Perhaps part of the explanation may be found in the concept of seeing and not seeing. Villagers talk about their village as being "on the outside" relative to Phnom Penh, which is located "inside"—the inside being the seat of power. They also recognize that the relatively wealthy urbanites (and the state itself) do not "see them," meaning there is little or no interpretive labor on the part of the urbanites toward their fellow citizens in the hinterlands, no empathy, and no real sense of communal relationship. They are cognizant that the wealthy and powerful consider them to be inferior, even seeing them as "others."

In the idealized vision of the festival, however, wealthy urbanites come to the festival and presumably see and experience the village in its exemplary state—a state of strong village identity with a vibrant connection to its ancestral past, comradeship, solidarity, and community. The urbanites, if they were to come and join, would be a part of the communal festival, and therefore the boundaries between those inside and those outside might at least temporarily be removed or lessened. In the ritual context, this seeming impossibility becomes possible, as rituals by their nature are counterintuitive. As Bloch (1989, viii) posits, "the cosmologies which may emerge from the analysis of ritual and similar phenomena as powerful *alternatives* [his emphasis] to everyday cognition, which are experienced by actors as governing [an] altogether different world." This alternative, like the alternative worlds presented in the stories above or in the realm of the virtuous ancestors discussed in Zani (2019), is a world of peaceful relations. Thus the potentiality found within ritual here is an emergent and flexible vision of peace and fraternity, a vision of what could be, in some ways mirroring the ancestral past where people lived equally, harmoniously, and were honest and faithful.

There is another dimension to this as well. The imaginings of cars and urbanites may also at the same time be a gesture toward placing their village community in the modern era alongside Phnom Penh and other provincial cities, similar perhaps to the way in which Thongchai Winichakul (2002) characterized late 19th-century Siam's (Thailand's) carefully crafted image formation of a "civilized" state in the World's Fair in an effort to be modern and belong to the cosmopolitan global community. As Siam sought to belong to the set of modern "civilized" nations, so too might the village community aspire to belong to the modern Cambodia of its compatriots (see also Gordon, this volume).

Elements of these different aspirations with some variance of interpretation across different members of the village community emerged in many conversations I had with villagers at the time of the festival and throughout the time I spent with them. Bon Dalien, as an imagined ideal, is capable of capturing the varying visions of how people ought to live together drawing from the moral world of the ancestors as well as incorporating the modern. In this manner, the ritual festival provides a means of both looking forward and looking back. These dual elements are present in the festival itself, in its combination of modern and traditional. Thus the festival together with moral stories and myths of enchanted worlds allows connection with the past, present, and future and creates an imaginary as a basis for a peaceful and more prosperous future.

Conclusion: Imagination and Recovery

This chapter has focused on the ways in which a Cambodian village community has drawn upon its imaginary as a source for meaning and moral guidance as its members take steps in mending the rupture to their social and moral world. These local imagined spaces and stories provide the necessary plasticity to absorb tentative forays into considerations of how to live together again in the aftermath of violence and rupture. These sites—whether a ritual, a set of tales, a vision of the modern world, or some other form of cultural knowledge or ideal—are integral to the process of recovery, whether they are explicitly identified as such or not, and are meaning producing. As such, as noted by Viktor Frankl (1992), they become a fountainhead for resilience to carry on and live with one another compassionately and humanely.

Underpinning this chapter is an argument that local forms of social and moral repair in the wake of mass violence have the potential to contribute to a sustainable and resilient peace. This is because these local practices touch on deeply held and enduring, yet flexible, belief systems and are part of everyday discourses and interactions, making them accessible, understandable, and pliable by individuals and communities. Moreover, in addition to traditional sources of ideals, visions, and morals, other ideologies in the present may also provide sources of inspiration for rebuilding lives as suggested above, and as drawn out more explicitly in Mieth's chapter and as apparent in the other chapters in this volume. Whether drawing from traditional sources or new ideologies or both, local communities locate pathways to reestablish a sense of ontological and existential continuity, create a foundation for coexistence, and build a vision for the future. While interventions from international human rights, justice, peacebuilding, and development agencies may assist the reconstruction and peacebuilding process, it should not be assumed that without the interventions there are no local resources available to meet these needs. Better understanding of the local resources being employed implicitly and explicitly by communities and societies in the wake of mass violence may lead to better and more nuanced interventions. These processes may not appear as obvious repair measures but listening to what local people say and observing what they do is paramount to understanding these processes. Moreover, more attention needs to be paid to the ways in which local practices may combine with externally derived ideologies and resources such as discourses of human rights.[35]

Finally, as the chapters in this volume indicate, rebuilding lives, communities, and societies after wars and genocides is particularly morally problematic.[36] The categories of good and bad and right and wrong are often complicated. Finding ways to live together again is challenging and difficult, and the aftermath of the upheaval of the treachery of the Khmer Rouge process echoed that truth. Nonetheless, as argued here, there exist sources of moral guidance, inspiration, and resilience that can help in the rebuilding process. It is through the remarkable power of the imagination that survivors may envision an alternative world and see themselves as part of something larger and transcendental that spans from the ancestors to their descendants and in horizontal webs of relationships across different circles of belonging. Whether these worlds emerge in ritual contexts, folk and religious tales and teachings, through myths, or other local beliefs, imagined worlds provide sources of meaning and guides on how to live in the chaotic and danger-fraught world of transitioning societies and help contend with painful and difficult violent histories.

NOTES

This chapter draws on earlier research that was published in part by the University of Hawai'i Press in 2013 under the title *Forest of Struggle: Moralities of Remembrance in Upland Cambodia*. The original research was funded by a generous grant from the Center for Khmer Studies. The description of the Bon Dalien festival also appeared in an article for the *Journal of Asian Studies*. Earlier versions of this chapter were presented at the Cornell University Southeast Asia Program Gatty Lecture (2016) and the Council of Southeast Asian Studies Brown Bag Seminar at Yale University (2016). I am very appreciative for the constructive comments on this paper I received in each of these events, as well as from the participants of the Reflections in the Aftermath of War and Genocide manuscript workshop (2017) held at Kean University.

1. The White Khmer (*Khmer Sar*) in this region was a renegade guerrilla military force under the leadership of Prince Chantaraingsay who fought against the Khmer Rouge. Arriving in the area just after the Khmer Rouge, the group recruited local

villagers. In interviews I was told that those who joined were killed by the Khmer Rouge.

2. Although there were economic development organizations working in the region, there were no foreign transitional justice or peacebuilding measures occurring within the village area between 2002 and 2003.

3. The idea that relationships manifest the foundation of the Cambodian social and moral order derives from Cambodian culture itself. See Zucker (2013), especially the conclusion. But the focus on human relationships as a key to peaceful coexistence is also found in the literature on peacebuilding, particularly in the work of John Paul Lederach (2005), who argues for "the centrality of relationships" in peacebuilding, seeing relationships as the locus for resources for a resilient and long-lasting peaceful coexistence.

4. Merriam-Webster online, https://www.merriam-webster.com/dictionary/imagination

5. Sociality is a somewhat elusive term, but I appreciate Long and Moore's (2012, 41) conceptualization of it as "a dynamic relational matrix within which human subjects are constantly interacting in ways that are co-productive, continually plastic and malleable, and through which they come to know the world they live in and find their purpose and meaning within it."

6. In the paranoid political climate of the Khmer Rouge, imagined enemies were everywhere; see Chandler (2000), Hinton (2004), and Zucker (2013, chapter 3).

7. The reexamination, contestation, and adoption of old and new moral frameworks in managing large-scale violence in the past has also been studied by Heonik Kwon (2008) for Vietnam. Kwon shows how old ancestral rituals reemerge to help tend to the ghosts of the war alongside state rituals of martyrdom.

8. The name of the village and the names of all persons who were interviewed in the village area for the research have been changed to protect their privacy.

9. In the war of independence against the French in the mid-20th century; in the civil war between the government and the Khmer Rouge in the late 1960s and early 1970s; and again in the second civil war between the Khmer Rouge and the government during the 1980s and 1990s.

10. Author interview, December 2002.

11. Author interview, December 2002.

12. Author interview, August 2003.

13. Author field notes.

14. Author interview, July 2003.

15. Paul Christianson (2019) and Mathew O'Lemmon (2014) have also written about the resurgence and flourishing of spiritual practices since the Khmer Rouge.

16. Author interview with Kheau, January 2003. Kheau lost her husband in the early years of the Khmer Rouge. Her husband was spied on by one of her neighbors who reported him to the Khmer Rouge for saying things deemed traitorous to the revolution. This was around 1973, before the Khmer Rouge fully controlled the country.

17. Author interview, January 2003.

18. Author interview, September 2003.

19. Author interview, October 2002.

20. The organization of the festival, however, was at times seen as less than ideal.

21. Clifford Geertz (1980) argues that the ritual spectacle in the 19th-century Balinese Kingdom was not a means to an end but rather *was* the end. By creating the exemplary ritual spectacle, the moral kingdom and universe is actualized.

22. The older of these two women's husband was executed by the Khmer Rouge after the other's (her niece) father allegedly reported him as a traitor. Despite this history the women were friendly with one-another.

23. Author interview, February 2003.

24. Although he did not attend this 2003 Bon Dalien, I learned from the villagers during subsequent fieldwork in 2010 that he later moved back to the village and attended the Dalien ceremonies in 2008 and 2009.

25. Victor Turner, *The Ritual Process* (1995), 96.

26. Turner, *The Ritual Process* (1995).

27. Author interview, September 2003.

28. For a comparison from anthropology, see Keith Basso's (1996) work on the Apache where features of the landscape and their associated moral tales are vessels containing cultural and moral knowledge.

29. David Chandler writing about such tales in *Songs at the Edge of the Forest* (1996) states, "They describe the gaps in the world between what ought to happen in the world, what often happens, and the 'normal'" (98).

30. See also Hansen and Ledgerwood 2008.

31. "In the logic of parallels, the perception of other realms of peace may be interpreted as evidence of the immorality of our political systems—while also indicating that alternative forms of politics are possible" (Zani 2019, 5).

32. Lambek is following Roy Rappaport here.

33. See Eve M. Zucker (2013), *Forest of Struggle*, and *From Soldier to Guardian Spirit: Cultural Resilience through Re-Enchantment* (2017), http://theasiadialogue.com/2017/08/10/from-soldier-to-guardian-spirit-cultural-resilience-through-re-enchantment, accessed December 27, 2018.

34. Author interview, July 2003.

35. See Lia Kent (2011) and Heonik Kwon (2013).

36. See for example Buruma (2013) and McElwee (2005).

REFERENCES

Anderson, Benedict. 1991. *Imagined Communities: Reflections on the Origin and Spread of Nationalism.* London: Verso.

Basso, Keith. 1996. *Wisdom Sits in Places: Landscape and Language Among the Western Apache.* Albuquerque: University of New Mexico Press.

Bloch, Maurice. 1989. *Ritual, History and Power: Selected Papers in Anthropology.* London: Athlone Press.

Bloch, Maurice. 2008. "Why Religion Is Nothing Special but Is Central." *Philosophical Transactions of the Royal Society B: Biological Sciences* 363 (1499): 2055–61. https://doi.org/10.1098/rstb.2008.0007

Buruma, Ian. 2013. *Year Zero: A History of 1945.* New York: Penguin Press.

Chandler, David P. 1996. "Songs at the Edge of the Forest." In *Facing the Cambodian Past.* Chiang Mai: Silkworm Press.

Chandler, David P. 2004. *Voices from S-21: Terror and History in Pol Pot's Secret Prison.* Berkeley: University of California Press.

Christianson, Paul. 2019. *"We Will Never Get Rich if We Follow Buddhism": The Rise of Brahmanism in Cambodia*. GISCA Occasional Paper Series. No. 24.

Frankl, Viktor. 1992. *Man's Search for Meaning: An Introduction to Logotherapy*. Boston: Beacon Press.

Geertz, Clifford. 1980. *Negara: The Theatre State in Nineteenth-Century Bali*. Princeton: Princeton University Press.

Graeber, David. 2006. "Dead Zones of the Imagination: On Violence, Bureaucracy, and Interpretive Labor." The 2006 Malinowski Memorial Lecture. *HAU: Journal of Ethnographic Theory* 2, no. 2: 105–28.

Hansen, Anne R. 2008. "Gaps in the World: Harm and Violence in Khmer Buddhist Narrative." In *At the Edge of the Forest: Essays on Cambodia, History, and Narrative in Honor of David Chandler*. Ithaca: Cornell University Press.

Hansen, Anne R., and Judy Ledgerwood, eds. 2008. *At the Edge of the Forest: Essays on Cambodia, History, and Narrative in Honor of David Chandler*. Ithaca: Cornell University Press.

Hinton, Alexander Laban. 2004. *Why Did They Kill? Cambodia in the Shadow of Genocide*. Berkeley: University of California Press.

Kent, Lia. 2011. "Local Memory Practices in East Timor: Disrupting Transitional Justice Narratives." *International Journal of Transitional Justice* 5, no. 3: 434–55. https://doi.org/10.1093/ijtj/ijr016

Kwon, Heonik. 2008. *Ghosts of War in Vietnam*. Cambridge: Cambridge University Press.

Kwon, Heonik, 2013. "Cold War in a Vietnamese Community." In *Four Decades On: Vietnam, the United States, and the Legacies of the Second Indochina War*, edited by Scott Laderman and Edwin A. Martini, 84–102. Durham: Duke University Press.

Lambek, Michael. 2000. "Anthropology of Religion and the Quarrel between Poetry and Philosophy." *Current Anthropology* 41, no. 3 (June): 311–12.

Lederach, John Paul. 2005. *The Moral Imagination: The Art and Soul of Building Peace*. New York: Oxford University Press.

Levi, Primo. 1986 [2017]. "The Gray Zone." In *The Drowned and the Saved*. New York: Simon and Schuster.

Long, Nicholas J., and Henrietta L. Moore. "Sociality Revisited: Setting a New Agenda." *Cambridge Journal of Anthropology* 30, no. 1 (2012): 40–47. http://www.jstor.org/stable/43610888

McElwee, Pamela. 2005. "'There is Nothing that is Difficult': History and Hardship on and after the Ho Chi Minh Trail in North Vietnam." *Asia Pacific Journal of Anthropology* 6, no. 3 (December): 197–214.

Merriam-Webster Online. "Imagination." https://www.merriam-webster.com/dictionary/imagination. Accessed December 1, 2018.

O'Lemmon, Matthew. 2014. "Spirit Cults and Buddhist Practice in Kep Province, Cambodia." *Journal of Southeast Asian Studies* 45, no. 1: 25–49.

Turner, Victor. 1995. *The Ritual Process: Structure and Anti-structure*. New York: Aldine de Gruyter.

Um, Khatarya. 2015. *From the Land of Shadows: War, Revolution, and the Making of the Cambodian Diaspora*. New York: New York University Press.

Winichakul, Thongchai. 2000. "The Quest for 'Siwilai': A Geographical Discourse of

Civilizational Thinking in the Late Nineteenth and Early Twentieth-Century Siam." *Journal of Asian Studies* 59, no. 3 (August): 528–49.

Zani, Leah. 2019. *Bomb Children: Life in the Former Battlefields of Laos.* Durham: Duke University Press.

Zucker, Eve M. 2013. *Forest of Struggle: Moralities of Remembrance in Upland Cambodia.* Honolulu: University of Hawai'i Press.

Zucker, Eve M. 2017. "From Soldier to Guardian Spirit: Cultural Resilience through Re-Enchantment." *Asia Dialogue* (August 10). Available at http://theasiadialogue.com/2017/08/10/from-soldier-to-guardian-spirit-cultural-resilience-through-re-enchantment

3 | "And to This New Life We Are Striving"

The Role of Imagination in Post-Conflict Sierra Leone

Friederike Mieth

"We have plenty of peace. What we need now is development." The man, well into his sixties, smiled firmly. It seemed as if he wanted to brush off any further questions about coexistence that my research assistant and I were asking. We were in Tombodu, a village in eastern Sierra Leone. That day, we encountered the group of eight or nine middle-aged men sitting in the shade of a thatched pavilion in front of a house, who spontaneously agreed to talk with us. The comment was rather surprising to me, as we had just discussed a range of difficulties that the civilian villagers experienced while living in coexistence with excombatants. But the group of men sitting around us indicated that their sentiments were the same.

The man's statement illustrates a typical situation in my ethnographic research in Sierra Leone. My aim was to investigate local ways of dealing with the past of the civil war that took place in the country from 1991 to 2002. Yet the research participants seemed to be more concerned with the future. Rather than talking about issues like memory, reconciliation, or post-conflict justice, the focus of our conversations was often on issues that were more relevant in people's immediate lives. The concept of "development" was almost omnipresent throughout the research, and the notion of "we need development" resonated widely in Sierra Leone at the time. A journalist in Sierra Leone's capital of Freetown wrote, for example, "[T]he war is over. Now is the time for development" (Bangura 2013).

These observations raise a range of questions with regard to dealing with the past in the aftermath of mass violence. For example, the preference for development over other forms of post-conflict intervention raises the question whether peacebuilding and transitional justice interventions should engage with development and related socioeconomic aspects. This has been widely debated in the transitional justice field over the last decade (see, e.g., Carranza 2008; De Greiff and Duthie 2009; Gready and Robins 2014; Mani 2008).

In this chapter, however, I would like to focus on what people were doing when they spoke about development: they were *imagining* a particular future. I ask, what does it mean when people in a postwar context want to talk about the future instead of how to reach justice, reconciliation, or memorialization? To this end, I will first examine what the concept of development entailed for the research participants, before looking at the role of imagination on both the collective and individual level. Specifically, I investigate how certain ideas about development inform practices and narratives of coexistence in Sierra Leone, as well as how, on an individual level, imagination plays a role in reframing memories and making sense of past (and present) suffering.

The analysis in this chapter is based on data gathered during eight months of ethnographic fieldwork that I conducted in Sierra Leone between 2010 and 2012. I conducted research in three research sites in different parts of the country: a small village in northern Sierra Leone (Madina), a mid-sized village in the diamond-rich east of the country (Tombodu), and the capital Freetown. While these locations differ substantially in terms of history, geography, and ethnicity of the people who live there, as well as different levels of violence experienced during the war, this research was not designed as representative of Sierra Leonean society generally. Rather, my intention was to grasp some of the complexities of individual and social recovery in the country by engaging with people from different backgrounds and in different surroundings. My initial research was split up in a five-month and a three-month phase; I later revisited the country for one month each in 2014 and 2016/17.

During my research, I used different ethnographic methods to collect data, such as participant observation, interviews, and informal conversations. I conducted a total of sixty-two interviews, forty-two with Sierra Leoneans of a wide range of backgrounds, such as farmers and traders, religious and community leaders, business professionals, university students, and urban and rural youth. Sixteen interviews were conducted with professionals in the area of peacebuilding and dealing with the past, and four interviews took the form of life stories of close friends and acquaintances.[1] I worked together with two research assistants who helped in organizing the research, translating during interviews and transcriptions, and reflecting on preliminary findings.[2]

By way of background, the small West African country of Sierra Leone has been the site of a brutal civil war (1991–2002) and a remarkable recovery from this violent period. The civil war was not an identity group conflict, meaning that fighting factions were not divided along political, ethnic, religious, or other lines. Rather, the rebel movement that began to enact violent acts in 1991 cited their frustration of ineffective and corrupt politicians and their wish to overthrow the government as the main motivation for armed struggle. The inability of the government to suppress the rebellion as well as economic factors such as fighting factions' access to and competition over diamond mining played a large role in expanding and prolonging the initially localized violence. The nature of the atrocities was mostly chaotic and at times anarchic, with fighting factions—rebels, soldiers, and a civil defense force, later also a group of rebels *and* rogue soldiers—turning against civilians in all parts of the country. It is estimated that more than 50,000 people were killed and 2.5 million people displaced, half of Sierra Leone's population. The use of captured fighters, including child soldiers, was widespread, and the violence unleashed on the population was exceptionally brutal.[3]

Since the formal end of the civil war in January 2002, which was brought about with the help of several international peacekeeping forces, Sierra Leone has been peaceful. It is now one of the safest countries in Africa to live in but ranks extremely low on all human development indicators (Afrobarometer 2015; Mo Ibrahim Foundation 2016; UNDP 2016). The immediate post-conflict years were characterized by a large international presence. A UN mission monitored the peace and many international NGOs were involved in post-conflict reconstruction efforts. Also, two transitional justice mechanisms were established to deal with the past of the war, a truth and reconciliation commission and the Special Court for Sierra Leone, a hybrid war crimes court.

Several of the research participants of this study described that, beginning at the time of the general elections in 2007, the overall mood in the country changed to a more hopeful atmosphere. The elected president promised to "run the country like a business," distinguishing himself from the former "NGO-president." In this period, Sierra Leoneans increasingly experienced economic and infrastructural development. In 2014, however, the country experienced several severe setbacks. The 2014–16 Ebola outbreak caused widespread suffering and many deaths in Sierra Leone and the neighboring countries of Guinea and Liberia. At the same time, the country's economic situation deteriorated significantly, and the hopeful atmosphere seemed to have given away to a more realistic outlook.

During my last visit in the country in 2016/17, I learned how many ordinary citizens were frustrated by high levels of corruption and a slow progress of economic development in the country (Mieth 2018).

Imagining Development

During my research, almost all respondents—of different ages and genders, and in all research locations—spoke about development in our interactions. For many, this was the absolute priority in Sierra Leone—for the country as a whole, for one's community, and ultimately for oneself—and they hoped that an improvement of the general socioeconomic situation would also have a positive effect on their lives. Already shortly after the war, Sierra Leoneans talked about development in this way, as Jackson (2004) noted:

> Then there was this question of "development." In both Freetown and in the north, people had impressed upon me the importance of "development." When I asked what they had in mind, I was told that improved roads would bring development, for along these roads would come the benefits of the outside world. The attitude was naive, if not magical. (Jackson 2004, 168)

In a similar way, the research participants of my study used the word so broadly that it is perhaps best defined by an improvement of the "entire situation." Yet what exactly did people mean by development?

In my research, the term came up in relation to two kinds of experiences, namely socioeconomic need and a sentiment of hope. Regarding the former, there was a dire need for socioeconomic development, because people experienced extreme poverty and suffering. This was often pointed out as an obvious fact by saying "look at the way we live here" or "just look at this place!" In this way, "development" did not need further explanation for the research participants. Similar to Jackson's (2004) observations, respondents talked about a range of concrete things that would contribute to development in their communities: roads, schools, electricity, water, and sanitation. They also described the inadequacy of basic services in Sierra Leone, first and foremost health care and education, but also the lack of infrastructure such as electricity. Finally, many mentioned that there is a lack of employment and other perspectives for the youth in Sierra Leone.

Indeed, human development standards in Sierra Leone are extremely low. The country ranked 179 out of 188 countries assessed by the Human Development Index 2016 (UNDP 2016b). Life expectancy in Sierra Leone is fifty years, the lowest in the world (WHO 2016). More than half of Sierra Leone's population is illiterate (UNDP 2016a). The World Health Organization also recently found Sierra Leone to be the most dangerous country on earth for young people to live in—not because of violence or lack of personal safety but because of the danger of dying from ordinary sicknesses and tropical diseases (Marés 2017; see also Graphic 2017). Finally, youth unemployment has been estimated as high as 70 percent (UNDP 2016a).

An example of what the research participants understood as "development" in this context of socioeconomic suffering was a project that was implemented in one of the research locations, Madina. Paid for by the International Labour Organization and in cooperation with the government, the so-called quick impact project entailed that the young men of the village broaden the road while the women were paid to cook meals for the workers. After this, while still not paved, the road was wide enough for cars and trucks. Since then, occasionally a truck would come to the village allowing the farmers to transport greater amounts of produce to the markets in bigger cities. This was identified by the Madina villagers as how "development" should work.

More subtly, development was mentioned in relation to a diffuse hope for the future, in the context of an overall positive atmosphere in the country during the time of my research. Considering the substantial changes that took place in Sierra Leone in the decade after the war, at the time of my research in 2010–12 there was, for the first time, a realization that a better future may actually be possible. "Yes, they have forgotten about the war because so many things are changing," summarized an NGO employee on the situation in one of my conversations in Freetown in March 2012.

Yet this hope was accompanied by feelings of impatience and frustration, particularly among younger people in urban locations. For example, many acquaintances were fixated on what they defined as a "modern" lifestyle: technology and gadgets, music, and their particular appropriations of a Western lifestyle. This was in sharp contrast with their living circumstances, given that living in slum-like conditions without running water or electricity, dropping out of school, being unemployed, and seeing the death of friends due to preventable diseases all belonged to the experiences in many young people's lives. In these circumstances, aspirations for a modern lifestyle, like owning the latest smartphone, became symbols for the discrepancy between the situation-as-is and an imagined better future.

The mother of a friend summed this up to me once by saying, "people are ahead of the country." Generally, the mood of the youth seemed restless and impatient.

These experiences in the present had an impact on the perception of the past. In light of many immediate and pressing needs, I often got the impression that the experiences and memories of the past violence seemed to fade into the background. Many of the respondents explained that they thought and talked about the civil war in specific moments, but that this past was not really relevant now, as everyone is concerned with making a living. Other research participants conflated the past and present, merging wartime violence and present experiences of poverty under the theme of suffering. An elderly man in Tombodu explained, for example, that for him the "war was not yet over" because he was still sleeping under a leaky roof. And others related development to practices of memory and forgetting: accordingly, people argued they had already "forgotten" about the war because of development (see Mieth 2014).

The concept of development in my research material is thus multidimensional: it alludes to the concrete suffering that people experienced. Yet it was also an expression of the hope that people shared. Both aspects reveal a strong focus on the present and future, and an awareness of the discrepancy between *what is* and *what could be*. In the following sections, I will investigate in more detail how imaginations of the future play a role in practices of dealing with the past.

Coexistence

After the war, Sierra Leoneans in many parts of the country faced the challenge of living together again. As mentioned above, the conflict was not fought among identity-based groups, so coexistence after the war concerned not so much the living together of particular ethnic, religious, or political groups but rather civilians and former combatants more generally.[4] In my research, this distinction played a more noticeable role in rural areas, for example in the village of Tombodu, where some of the former combatants had simply remained in the village after the war. In such contexts, some of the community members knew about the others' actions during the war. Depending on the particular circumstances of the research participants, this was at times described as a difficult situation.

Yet the situation of civilians and former combatants in Sierra Leone was unlike many other civil war contexts as the majority of combatants did not benefit in a material or other way from taking part in the conflict. In fact, many of my research participants pointed out that former combatants were now worse off than civilians, that they were poor, did not learn anything to obtain employment, or were simply "dancing" in the streets (a reference to persisting mental health problems due to widespread drug use during the war). Some research respondents even stated that what happened to the former combatants was a kind of karma. A man in his sixties in Tombodu explained that the former combatants were still fighting to get a livelihood, and that their condition was not better than that of civilians: "Those who were fighting, some of them are in a bad condition, some are crazy. Because they put their hands on something that is not for putting your hands."

It has to be seen in this context that in many interviews and conversations the research participants remarked on the commonality of the experience of suffering after the war—for both civilians and former combatants alike. For example, an elderly man in Tombodu mentioned that both civilians and former combatants were suffering after the war: "Still we are suffering. . . . We are all suffering together with the rebels, they are suffering, we too are suffering, what else can we do? Those who fought are not killing us now, but they are straining us. Because they too don't have food to eat, the gardens that we make they go and steal from us. Here, you see our sufferings?" He pointed out that the former combatants—"those who fought"—were not behaving correctly by stealing from other community members. Immediately, however, he gave an explanation for it by saying that "they too don't have food to eat," an indication of his ability to imagine their situation.

As McGrew (this volume) writes, this recognition of the other's experience is a crucial part of empathy and ultimately plays a role in peaceful coexistence. In Sierra Leone, empathy can further be traced in the particular language that people used to describe their situation. I noticed, for example, how some research respondents spoke of "brothers and sisters" when referring to former combatants, or of "family" when referring to the community. For example, a young businessman in the village of Madina, northern Sierra Leone, described how the shared suffering made everyone "equal":

Why I said we are one big family now? They suffered, and we too suffered. I mean right now, they are suffering, and we are suffering. All what they did, they've done their best, but for now, we are all equal.

This man separated the suffering of the past with the suffering of the present, but similarly to the earlier quote he acknowledged that suffering was experienced by everyone in Sierra Leone, no matter their personal histories. In the same vein, Millar (2012) refers to a lack of "otherizing" in Sierra Leone, based on research done in the city of Makeni.

The term *development* did not only arise in our discussions about people's perception of their own and other's situations. It was also indicative of a forward-looking attitude of the research participants. It was common, for example, that respondents suggested to us that it was not helpful to focus on the past too much, for doing so would hamper the chances of achieving development. In interviews, when we discussed the relationship between civilians and former combatants, research participants often shifted our discussion to development. During a long conversation about a recent reconciliation project, an elderly man in Tombodu explained how difficult it was for him to live in the town with former combatants. "[The people] will never forget," he finished his statement, "so many things. Most of the rebels are still around." This fact surprised my research assistant, who was from the area but did not know Tombodu very well. "Really?," she asked. The man answered,

> Yes, some are here. But when they said peace, you don't have to take the law into your hands. You have to sit down, you form another life. And to this new life we are striving. They have damaged the area, done all kinds of things here, so we are looking toward a new life. Class 1. Like this we don't reach development.

Similar to other research participants, by mentioning a "new life" and "class 1"—to start from scratch again—this man seemed to signal that he saw little use in dwelling on the past and thought that people should focus on development instead.

What emerged from such conversations was that the research participants assumed that development was a common goal that everyone in Sierra Leone was hoping and striving for. In an interview with the appointed youth leader in Madina, a thoughtful man in his late twenties, we discussed possible reasons for the current peace in Sierra Leone. I mentioned that there were many countries that have struggled not to return to violence in the immediate phases after the conflict and asked why he thinks the peace holds in Sierra Leone. "Well, for one, this is a small country," he said, "and second, we, the people, are so poor. So, for us it fits that when they say, 'forgive and forget' we do not refuse."[5] He further noted:

We all need to get development, so it does not help to have grudges against each other, it will not make us developed. That is why you cannot compare us to other countries. Even though we have [natural] resources here, we, the people, are poor. So, we don't need to follow other countries [in not reconciling], it will not make the country developed.

There was also an implicit idea that it is the duty of community members to actively support the greater goal of development. A young man from Madina asserted that people should agree to development, even if this brings short-term losses. He referred to the aforementioned road building project that was going on in the village at the time, during the course of which some households were forced to cut some of their trees:

Like, if they uproot the mangoes, your garden, or your palm kernel tree, you should agree to that because they are making the road. You should accept that. If it was the time of the war, he! People would start to say, "I will not allow that, I will not accept that they come and destroy my plantation!" But being that all of us are one people now, all of us have to come together. . . . You will not say anything when they uproot your mango tree, as they make the area look nice.

This man contrasted the time of war, a time of noncooperation, with the time of peace, in which people should contribute to the greater good. Similarly, in Waterloo, a former refugee community near Freetown, a middle-aged woman suggested that the already visible signs of development were a reason not to start fighting again: "If we do bad, we will spoil our country. Just like how we spoiled it before. And now they are trying to make it [look good] again."

To conclude, my aim here is not to suggest that people's hopes for development was the cause of peaceful coexistence in postwar Sierra Leone, as there are several other aspects to consider. Rather, I argue that these ideas help us understand why so many people in Sierra Leone were *willing* to live in coexistence, even if it was connected with negative emotions.

Narratives

The idea that coexistence will help a community, and the country more generally, to obtain development was part of a greater shared narrative in Sierra Leone. Although the context and conditions different significantly in the various sites of my research, the notion that "we need to get development" emerged in my data from all locations. Such narratives can help people make sense of events, providing both a commonly accepted explanation for the past violence and ideas of how to move on from this past.

In the Sierra Leonean case, it is particularly interesting that the narrative "we need development" also spoke to the specific form of historical injustice. To begin with, the origins of the wish for development can be traced to the time before the civil war, and development, when imagined as a redress, therefore goes beyond redressing the injustice experienced during the civil war. It is widely agreed upon by Sierra Leoneans and observers alike that one of the root causes of the war was a deliberate "underdevelopment" of large regions of the country, which left large parts of the population increasingly marginalized (Keen 2005). This underdevelopment had its roots in the country's colonial history and postindependence politics. Thus, similar to many other African societies, the decades after the country's independence in 1961 were characterized by socioeconomic *decline* rather than modernization.[6] The political climate became increasingly repressive in the 1970s and 1980s, when a corrupt and nepotistic elite controlled the economy and denied or withheld education and employment opportunities to those outside of their circles. By the end of the 1980s the country was in deep economic crisis (see Abdullah 2004; Keen 2005).

This scenario provided a fertile ground for the civil war in several ways. The rebel group that started the war in 1991 claimed that they would overthrow the corrupt government to bring economic justice, employment, and education for all (Richards 1996). Initially, the group received some support from Sierra Leonean civilians. A friend in Freetown told me, for example, that when the rebellion started in the rural areas, some mumbled, "well, maybe a war will bring some change." It is also widely agreed upon by scholars and observers that the devastating situation of young people contributed to the ease with which several armed groups could recruit new fighters (see, e.g., Peters 2011; Shepler 2014). Some of the fighters also saw joining the armed groups as an educational and income opportunity in itself (Nuxoll 2015). What is interesting here is that several of my respondents empathized with those who joined the armed groups, explaining to me that they may have had no other alternative to survive in that situation. From this perspective, thus, it seemed fitting to them to label a "lack of development" as one of the root causes of the war.

Looking back, many people in Sierra Leone perceive the decade of the war as utterly senseless (King 2007). The violence perpetrated during the civil war stood in no relation to the goals that the rebel movement stated in the beginning. It became clear that the rebel group perpetrated brutal and erratic acts of violence, and with time other fighting factions—the national army as well as a paramilitary group—also attacked civilians. Typical attacks on villages were perpetrated by all armed groups in a "hit and run" style, and many of my respondents did not know who attacked them. The creation of the word *sobels* is illustrative: it was used to refer to soldiers who, during the nights, disguised themselves as rebels to plunder villages. Similar to the idea that "we all suffered," the concept of the "senseless war" was brought up by my respondents to argue that it is better to draw a line under the past and move on.

Against this background, it is not surprising that development has been central in Sierra Leonean political discourses in relation to the war. At the signing of a peace agreement in Lomé, Togo, then-president Kabbah immediately turned the attention to the future: "For Sierra Leoneans, war should now be against ignorance, poverty and disease" (BBC 1999). After the end of the conflict, a number of politicians reinforced the notion that development is a national priority and reinterpreted the experience of the war into a "lesson learned," seeking to unite the country under this banner. For instance, in one of her speeches during the campaign for the 2002 elections right after the war, presidential candidate Zainab Bangura stated, "We know that this war was ours, that it was a war which all of us bear some responsibility for and we have resolved to learn its lessons and to rebuild our country by constructing strong, loyal, transparent and patriotic institutions, promoting prosperity for all our citizens . . . ." (Bangura cited in Steady 2006, 57). As with the statements of many of my research participants, the emphasis in such speeches is on the most basic, unifying aspects of the war: the shared experience of suffering and the focus of (re)building the country.

To recapitulate, in Sierra Leone the imagination of a future in which all citizens can benefit from socioeconomic development relates directly to the root causes of the violence. Such narratives can have a positive impact on coexistence, as the wish for development can be shared by former combatants and civilians alike.

Reframing the Past

So far I have examined how imagination plays a role on the collective level. In the remainder of the chapter I will now look at processes that concern the individual level. Looking at psychological literature has been illuminating here because to understand how societies come to terms with an atrocious past, we also have to consider how individual ways of coping are intertwined with the specific societal forms of dealing with the past in a given context.

On an individual level, imagination is in many ways related to processes of coping with adversity.[7] Psychologists have defined imagination as "the ability to conjure up images, stories, and projections of things not currently present and the use of those projections for entertaining the self, planning for the future, and performing other basic tasks of self-regulation" (Taylor et al. 1998, 429). The authors continue: "By imagining how things are likely to be or, alternatively, how one wants them to be, one achieves some ability to comprehend what the future will be like." Discussing the case of postwar Mozambique, Nordstrom (1997, 192) states that imagination can be a link between one's inner feeling and one's being in the world, as well as that between "the given and the possible." Moreover, imagination is directly linked to hope: in order to have hope, one must have imagination (Bar-Tal 2001, 604). Hope is thus the result of, or related to, a *positive* imagination of the future.

Imagination is relevant in processes of dealing with the past because it can help individuals and societies in making sense of past and present suffering. Nordstrom (1997) describes how Mozambicans (re-)create their world in the wake of mass violence. At the end of the civil war, Mozambique was so utterly destroyed that imagining a future became an "act of pure creativity" (191). Mozambicans used imaginative acts such as parables, myths, or stories to spread knowledge of how it is possible to endure and survive violence, as well as how to unmake it (204). Nordstrom writes, "it is the imagination—creativity—that bridges the abyss, if not to reconstruct the past, to make the present livable" (190). Similarly, in this volume, Zucker describes how in Cambodia people's imaginations of their relations with enchanted objects or ancestral spirits provides a background potentiality against which people negotiate social change.

Furthermore, as implied in Nordstrom's work, imagination also plays a role in transforming memories of the past. Writing about a Pentecostal church group in postwar Freetown, Shaw (2007) demonstrates how imagining a better life in fictional stories allowed young people to work on and transform traumatic memories of violence, displacement, and dependency. She describes how a youth group practiced and performed a theater play, which revolved around a male character who was in a happy marriage with an amiable woman, in a stable job, and financially independent—thus a situation virtually impossible for many young Sierra Leoneans. By depicting the protagonist in this way, Shaw argues, the youth imprinted their own aspirations on the figure. During the play the young couple have to defend themselves against the man's mother who reverts to sinister spirits to draw them apart. The subsequent fight of the devotedly Christian couple against the demonic spirit and the Underworld may be reimaginations of the war itself, writes Shaw, and winning over the dark forces then symbolizes the transformation of these experiences. Hence by narrating both suffering and healing the play was ultimately an encouraging experience for the youth (88).

An example from my own research shows how the reframing of past events can transform memories of violence and, similarly to Shaw's analysis, decontextualize them. In 2012, a Sierra Leonean movie was released, called *State Crime*. The film focused on the life of a young army commander, who encountered and overcame a number of troubles in his professional and personal life. Some of the scenes were unmistakably inspired by the actual civil war: there was a rebel attack on a village, with an army battalion trying to free civilians; the on-screen rebels were shown in the kind of attire the rebel group wore during the war; they were taking drugs; women were raped; and there were scenes of arbitrary killings of innocent civilians. Later the plot evolved around the main actor's personal life, and the focus drifted away from the war scenes.

Yet what was remarkable about the film was that it began with a foreword by the producer, who also played the main character. Addressing the audience directly, he explained how this was the first action film ever produced in Sierra Leone and that this was something the viewers should be proud of. In a lengthy presentation, he recounted all the troubles of making the film, from obtaining original military outfits to creating special effects. The foreword painted a story of success, and the producer expressed his wish that his work could be an encouragement for other filmmakers in Sierra Leone. With this framing, the film was not merely a reminder of the horrible violence that happened in the country but, on a different level, proof of just how professional a Sierra Leonean movie could look. It thereby became a part of Sierra Leone's future rather than renarrating the past.

To recapitulate, acts of imagination such as cultural productions can reframe, recontextualize, or challenge the way we think about the past. Rather than prescribing a certain narrative about the past, they can help the audience realize that there are more options of how to view the past or engage with it. As Shapiro-Phim (this volume) discusses in-depth, cultural productions therefore engage both performers and audience in imagining alternatives and can therefore be a powerful arena in which to think about both past and future.

Imagining a Purpose

Finally, the act of imagining can also serve as a coping strategy. The manner in which the research participants of my study thought about development emphasized an active role of individuals. I had the impression that it provided people with a larger purpose, to which everyone could contribute. Many of my respondents used the narrative of "now we need development" to draw attention away from their experiences of violence and suffering, as mentioned earlier, and to actively turn to "better things." For example, a middle-aged woman from Tombodu pointed out: "We don't have problems with them [excombatants], actually. Because those things already happened. There is no other way. When I get money, I will be able to live fine with my family, is it not so? This we think of, nothing else." Some of the respondents also said that they tried not to "think too much" about the past and instead focus on finding ways to make a living in the present.

According to psychological research, focusing on action is an effective way of dealing with adversity. Explaining the title of their book *Don't Hope, Cope!*, Ungerer and Hoellen (2008) describe that they do not want to discredit hope but rather emphasize how crucial it is that hope is accompanied by action. In other words, a person is helped much more if they not only find hope—the positive imagination of the future—but concentrate on doing something about their situation immediately and practically. Thus the physical and mental benefit of hope becomes most relevant in scenarios that are action and goal oriented. In a similar vein, Taylor et al. (1998) point out that mental stimulation is more effective if not only a certain goal is envisioned but also the challenges that need to be overcome to reach that goal.

This resonates with studies on post-conflict recovery, where the resumption of everyday activities has been found to provide meaning in the aftermath of potentially traumatizing events (Almedom et al. 2005;

Summerfield 2004). Almedom et al. (2005) discuss the link between meaningful daily activity and increasing hope in Eritrea. Llanos and Velasco (this volume) also provide illuminating examples of how engaging in meaningful action can be an empowering experience for survivors of human rights violations.

In my research, what the imagination of development "added" to the lived experiences of the research participants was thus the idea that there was a larger purpose, which ultimately also contextualized their suffering. In the research locations people explained to me that it was their responsibility to make a living and take care of their families, as well as to contribute to development of their communities, as illustrated by the mango tree anecdote mentioned earlier. This should not give the impression that the people I met were not suffering on an everyday basis. Rather, the contextualization of that suffering makes a difference for one's well-being: Frankl (2006) describes it as the ability to place suffering into a greater context, such as seeing it as a step toward a certain goal or refocusing one's attention by dreaming of what one can do *after* the suffering, that allows a person to live through situations of extreme hardship.

Concluding Thoughts

In this chapter I hope to have shown how imagination can play a role in both collective and individual processes of coming to terms with an atrocious past. In Sierra Leone, eight to ten years after the war, the focus was firmly on the future, rather than on the past. In my research, I have found that this orientation to the future was less the result of a denial of the past or a repression of painful memories but revealed a range of strategies to deal with the difficult past of the civil war.

Most remarkable is the way in which the research participants discussed how development after the war was a priority for all Sierra Leoneans, civilians and former combatants alike. As a common vision, then, development was something that could address the structural violence of the past as well as unify Sierra Leoneans on the basis that they have similar hopes for the future. Everyone was suffering, was a commonly held perspective I encountered, so everyone needed development. This common vision spoke of the research participants' ability to have empathy for others, and notably for former combatants.

At the same time, imagination plays a crucial role in individual ways of dealing with the past. In Sierra Leone, people engaged with the future by hoping for development, which they imagined would allow not only the country to progress but ultimately to improve their personal lives. What makes this an effective way to cope with the past is that many research participants did not wait for development to magically "happen" but saw their own role in it, for example, by tolerating former combatants in their community or by focusing on earning an income for themselves and their family. "You have to sit down, you form another life," as the elderly man in Tombodu explained it so aptly to my research assistant and me. "And to this new life we are striving."

NOTES

Ishiatu A. Koroma and Doris B. Lebbie provided research assistance in Sierra Leone. The German Research Foundation (DFG) generously provided funding for fieldwork in 2010–12. The Robert Bosch Foundation funded an additional research trip in 2016–17.

    1. Unless otherwise specified, the quotes in this chapter are drawn from interviews conducted in the following time periods: Madina (November and December 2010) with Ishiatu A. Koroma, Tombodu (January and February 2011) with Doris B. Lebbie, and Freetown (between January and April 2012).

    2. The *lingua franca* of Sierra Leone is Krio, an English-based creole, which is widely spoken in the larger cities. In Madina, most villagers belonged to the Temne ethnic group and spoke only Temne; in Tombodu, most of the villagers belonged to the Kono ethnic group and spoke Kono and a rudimentary Krio. Interviews were conducted in the language preferred by the interviewee.

    3. See, *inter alia*, Abdullah (2004), Gberie (2005), and Keen (2005) for analyses of the civil war.

    4. I acknowledge that these categories are very blurry and should be treated with caution as the postwar reality is more complex than the two labels suggest.

    5. "Forgive and forget" was a popular slogan after the war that was taken up by civil society and religious leaders and spread to all parts of the country.

    6. Ferguson (1999) illustrates in great detail what such a decline means for the people who experience it.

    7. I acknowledge that coping is a Western concept, so my use here should be understood in a more general way, describing the ability to deal with adversity in an effective or functional way. In Sierra Leone, perhaps the closest translation would be the word "manage," which was often used in situations where people described their suffering but wanted to express that they were not giving up: "I'm managing." When in a lighter mood, people sometimes added the obvious joke, "you know, we are all managers."

REFERENCES

Abdullah, I., ed. 2004. *Between Democracy and Terror: The Sierra Leone Civil War.* Dakar: CODESRIA.

Afrobarometer. 2015. Summary of Results, Afrobarometer Round 6. Retrieved January

7, 2016, from http://afrobarometer.org/sites/default/files/publications/Summary%20 of%20results/srl_r6_sor_en.pdf

Almedom, A. M., B. Tesfamichael, Z. S. Mohammed, C. G. N. Mascie-Taylor, and Z. Alemu. 2005. "Use of 'Sense of Coherence (SOC)' Scale to Measure Resilience in Eritrea: Interrogating Both the Data and the Scale." *Journals of Biosocial Science* 39: 91–107.

Bangura, S. 2013. From War to Democracy: Reframing Sierra Leone. Retrieved January 6, 2013, from http://newint.org/blog/2013/01/06/development-democracy-sierra-leone-freetown-anniversary/

Bar-Tal, D. 2001. "Why Does Fear Override Hope in Societies Engulfed by Intractable Conflict, as It Does in the Israeli Society?" *Political Psychology* 22, no. 3: 601–27.

Basu, P. 2008. "Confronting the Past? Negotiating a Heritage of Conflict in Sierra Leone." *Journal of Material Culture* 13, no. 2: 233–47.

Bolten, C. 2012. *I Dit It to Save My Life: Love and Survival in Sierra Leone*. Berkeley: University of California Press.

Carranza, R. 2008. "Plunder and Pain: Should Transitional Justice Engage with Corruption and Economic Crimes?" *International Journal of Transitional Justice* 2, no. 3: 310–30.

Coulter, C. 2009. *Bush Wives and Girl Soldiers: Women's Lives through War and Peace in Sierra Leone*. Ithaca: Cornell University Press.

De Greiff, P., and R. Duthie, eds. 2009. *Transitional Justice and Development: Making Connections*. New York: Social Science Research Council.

Frankl, V. E. 2006. *Man's Search for Meaning*. Boston: Beacon Press.

Gberie, L. 2005. *A Dirty War in West Africa: The RUF and the Destruction of Sierra Leone*. London: C. Hurst & Co.

Graphic. 2017. Sierra Leone: Statistics on Diseases, Injuries, and Risk Factors. Retrieved August 30, 2017, from http://global-health.healthgrove.com/l/261/Sierra-Leone

Gready, P., and S. Robins. 2014. "From Transitional to Transformative Justice: A New Agenda for Practice." *International Journal of Transitional Justice* 8: 339–61.

Jackson, M. 2004. *In Sierra Leone*. Durham and London: Duke University Press.

Keen, D. 2005. *Conflict and Collusion in Sierra Leone*. Oxford: James Currey Ltd.

King, N. 2007. *Conflict as Integration: Youth Aspiration to Personhood in the Teleology of Sierra Leone's "Senseless War."* Uppsala: Nordiska Afrikainstitutet.

Mani, R. 2008. "Dilemmas of Expanding Transitional Justice, or Forging the Nexus Between Transitional Justice and Development." *International Journal of Transitional Justice* 2, no. 3: 253–65.

Marés, C. 2017. "Where is the world's most dangerous country for young people?" *The Guardian*. Retrieved from https://www.theguardian.com/inequality/2017/aug/21/where-is-the-worlds-most-dangerous-country-for-young-people

Mieth, F. 2014. *No Condition Is Permanent: Moving on After the War in Sierra Leone*. PhD thesis. Philipps University Marburg, Marburg.

Mieth, F. 2015. "'What Is the Use of Talking-Talking?' Reflections on Talking, Silence, and Resilience in Sierra Leone." *Acta Academica* 47, no. 1: 38–59.

Mieth, F. 2018. "Linking Transitional Justice and Social Transformation: Reflections from Sierra Leone and South Africa." *Swisspeace Working Paper* 4/2018.

Millar, G. 2012. "'Our Brothers Who Went to the Bush': Post-identity Conflict and the Experience of Reconciliation in Sierra Leone." *Journal of Peace Research* 49: 717–29.

Mo Ibrahim Foundation. 2016. A Decade of African Governance 2006–2015: 2016 Ibrahim Index of African Governance. Retrieved May 15, 2017, from http://s.mo. ibrahim.foundation/u/2016/10/01184917/2016-Index-Report.pdf?_ ga=2.92741853.1386445771.1494386199-614302487.1494385905

Nordstrom, C. 1997. *A Different Kind of War Story*. Philadelphia: University of Pennsylvania Press.

Nuxoll, C. 2015. "'We Listened to it Because of the Message': Juvenile RUF Combatants and the Role of Music in the Sierra Leone Civil War." *Music & Politics* 9, no. 1: 1–25.

Peters, K. 2011. *War and the Crisis of Youth in Sierra Leone*. New York: Cambridge University Press.

Peters, K., and P. Richards. 1998. "'Why We Fight': Voices of Youth Combatants in Sierra Leone." *Africa: Journal of the International African Institute* 68, no. 2: 183–210.

Reno, W. 2003. "Political Networks in a Failing State: The Roots and Future of Violent Conflict in Sierra Leone." *International Politics and Society* 2: 44–66.

Richards, P. 1996. *Fighting for the Rain Forest: War, Youth & Resources in Sierra Leone*. Oxford: James Currey.

Shaw, R. 2007. "Displacing Violence: Making Pentecostal Memory in Postwar Sierra Leone." *Cultural Anthropology* 22, no. 1: 66–93.

Shepler, S. 2014. *Childhood Deployed: Remaking Child Soldiers in Sierra Leone*. New York and London: New York University Press.

Sierra Leone Web. 2016. Address by the Chancellor, His Excellency the President, Ernest Bai Koroma at the Congregation of the University of Sierra Leone, Fourah Bay College, 22 December 2007. Retrieved May 15, 2017, from http://www.sierra-leone.org/ Speeches/koroma-122207.html

Steady, F. C. 2006. *Women and Collective Action in Africa: Development, Democratization, and Empowerment, with Special Focus on Sierra Leone*. New York: Palgrave Macmillan.

Summerfield, D. 2004. "Cross-cultural Perspectives on the Medicalisation of Human Suffering." In *Posttraumatic Stress Disorder: Issues and Controversies*, edited by G. M. Rosen, 233–45. New York: John Wiley & Sons.

Taylor, S. E., L. B. Pham, I. D. Rivkin, and D. A. Armor. 1998. "Harnessing the Imagination: Mental Simulation, Self-Regulation, and Coping." *American Psychologist* 53, no. 4: 429–39.

UNDP. 2016a. About Sierra Leone. Retrieved August 30, 2017, from http://www.sl.undp. org/content/sierraleone/en/home/countryinfo.html

UNDP. 2016b. Human Development Report 2016: Human Development for Everyone. Retrieved May 15, 2017, from http://hdr.undp.org/sites/default/files/2016_human_ development_report.pdf

Ungerer, T., and B. Hoellen. 2006. *Don't Hope, Cope! Mut zum Leben*. Tübingen: dgvt-Verlag.

4 | Imagining Alternatives

Cambodia, Accountability, and Compassion

Toni Shapiro-Phim

In 2008, choreographer Sophiline Cheam Shapiro published an essay in which she wrote that "[classical Cambodian dance] has always been a possession of the powerful—in the Hindu temples of Angkor, the royal palace, the Ministry of Culture—and [the danced] stories have supported [that] power. But . . . I have claimed 'ownership' of my art, choreographing new work that speaks, not of the greatness of princes and the harmony of the heavens, but of the conditions of the world as I see it and the state of the Cambodian spirit" (Shapiro 2008, 166).

Sophiline is a survivor of the genocide perpetrated by the Khmer Rouge regime between 1975 and early 1979 and part of Cambodia's first generation to study and re-create the country's mythohistorical classical dance-dramas and ceremonial dance pieces under the guidance of the relatively few accomplished dancers who hadn't perished in those nearly four years of terror and loss. She became a teacher herself in 1989 and, ten years later, a choreographer. In a tradition in which what is handed down generation to generation is sacrosanct, and in which only royalty or others in positions of authority were generally perceived to have the right to create new work—work always based solidly in received stories and patterns of movement—Sophiline's innovative dances sparked controversy from the start. In this essay I trace the trajectory of her oeuvre, highlighting moments and ways in which she calls those in power to task, including the royal and political elite as well as leaders of the Khmer Rouge. Hers is a set of creations that presents her compatriots with an opportunity to contemplate other—more just and equitable—ways of being, particularly in terms of power dynamics and violence.

Sophiline is the most prolific and renowned classical dance choreographer of her generation.[1] She and I have collaborated on research, documentation, and performance projects over the decades. She is also my sister-in-law. When she married my brother, we added an additional layer to our relationship. Though we are family, I still feel compelled, as a scholar of Cambodian culture, to highlight her contributions to engaging with the aftermath of mass violence in her country because of her unique vision and virtuosity as a choreographer and artistic director. Her work has changed the performative storytelling landscape in Cambodia, opening a path for others to engage with complex legacies and imagine alternatives for their future. Sophiline's case is one of an individual whose professional life has been dedicated to devising creative—sometimes subtle, sometimes subversive—ways to shift societal expectations away from the abuse of power, to equity and peace in a post-mass violence setting. Dance historian Alexandra Carter (2003) identifies "dance as a significant hegemonic practice; as such, dance not only reinforces but has the potential to challenge and subvert the cultural norms of society" (250). This certainly holds true for Cambodia. I aim here to fill in some gaps in the record of conflict transformation and peacebuilding efforts in Sophiline's country by adding documentation of her work.[2]

Ceremony

The year was 2011. *The Lives of Giants*, a dance-drama created in the classical dance style of Cambodia, was about to premiere in the country. Days before the story's first performance there, the artists involved in the production held an elaborate ceremony to ask for blessings. Offerings of flowers, candles, incense, selected meats, fruits and sweets, and more were presented by the dancers and musicians to the spirits as well as to living teachers of the arts, to ensure a safe and beautiful performance, one worthy of its lineage.

The master of ceremonies stood before a low table topped with shimmering headdresses and fierce masks representing the central characters and character types, as well as accoutrements from beloved dances. He called the spirits to attend, each being announced through its own sacred melody played by the *pin peat* ensemble—the orchestra that accompanies classical dance.[3] Dancers sat on the ground, legs folded under and to the side, hands lifted with palms together in a position of reverence. At one point, they rose to perform an excerpt from *The Lives of Giants*, presenting the piece for celestial protection and acceptance. At both the beginning and the conclusion of the ritual, dancers and musicians approached their elders to receive individual blessings.

This was a *sampeah kru* ceremony: in Khmer[4] the word *kru*, related to the Sanskrit *guru*, means spirit, teacher, and healer. Through this syncretic rite combining elements of local animism, Hinduism/Brahmanism, and Buddhism, artists honor the spirits of the land and the arts, teachers who have passed, and present-day teachers who embody valued cultural knowledge and skills that they have been generous enough to share.

The particular ceremony I describe set the stage for the presentation of a story about the devastating and injurious implications of cycles of violence and revenge that have plagued Cambodia, with a special emphasis on the Khmer Rouge years and their legacy.

A Choreographer

The Lives of Giants is one of a number of pieces choreographed by Sophiline.[5] She has created discrete dances and layered dance-dramas, many of which explore political and cultural vicissitudes in Cambodia, reflecting recent history and its implications for her and her fellow Cambodians. In addition to restaging traditional pieces handed down through the generations, she also makes "new dances that reflect my personal concerns about the world as I have experienced it. Being a child of war, poverty and cultural isolation, my work is often critical rather than celebratory," an approach at variance with much of the classical Cambodian dance repertoire, and "one that is relevant to my audiences" (Shapiro, personal communication 2017). Her dance-dramas propose that audiences envisage political endings and transitions outside of those they've experienced thus far in their lives. With the Khmer Rouge leadership as a special focus, Sophiline demands examination of rhetoric and action. Which leaders, when in power, have (ever) in fact truly prioritized the well-being of Cambodia's people? Who, among those who have governed the country, has ever attended to the shattering of trust,[6] the rupture of cultural continuity, and the unfathomable loss inflicted by a regime predicated on mass violence?

Peace Studies scholar and practitioner John Paul Lederach (2005) writes that "creativity and imagination . . . propose to us avenues of inquiry and ideas about change that require us to think about . . . what in the world is possible." He continues, "What we will find time and again in those turning points and moments where something moves beyond the grip of violence is the vision and belief that the future is not the slave of the past . . . [through] a journey guided by the imagination of risk" (39).

The imagination of risk involves a willingness to delve into the unknown, a move that can be treacherous, as the unfamiliar often offers no safety net. Mieth (this volume) argues that discussions and imaginings of the future in the context of aftermaths of mass violence, in her case, in Sierra Leone, need to be taken more seriously by scholars and practitioners than they have been up to this point. This argument is also made by Zucker (this volume), who notes the power of the Cambodian enchanted imaginary as a site for recovery. In this chapter I demonstrate the crucial role imagination plays through Cambodian theater in helping survivors of the Khmer Rouge grapple with their difficult past and its legacies.

Four years after Sophiline introduced Cambodian audiences to *The Lives of Giants*, the United Nations Special Rapporteur on Transitional Justice, Pablo de Greiff, acknowledged in an official report the need to honor and engage with aspects of local culture as part of society's process of moving forward following large-scale violence:

> In addition to interventions in the domains of official State institutions and in civil society, those in the domain of culture and individual spheres are required for long-lasting transformations, including non-recurrence. . . . Cultural interventions . . . have the capacity to affect not only victims but also the population at large. In addition to the capacity to engage empathy, there are artistic and cultural interventions that are ideally suited to "make visible" both victims and the effects of victimization, to account for the very complex ways in which violations affect the lives of individuals and of communities, especially over time. Furthermore, some artistic media provide space for victims to articulate their experiences and even, emphasizing the interventions' enabling potential, to try out new identities, including the identity of a rights claimant. (de Greiff, 2015)

The formidable range and variety of challenges facing Cambodians at the end of decades of violence (from the civil war that started in the late 1960s through the genocide of the 1970s to renewed war in the 1980s and early 1990s) is familiar to those who have studied or experienced similar strife: crumbled infrastructure; fractured intra-village and even intra-familial relationships; anger and distrust; extensive loss of property and ways of life; widespread bereavement and displacement; damaging psychological, emotional, and physical effects of the violence perpetrated on individuals and discrete groups; a shattered economy; and so on. It is an enormous task for communities to assess all that has taken place, and then to begin to reform and rebuild—in social, political, economic, and spiritual and other cultural spheres—in such overwhelming circumstances. Sophiline, who survived the genocide and ensuing war, has been shining a light on what might be beyond words, while also helping her fellow Cambodians imagine alternatives to repeated viciousness that leads to further suffering.[7] Through her art, she harnesses the aesthetic and moral potency of expressive culture, opening up new possibilities for her audiences while acknowledging the treachery of the past.

The Dance

When presented as a part of a sacred ritual, Cambodian dance of the court tradition—also called classical or royal—is believed by many Cambodians to impact the world. The performance of hallowed stories and melodies nurtures the fertility of the land and the well-being of the people. Annually, for example, Cambodia's royal dancers perform a tale of a giant and a goddess whose tussle in the heavens sends thunder rumbling overhead and lightening coursing through the sky, harbingers of the rainy season to come. This dance-drama is staged during Cambodian New Year at the behest of the royal family in an effort to encourage the rains needed to nourish the country's farmland and provide an abundant harvest. Dancers themselves embody the sacred. Emulating the sacred serpent (*naga*), they speak of re-creating its curves through their gestures and postures, and tracing the serpent's movement through figure-eight choreographic patterns. Since the mid-twentieth century, theatrical (non-sacred) classical dances have graced stages as well, *The Lives of Giants* being one of them. The choreographer, dancers, and musicians nonetheless maintain a vital spiritual connection to their teachers and the spirits of the dance, the *kru*, through ceremonies and individual ritual gestures that honor received cultural knowledge and protect the artists and a story's performance.

The Country

Sophiline was born in the capital city of Phnom Penh in the Kingdom of Cambodia in 1967. When she was three years old, the royal government was ousted in a coup d'état orchestrated with the support of the United States government. Lon Nol became prime minister. The civil war, fought between Khmer Rouge communists and government forces, had begun in the late 1960s and intensified during the early 1970s. The spillover of the war in Vietnam into Cambodia brought additional hardships including US bombing raids.[8]

In 1975, the Khmer Rouge declared victory. Ruling over a nation they called Democratic Kampuchea, they forced most of the urban population into the countryside where communally organized living and working conditions, lack of resources, and seething distrust and violence resulted in mass starvation and death from disease, torture, and execution. They labeled city dwellers and others with ties to the royal or republican regimes that had previously held power as enemies and turned children against their parents. For the most part, schooling was eliminated, as were markets and any form of religious worship. All loyalty was to be paid to a kind of amorphous anonymous entity, *Angkar*, which literally means "organization." By the end of almost four years of Khmer Rouge rule, between a quarter and a third of the country's population had perished. Both of Sophiline's brothers died, as did her father; however, her mother and her sisters survived.

In 1979, Vietnamese forces, along with former Khmer Rouge soldiers who had defected earlier, liberated Cambodia from the Khmer Rouge. Under the newly established People's Republic of Kampuchea, a Soviet-style communist regime (as opposed to the Maoist Khmer Rouge), a call went out to rebuild the country on many fronts, including the arts. The nation was in ruins—roads, electricity, schools, factories, irrigation schemes—most nonfunctioning or gone. Because the country was communist, and being run in collaboration with Vietnam, the United States placed an embargo on Cambodia; aid came from the Soviet Union and its allies. Meanwhile, war took root as forces loyal to all the regimes that had once ruled the nation (royalists, republicans, Khmer Rouge) fought from bases on the western border with Thailand to retake the country from the Vietnamese-backed regime in place.

In the midst of this ongoing conflict, the arts were beginning to thrive anew. An estimated 80–90 percent of the nation's professional performing artists—dancers, musicians, singers, actors—had perished in the Khmer Rouge years. Dance and music under the Khmer Rouge, much of it stylistically unrecognizable to Cambodians, served only the cause of the revolution. Those active as artists before the revolution, who by 1979 had managed to survive, together with Sophiline's generation, were eager to revive the arts, which they considered vital to the existence of their country, their people, and themselves. They were eager to dance, to make music, to perform (Shapiro 1994).

Art and War

Within months after the fall of the Khmer Rouge, surviving artists began crafting responses to the horrors they had just endured. Those who regrouped in Cambodia's western Battambang province, for example, created and performed *Jail Without Walls*, a play about life under that genocidal regime. In the midst of the civil war between the Khmer Rouge and the Vietnamese-backed communist government, and within constraints dictated by those in power, popular songs recalled, in harrowing detail, death and loss. Primary school children learned refrains about the murderous Khmer Rouge.

In times of war, journalist Chris Hedges (2002) writes, the nationalist narrative takes precedence over everything else. So we find songs, classical and folk dances, and traditional and new theater pieces extolling the friendship (at that time) of Vietnam, Cambodia, and Laos, and the cruelty and horrors of the Khmer Rouge years. Even well-known tales were reinterpreted to make a statement about the then-current political situation. One could say that staged or sung representations of the Khmer Rouge era served a political purpose—aiming to strengthen people's will to keep the fight going to prevent the Khmer Rouge from taking power once again. Indeed, when I started interviewing people in Cambodia in 1990, some told me that they had sent one child to be a soldier in the army and the other to be a dancer because both were fighting for the nation. Dance and theater students and teachers at the School of Fine Arts took dangerous trips by bus to contested territory throughout the country in the 1980s, staging productions at the frontlines (*samaraphum*) as, in their words, part of the battle.

But woven into or alongside the strands of political oversight were the threads of individual and communal need or desire to tell or dramatize or sing about the devastation people had all just been through, and its ongoing impact on their lives. By doing so, they were rejecting beliefs about victimhood—making a statement against inhumanity not only by exposing it but also by creating something thoughtful, perhaps entertaining, perhaps beautiful. They were making art. Velasco, Burnet, and Zucker in this volume also speak to the importance of narrative in processes of social recovery after mass violence—as ways to activate imagination, to provoke empathy, or to move toward coexistence.

In 1991, peace accords were signed between all of Cambodia's warring factions. The royalty returned, including Princess Norodom Buppha Devi, who had been a star of the royal dance troupe in the 1960s. Elections were held under United Nations auspices two years later. Cambodia became, once again, officially, a Kingdom.

The Imagination of Possibilities

It wasn't until 1999, however, that the Khmer Rouge completely disbanded. (By then all major Khmer Rouge leaders had defected to the Royal Government, been arrested, or died.) In that same year, Sophiline started asking—publicly, through dance and music—how those in positions of power can be so ruthless and so shortsighted. How can they repeat cycles of violence and destruction, not taking heed of their predecessors' mistakes? Why don't they attend to the needs of the people for whom they are in a position to make life-altering decisions?

Writer, historian, and activist Rebecca Solnit (2016) examines how hope can exist even in the aftermath of disaster and destruction. "Hope locates itself in the premises that we don't know what will happen and that in the spaciousness of uncertainty is room to act" (xiv). Hope, which Solnit says often initially percolates in the margins of society, is also located in the notion that we haven't given up all efforts toward creating meaning and finding dignity, even while grieving loss. The year 1999 was pivotal in Cambodian dance history and practice. Whereas in the immediate aftermath of mass violence Cambodians had both celebrated with social dancing on the street and engaged with the atrocities through performances that re-created aspects of that brutality, Sophiline was the first Cambodian choreographer to wonder aloud through movement, while still reeling from the hurt and damage of the genocide and the decade of war that followed, about other ways of being in the world beyond the inhumanity she and her fellow citizens experienced. She was the first to take this kind of imagining of possibilities to the stage.

Sophiline's first choreographed dance-drama was a Cambodian classical dance adaptation of Shakespeare's *Othello*, which she entitled *Samritechak*. *Othello* is a story of an outsider, of racism, and distrust and betrayal.[9] She has spoken of how she laments the lack of responsibility that leaders—those in her own country as well as elsewhere—take for their actions. In particular, she aimed her angst at the Khmer Rouge leadership who proclaimed their innocence regarding the genocide that shattered Cambodia and Cambodians. In Sophiline's *Samritechak*, the prince, once acknowledging responsibility for his crime—he had killed his wife (who was innocent of any wrongdoing) in a misplaced jealous rage—pleads for punishment. He models the actions of a powerful leader with the strength to concede the folly of his ways. Cloaked in a foreign story, this calling out of Khmer Rouge leaders for their crimes against humanity coincided with the first official accusation in the eventual development of the Khmer Rouge Tribunal: in September 1999, the Khmer Rouge senior military figure Chhit Choeun (aka Ta Mok) was charged with genocide and other crimes. Also, Kaing Guek Eav (aka Duch), the director of the infamous prison Tuol Sleng, was charged with murder and membership in an outlawed group. The Khmer Rouge Tribunal, officially known as the Extraordinary Chambers in the Courts of Cambodia (ECCC), became fully operational in 2007.[10]

Sophiline continued her prodigious output of choreographic works, many of which relate to the theme of leadership, and all of which engage with the imagination of possibilities. In *The Lives of Giants*, mentioned earlier in the chapter, she addresses the futility and destructiveness of cycles of revenge, taking as her starting-off point her own lived experience under various Cambodian regimes, including the Khmer Rouge. In the printed program for *The Lives of Giants* Sophiline states:

> Having grown up in a country where political systems changed frequently and often in violent ways, I have long recognized the persistence of corruption, arrogance, rigidity and loss of compassion that those with power resort to. . . . The abused become the abusers. . . . I believe compassion [may be] an antidote. When we acknowledge our own and our enemies' humanity, we create room to step away from inhumane behavior. I'm a realist and recognize that this is a difficult task. Compassion often loses out to adrenaline-fueled revenge. But I hope an alternative path exits. "What might have been" can become "what can be." (Shapiro 2010)

The Lives of Giants is a retelling of a rarely performed episode from the *Reamker*, the Cambodian version of the *Ramayana* epic of Indian origin. Akaeng Khameaso is a "giant"[11] in Preah Eyso's (Shiva's) heavenly realm.

Fig. 4.1. *The Lives of Giants*, Sophiline Arts Ensemble, Bryn Mawr College (United States, 2010). Photo by Chan Sopheap.

From the time of his childhood, Akaeng Khameaso has been the target of relentless taunting by a band of mischievous angels who tease him and knock on his head so many times that he eventually becomes bald. When he can no longer stand it, he complains to Preah Eyso about his plight and Preah Eyso gives the giant a magic finger with which to protect himself. When the angels return and resume knocking him on the head, he points his finger in their direction, injuring them. Drunk with power, he lays waste to heaven. The angels plead for Preah Eyso's help, but, worried for his own safety, he flees. Uma, the wife of Preah Eyso, turns to Preah Visnu (Vishnu) for help. Preah Visnu declares that the only solution is to kill Akaeng Khameaso. But Uma disagrees. She wants to teach Akaeng Khameaso compassion so that he'll renounce violence and use his power for the benefit of others. Uma draws Akaeng Khameaso in with a dance, but Preah Visnu becomes impatient and attacks, grabbing his adversary's finger and pointing it inward toward the giant who then inadvertently injures and incapacitates himself. Akaeng Khameaso, enraged, declares that he will be reborn with even more power in his next life so that nobody will be able to defeat him. He dies.

In *The Lives of Giants*, Uma, foreseeing the coming violence, laments the triumph of aggression and revenge over compassion and reconciliation:

> Now let's start to behave
> And be considerate to each other
> This is not karma
> This problem is caused by you
> You play with other people's misery
> And cause disaster
> And now my life is ruined, too.

Sophiline, as choreographer and lyricist, explains:

> In the original story, Uma did not play much of a role; she was just Shiva's consort. She didn't give any input into how to solve the problems. In my version I have her play an important role. After Shiva left, she had to carry this responsibility on her shoulders. In real life, so many women . . . carry responsibility, running families as well as contributing to society. . . . [Uma's] actions are a reflection of the ways in which women solve problems. (Shapiro in Buck et al. 2016, 74–75)

Ultimately, in the *Reamker*, Akaeng Khameaso is reborn as the ten-headed giant Reab (Ravana), and the cycle of war and revenge does continue. But in *The Lives of Giants*, Uma has at least made her plea.

Ethnomusicologist Thomas Turino writes of the arts—visual, literary, and performing—as:

> a type of *framed* activity where it is expected that the imagination and new possibilities will be given special license. As a result, the arts are a realm where the impossible or nonexistent or the ideal is imagined and made possible, and new possibilities leading to new lived realities are brought into existence in perceivable forms. (emphasis in original)[12]

Sophiline's dances and dance-dramas do this by unmasking or reconfiguring relationships of power.

Durational Aftermaths

Working toward a constructive future following mass violence is a long-term and multipronged undertaking. The immediate and extended "aftermaths" of that time of despair and wretchedness in Cambodia offer different contexts. It was two decades following the ouster of the Khmer Rouge from power that—on stage—Sophiline staked a claim for all Cambodians to a different kind of future. In a publication on the primacy of contextual considerations in proposing or understanding policies and practices during times of transition from mass violence and/or authoritarianism, Roger Duthie (2017) writes that "[i]nstitutions and structural inequalities can take decades to change, and political contexts can carry divisions and violence over from conflict to peace. . . . The tension between human rights principles and contextual opportunities must always be kept in mind" (12). Cambodia was just two years beyond a 1997 coup d'état as Sophiline built characters, story, and movement sequences around a crisis of leadership.

While Sophiline's *Samritechak* was a cry for Khmer Rouge accountability, her work since the premiere of that piece has continued to shine a light on the destructive legacies of the Khmer Rouge era and the depravity of political leaders' choices, as well as the absence of women's experience in the historical record, all in a context of government silencing of opinions and information that oppose the official line. Rather than seeking to antagonize government officials, believing that would be counterproductive, she hopes to inspire conversations and new perspectives among audience members, whether or not they are positioned to change policy, as a means of contributing to "an informed democracy" (Shapiro, personal communication, 2009). Because it is considered by many to be a valuable aspect of Cambodian culture, classical dance allows her to stimulate discussions in a nonthreatening way, which is thus at times subversive.[13]

Art and Peacebuilding

An emergent field of theory and practice related to the peacebuilding potential of the arts provides evidence of the depth and range of individuals' and communities' engagement with visual and expressive culture as part of post-conflict transitional justice and reconciliation endeavors. As Pablo de Greiff noted in the report cited earlier, legal, legislative, and civil society efforts alone cannot necessarily address a society's need for constructive attitudinal, behavioral, and affective/emotional changes following mass violence.

Engagement with the arts—as creative force (the composer, choreographer, playwright, painter, etc.), or performer, audience member, or other participant—has the potential to help people mourn losses and empathize with the suffering of others. Perhaps it may call the world's attention to the injustices portrayed and seek accountability while also imagining new possibilities for the future. This outline of the arts' potential in the aftermath of mass violence is drawn from *Acting Together: Performance and the Creative Transformation of Conflict*, a collection that illuminates the transformative potency that rests at the nexus of the performing arts and peacebuilding ventures.[14] The arts have the power to do this because they are often invested with a moral force that exceeds that of other communicative forms. This is especially true of certain genres of aesthetic practice within certain cultures, such as the classical dance of Cambodia.

Lederach (2005) notes that "[t]ime and again, social change that sticks and makes a difference has behind it the artist's intuition: the complexity of human experience captured . . . in a way that moves individuals and whole societies" (73). One key to nurturing such a prospect is recognizing what people already do and what communities already value.

> [A]rtists . . . , attuned to the needs and issues of their communities, intentionally choose topics, themes, or questions that address the experience of violence and its consequences and causes: the suffering of victims and survivors, the complicity and shame of perpetrators; the stereotypes and fears that impeded trusting relationships; and the hopes for a more equitable, just, and inclusive social order. . . . Audience members, witnesses, and participants correspondingly bring conflict dynamics into the creative space, as performances invite and support them to attend to memories, questions, emotions, dilemmas, fears, and hopes. (Cohen et al. 2011, Vol. II, 166)

During the Khmer Rouge years, dance, as recognizable to Cambodians, was forbidden. Only formulaic revolutionary pieces were allowed because classical dance was a threat: it creates bonds to spirits, gods, and goddesses, and forges continuity with the past, both kinds of relationships officially intolerable to that regime. Yet in private, traditional dance was so important to some Khmer Rouge cadres that they provided extra food to dancers who would perform for them without others knowing. Dance mattered. In the god-forsaken refugee camps in active war zones, Cambodians danced. They jumped off makeshift stages into trenches when artillery shells rained down. Then got back up and finished the shows for the thousands of fellow refugees standing in the tropical sun to watch. Dance mattered that much. Today, ritual dances help secure sufficient rainfall and pass on stories with lessons about morality to the next generation as they did in the pre-Khmer Rouge past. As for theatrical dances, their creators, the choreographers, continue to practice their trade but occasionally are questioned by the authorities for innovations in casting and costuming that, elsewhere, might seem quite benign.

Dance and music of the classical form have historically, in Cambodia, communicated ideas of appropriate social behavior, played out through nuances of loyalty, jealousy, and honor. The *Reamker* itself has even been a source for fortune-telling (Pech 1993, 16).[15] Thus Sophiline's embrace of an expressive medium that resonates broadly offers a platform for the inspiration of conversations about constructive change. And her innovations in selecting who can play what role (she was chastised by the government and threatened with not being allowed to take the performance on tour for casting men in certain roles in one of her dance-dramas), gesture and movement, attire, set design and music, stir further thoughtful engagement. "I look into carrying on the best practice, the best choreography, and the best music of the past. I try to focus on a continuity of spirit and creativity. I also question weaknesses within the canon and ask, can we make it better? We look for opportunities to do what has never been done before" (Shapiro, personal communication, 2017). Sophiline's breaking of convention rests on a platform of brilliant command of form upon which she innovates respectfully and imaginatively.[16]

Following the 2000 Cambodian premiere of Sophiline's *Samritechak*, two young men from the audience approached her. They wanted to know why the general (Othello) had committed suicide. "Because," Sophiline answered, "he had killed his wife for no good reason." "But generals don't kill themselves," they countered. Sophiline had turned the fact that no Khmer Rouge leaders had taken responsibility for their crimes on its head by exploring crises of leadership through a European story refashioned as a Cambodian dance-drama. *Samritechak* traveled to venues in Cambodia and the United States, including some cities with substantial diasporic Cambodian communities. In conversations with audience members, this relationship of power to responsibility was front and center.[17] People's next steps in terms of expectations or demands (if there were any) of political and other leaders remain unknown. We do know, however, that some seeds of thought were planted.

Theater director and scholar Roberto Gutierrez Varea (2011) has written:

> Whenever we have had to understand our world, our place and time, our sense of self and of belonging in a community with others, we've had to tell stories. . . . Perhaps nothing threatens our ability to create meaning more than becoming victims of violence. In its many shapes and forms, violence interrupts the telling of the story and our ability, as survivors, to make sense of it. . . . It is in these moments that we need our storytellers most. (153–54)

Stories and storytellers can, of course, be co-opted by and harnessed to benefit evil, too. Here, however, we are talking about storytellers who acknowledge people's dignity, putting pieces (back) together in ways that allow for and cultivate the capacity for rehumanizing oneself and others and for the rebuilding of relationships. Burnet's and Kahn's discussions (in this volume) of the stories told by rescuers speak to the important role of reclaiming dignity of victims and perpetrators, as both might eventually see the humanity in each other after the horrors of mass violence. Recognizing a common humanity is also an important aspect of empathy as described by McGrew (in this volume) when she writes about a Buddhist monk who shares narratives focused on compassion and humanity from a revered Buddhist leader.

In 2012, Sophiline was presenting her ensemble's version of an old dance-drama to her revered teacher Soth Sam-On, under whose guidance much of the re-creation of traditional dances had been done following the fall of the Khmer Rouge. Then ailing and weak, Soth Sam-On had just whispered her appreciation for the caliber of the dancers Sophiline was training and the quality of the choreography. "This is where the hope for Cambodian dance lies," she said before lifting her frail chest and head to the sky and letting loose a mournful cry, "They took all my friends away!"

"She was angry at the Khmer Rouge," Sophiline explains. "She was really angry at them for all they had taken away—the accomplishments of the arts of the 1960s and 1970s—and then it was all gone. When I saw her in that state, I started thinking about . . . how Cambodian dance might have advanced had we not lost so many and so much knowledge that they carried within them. I was angry, too. Every time I encountered loss and destruction I thought about [a] story that would allude to the depths of such damage and be a wake-up call regarding choices for the future" (Shapiro, personal communication, 2014). Sophiline is a storyteller whose work, like that of others facing or following unchecked violence anywhere in the world, though "rooted in grief and rage," nonetheless "point[s] toward vision and dreams."[18] The American composer Leonard Bernstein, grieving in the immediate aftermath of the assassination of US president John F. Kennedy in 1963, said, in "An Artist's Response to Violence":

> It is obvious that the grievous nature of our loss is immensely aggravated by the element of violence involved in it. And where does this violence spring from? From ignorance and hatred. . . . This must be the mission of every man of goodwill: to insist, unflaggingly, at risk of becoming a repetitive bore, but to insist on the achievement of a world in which the mind will have triumphed over violence.
>
> We musicians, like everyone else, are numb with sorrow at this murder, and with rage at the senselessness of the crime. But this sorrow and rage will not inflame us to seek retribution; rather they will inflame our art. Our music will never again be quite the same. This will be our reply to violence: to make music more intensely, more beautifully, more devotedly than ever before. (Bernstein 1963)

During the question-and-answer session with the artists following a performance of *The Lives of Giants* that I attended in the United States, a Cambodian American audience member asked if Sophiline was planning to write this story down. "It's so important that we Cambodians talk about these things. I mean these cycles of violence and revenge. We destroy our own futures. So will you publish this in writing? We all need to consider how to change things." Then another person in the audience stood up to reply: "But this is *Neak Kru* [Teacher] Sophiline's way of 'writing' it down. She's a dancer. She creates dances. This is a danced story that we can talk about. We don't need it in a magazine or book. Now that you are inspired, and so am I, we need to do something. Let's think about who we can talk to. What's our first step?"[19]

In 2016, Sophiline choreographed *Phka Sla* (Areka Flower), a stark dance-drama that shares actual stories of individuals forced to marry partners selected for them by the Khmer Rouge in a practice that was, in fact, institutionalized rape. As this chapter was being written (2018), this dance was touring Cambodia, adding to the historical record and engendering empathy (*anit aso*, in Khmer) for those who had survived the violence and indignity of forced marriage. Following many of the performances, formal discussions were facilitated about contemporary gender relations (and violence) as a means of building constructive futures.[20]

Conceived in concert with Cambodian nonprofit organizations address-ing trauma and peacebuilding, and with survivors themselves, *Phka Sla* was drawing crowds of hundreds at each performance.

All these years after the fact, the stories remain potent. Sot Sovanndy, a dancer in Sophiline's ensemble, shares that "even though this all happened so long ago, for the people of Cambodia, it's as if it just occurred yesterday. You could even consider forced marriage, in some sense, as worse than death. The suffering persists their entire lives." She explains that some of their audiences have been made up mostly of people whom the Khmer Rouge matched with a spouse against their will, including her mother, "who was only 17 at the time, and didn't know anything. . . . Many of those who were wronged in this way have never told their stories. They are ashamed or didn't think it would bring them any benefit in terms of dig-nity or respect" (Sot, personal communication, 2017). The four couple's stories in *Phka Sla* amplify the voices of these survivors.[21]

Kang Rithisal, executive director of Amrita Performing Arts, an orga-nization focused on contemporary Cambodian performance, recognized "that the performers were trained in the classical form, but with bodily possibility to do more. The ingenious choreography executed with superb technique, along with powerful narration, made for such intense mean-ing." Sophiline opened the event by ritually acknowledging the presence of forced marriage survivors who sat on mats in front of the rest of the audience. Kang explains:

> She bowed towards them three times, with her hands in a gesture of prayer and respect, which was profoundly moving. And then, for the entire performance, I found myself watching both the amazing choreography and the reaction of the audience members, many of whom were weeping openly, and being comforted with pats on the back or whispers into their ears by staff of the organizations who helped develop the project. (Kang, personal communication, 2017)[22]

Phka Sla exhibits innovative music as well as choreography. Him Sophy, the composer, received a PhD in music composition in the Soviet Union and has pioneered the expansion of possibilities for the *pin peat* ensemble. For this piece, he played with meter, instrumentation (includ-ing a *tro*—upright fiddle—from the Cambodian wedding ensemble), and quiet versus stridency in the soundscape. When Sophiline asked him to collaborate on the project, he "quickly agreed to do it, strongly believing that when I composed the music, remembering that time, my emotions will come out [through my composition] in response to the story that Sophiline wrote." Because, he explains, sometimes there are "no words to describe all the tragedies experienced under the genocidal regime, as artists we can create work to show the younger generation in a way they can understand" (Him, personal communication, 2017).

After every performance, male and female survivors of forced marriage—some still married to each other—tell the choreographer and dancers that they saw themselves and their experiences on stage, and that they are grateful. Some share that they brought family members to the show as a way of opening up about their pasts.

Kang Rithisal experienced the performance as an opportunity to empathize with and feel compassion for others, something critical not only for better understanding survivors of the Khmer Rouge but also for nurturing a more loving society moving forward.

> When one experiences the interaction of audience and performers, one feels compassion for the characters on the stage as well as the people watching. That compassion is like a vitamin that nourishes one's soul, a community's soul. When youth see that show, they get a lesson in compassion that I hope transcends the theater: I hope it helps them be more caring, in general, about others in their midst. (Kang, personal communication, 2017)

As it was becoming apparent in mid-2017 that the ECCC (Khmer Rouge Tribunal) might soon cease functioning, Youk Chhang (2017), executive director of the Documentation Center of Cambodia, published a statement declaring:

> Legal justice is not a replacement for historical enquiry, debate or education, and the latest announcement [of a permanent stay of proceedings at the Court] . . . does not end our country's responsibility to the survivors of this history and the next generation. . . . Truth must never become a prisoner of political circumstance, legal process or time. . . . Our obligation is not just to ourselves, to victims or to our society, but to the world, where our work will resonate either as proof of impunity or of mankind's resolve.

Each of Sophiline's projects aligns with that sense of obligation. All of them push some received knowledge aside and ask hard questions in the ongoing aftermath of genocide, thus contributing to efforts to both envision and work to realize communities of compassion and accountability. They also, in Sophiline's words, "make it impossible for genocidal people to complete their mission to eliminate the spirit of Cambodians from the face of the earth" (Shapiro, personal communication, 2014).

The dancers in her all-female ensemble have received training in choreography as well, gaining and displaying agency and critical thinking and technical skills. With their teacher as a model, they have begun to tackle questions of intergenerational mistrust, gender inequity, and environmental destruction through innovative movement, centered on classical dance aesthetics, but with the freedom and encouragement to experiment with the form. Some have even explored issues of power imbalances in Cambodian society.

Chey Chankethya, an accomplished choreographer (not affiliated with Sophiline's ensemble) who is a generation younger than Sophiline, with feet firmly planted in both classical and contemporary (Western-inspired) dance, was one of the first in Cambodia after Sophiline to pay attention through choreography to what an inheritance of the Khmer Rouge experience has wrought. A child of genocide survivors, her study of her relationship with her mother and her dance teacher, *My Mothers and I*, is nuanced and complex. In addition to acknowledging the brutality her mother and teacher endured, Chankethya presents the intimate impacts of its aftermath.[23] As does Sophiline, Chankethya, too, asks the audience to ponder implications of horrific violations of one's humanity for their lives today and in the future, and to consider what they (each/all) can do to take their society in new, more constructive directions.

Chankethya and other contemporary choreographers—originally trained as classical or folk dancers in Cambodia's School of Fine Arts with Sophiline and her peers as teachers—have had myriad opportunities to expand their knowledge and practice. Some have studied abroad; others participate in workshops and projects with international choreographers, composers, and artistic directors. Sophiline helped pave an initial path for their (eventual) radical breaks with tradition.

Whether as ritual, stage entertainment, or vernacular expression, presenting and inspiring an imagining of possibilities in the aftermath of mass violence through performance may challenge the status quo or open opportunities for the contemplation of alternative paths to reconciliation, peacebuilding, and community well-being. Gripping, sometimes humorous, and often dangerous—theater and social justice work that deals not only with history and memory but also with ongoing struggles such as racial, ethnic, and domestic violence, economic injustice, and indeed war, is underway across the globe. This chapter shines a spotlight on one artist in one particular context.

In Cambodia, to speak truth to power through a symbolic poetic language of movement, to explore the travesty of cycles of revenge and refusal of responsibility for what amounts to evil, to counter prevailing norms, reformulate traditional stories and thereby reflect upon personal or communal struggles (gender expectations, gender violence, a crisis of leadership), to speak in one's own defense when Ministry of Culture officials question your loyalty to country and tradition, and to innovate within tradition, are each revolutionary acts. Such acts, with their aesthetic, social, and political potency, call into question the existing state of affairs and model ways to take a leap into the unknown with a first step of imagining alternatives to continued violence and injustice.

NOTES

1. Inside Cambodia, she has served as an advisor to the Ministry of Culture and the Secondary School of Fine Arts; younger choreographers ask her for guidance and critique. Her honors outside the country include Guggenheim and Irvine Foundation Fellowships, the Nikkei Asia Prize for Culture, the US Artists Knight Fellow Award, and a National Heritage Fellowship from the United States National Endowment for the Arts. Her dances have been performed throughout Cambodia and elsewhere in Asia as well as across North America and Europe, including *Samritechak* at the Venice Theatre Biennale in 2003 and *Pamina Devi: A Cambodian Magic Flute* at the 2006 New Crowned Hope Festival in Vienna, honoring the 250th anniversary of Mozart's birth.

2. In an earlier essay, I address how Cambodian and Liberian dancers—separately, during years of civil and international war—harnessed their arts' significance to nurture shifts in attitude and even, in the Liberian case, the actual laying down of arms. "While constrained within the larger complex web of a specific protracted conflict, the individuals and troupes I discuss were inspired and determined to make a difference—to foster change—through what they knew to have resonance in their cultural, historical, political, and aesthetic contexts" (Shapiro-Phim 2013, 200).

3. The *pin peat* orchestra also accompanies Buddhist ceremonies and shadow puppet plays, among other forms of cultural expression.

4. Khmer is the name of the official language of Cambodia and the name of the country's majority ethnic group, though the words "Khmer" and "Cambodian" are often used interchangeably.

5. Sophiline began work on *The Lives of Giants* in 2009. Its world premiere was in 2010 in the United States. It is performed solely by the Sophiline Arts Ensemble, which Sophiline founded in Cambodia (originally as the Khmer Arts Ensemble) in 2006.

6. For more on trust and distrust before and after the Khmer Rouge see Eve Zucker, 2013, *Forest of Struggle*, Honolulu, University of Hawai'i Press, ch. 3.

7. Chérie Rivers writes about arts initiatives in the Democratic Republic of the

Congo where, "in instances of collective trauma, [and] where cultural mores limit processing of events, film can break the silence by speaking the 'unspeakable,' creating both a model and a space for conversation and healing" (2017, 253).

8. "The United States dropped . . . 2,756,941 tons of ordnance in 230,516 sorties on 113,716 sites [in Cambodia]." This amounts to hundreds of thousands of tons more than were dropped in World War II by all the allies combined (Owen and Kiernan, 2006).

9. The themes resonated with Sophiline when she studied this tragedy in college in the United States. She moved to California in 1991 and returned to Cambodia to set *Samritechak* on dancers at the Royal University of Fine Arts in 1999. Later, in 2006, she moved back to Cambodia permanently.

10. Ta Mok died in prison in 2006. Kaing Guek Eav was tried and, in 2010, found guilty. Two other senior officials of the Khmer Rouge regime were sentenced to life in prison in 2014 for crimes against humanity. Their second trial at the ECCC ended with guilty verdicts in 2018 for both on the charge of genocide. Both have publicly rejected responsibility for any wrongdoing.

11. In classical dance-dramas of Cambodia, the four main character types are the giants, princes or gods, princesses or goddesses, and the monkeys.

12. (Turino, 2008, 17–18). "Music, dance, festivals, and other public expressive cultural practices are a primary way that people articulate the collective identities that are fundamental to forming and sustaining social groups, which are, in turn, basic to survival. The performing arts are frequently fulcrums of identity, allowing people to intimately feel themselves part of the community through the realization of shared cultural knowledge . . ." (2). The imagining of an impossible or not-yet-existent ideal is also present in Zucker's chapter (this volume) in her discussion of the imaginary ancestral past as well as in the magic of the *Bon Dalien*.

13. Over the years she has been called out by different ministries for what the authorities read as misrepresentations of Cambodia and its classical dance.

14. Examples from across the globe include stage, street, and ceremonial practices both in the midst of crises of mass violence and in their aftermath. Cohen et al., 2011. See also Thompson et al., 2008; Jackson and Shapiro-Phim, 2008; O'Connell and El-Shawan Castelo-Branco, 2010, and LeBaron et al., 2013.

15. A version of a 1903 text of the *Reamker* is included in Chet, 2002.

16. In a book on music and social change, Rosenthal and Flacks (2012, 57) contend that, "[i]f working within a genre presents a framework that is one factor in guiding a listener's (and artist's) interpretation of meaning, challenging those conventions may be an even more obvious pointer for message and meaning. . . . The breaking of convention encourages the listener (and the artist in the act of creation) to work harder, interpreting the unexpected. . . ." Dance scholar and choreographer Ananya Chatterjea (2004, 47) writes about the "resistive choreographies" of Indian artist Chandralekha for whom, just as for Sophiline, there is a search "to understand the possible relevancies of these [classical dance] legacies of the body in contemporary times, how they come to be figured in today's world. Here, where the radical . . . is based on a recycling and revisioning of older cultural practices, past history and present creation coalesce and comment upon each other."

17. This is something I noted at performances I attended. It was also reported to me by dancers and by Sophiline.

18. Patrice Cullors, in King (2014), uses these words in speaking of the Black Lives Matter movement in the United States.

19. Postperformance discussion, Bryn Mawr College, United States, 2010.

20. Llanos in this volume also speaks to the importance of sharing public narratives of gender-based violence as a way to open discussions, build networks, and to imagine new futures.

21. This resonates with Ricardo Velasco's description (this volume) of the situation for some in Colombia, reminding us to ask whose voices aren't being heard and what are the structural and/or symbolic obstacles to their inclusion in testimony and discussion focused on memorialization and/or any other aspect of post-mass violence initiatives. The *Phka Sla* initiative was a collective and moral reparation project of the ECCC. Reparation undertakings are meant to contribute to the betterment of conditions for survivors. In this case, the court acknowledged the crimes against survivors of forced marriage and dignified them with a presentation in a highly regarded art form plus forums for discussion, especially with younger generations. The court thus also honored the resonance of classical dance for communities across Cambodia.

22. Kdei Karuna (a peacebuilding organization) and the Transcultural Psychosocial Organization (a mental health agency) were among the collaborating entities, which also included Bophana Audiovisual Resource Center (responsible for documentation) and the Sophiline Arts Ensemble.

23. Chey Chankethya choreographed *My Mothers and I* in 2012. She participated in a forum that I organized and moderated the following year, during which she discussed her approach to this dance: "Body Destroyed/Body Remembered: Genocide, Civil War and Performance," Performing Diaspora Symposium, CounterPULSE, San Franscisco, August 2013. A number of additional gifted choreographers are at work in Cambodia as well. Some are inspired by abstractions such as form, shape, and sound; others by concerns about pressing social justice issues, forbidden love, or simply good storytelling, whatever the topic. For the most part, these choreographers create and perform what they call contemporary, as opposed to classical, dance. One exception is Prumsodun Ok whose Prumsodun Ok & NATYARASA dance ensemble, Cambodia's first gay dance troupe, restages Khmer classical dances and creates new ones.

REFERENCES

Bernstein, Leonard. 1963. "An Artist's Response to Violence—Memorial to John F. Kennedy, Night of Stars, Madison Square Garden, November 25, 1963." https://leonardbernstein.com/lectures/speeches/jfk-memorial-speech

Buck, Ralph, Nicholas Rowe, and Toni Shapiro-Phim. 2016. *Talking Dance: Contemporary Histories from the South China Sea.* London: I. B. Tauris.

Carter, Alexandra. 1998 [2003]. "Feminist Strategies for the Study of Dance." In *The Routledge Reader in Gender and Performance*, edited by Lizbeth Goodman with Jane de Gay, 247–50. London: Routledge.

Chatterjea, Ananya. 2004. *Butting Out: Reading Resistive Choreographies Through Works by Jawole Willa Jo Zollar and Chadralekha.* Middletown, CT: Wesleyan University Press.

Chet Chan. 2002. *The Reamker, Painted by Chet Chan.* Edited by Ly Daravuth and Ingrid Muan. Phnom Penh: JSRC Printing House.

Chhang, Youk. 2017. "Cambodians Must Find Their Own Justice as Khmer Rouge Tribunal Breaks Down." *Southeast Asia Globe*, June 15. http://sea-globe.com/category/cambodia

Cohen, Cynthia E., Roberto Gutiérrez Varea, and Polly O. Walker, eds. 2011. *Acting Together: Performance and the Creative Transformation of Conflict*, Volumes I and II. Oakland: New Village Press.

de Greiff, Pablo. 2015. *Report of the Special Rapporteur on the Promotion of Truth, Justice, Reparation and Guarantees of Non-recurrence*, Human Rights Commission. A/HRC/30/42 VI. 92 [plus] VI. B. 95, pages 21–22, September 7, 2015. Accessed January 10, 2017, http://www.ohchr.org/Documents/Issues/Truth/A-HRC-30-42.pdf

Duthie, Roger. 2017. "Introduction." In *Justice Mosaics: How Context Shapes Transitional Justice in Fractured Societies*, edited by Roger Duthie and Paul Seils. New York: International Center for Transitional Justice. https://www.ictj.org/justice-mosaics

Hedges, Chris. 2002. *War Is a Force that Gives us Meaning*. New York: Public Affairs.

Jackson, Naomi, and Toni Shapiro-Phim, eds. 2008. *Dance, Human Rights, and Social Justice: Dignity in Motion*. Lanham, MD: Scarecrow Press.

King, Jamilah. 2014. "Facing Race Spotlight: Organizer Alicia Garza on Why Black Lives Matter." *Colorlines*, October 9. http://www.colorlines.com/articles/facing-race-spotlight-organizer-alicia-garza-why-black-lives-matter

LeBaron, Michelle, Carrie MacLeod, and Andrew Flower Acland, eds. 2013. *The Choreography of Resolution: Conflict, Movement, and Neuroscience*. Chicago: American Bar Association.

Lederach, John Paul. 2005. *The Moral Imagination: The Art and Soul of Peacebuilding*. Oxford: Oxford University Press.

O'Connell, John Morgan, and Salwa El-Shawan Castelo-Branco, eds. 2010. *Music and Conflict*. Chicago: University of Illinois Press.

Owen, Taylor, and Ben Kiernan. 2006. "Bombs Over Cambodia." *The Walrus*, October: 62–69. Yale University Genocide Studies Program. http://gsp.yale.edu/sites/default/files/walrus_cambodiabombing_oct06.pdf

Pech Tum Kravel. 1993. *Sbek Thom: Khmer Shadow Theater*. Ithaca: SEAP Publications, Cornell University.

Phim, Toni, and Ashley Thompson. 1998. *Dance in Cambodia*. Oxford: Oxford University Press.

Rivers, Chérie. 2013 [2017]. "Beyond 'Victimology': Generating Agency Through Film in Eastern Democratic Republic of the Congo." In *Art and Trauma in Africa: Representations of Reconciliation in Music, Visual Arts, Literature and Film*, edited by Lizelle Bisschoff and Stefanie Van de Peer, 251–71. London: I. B. Tauris.

Rosenthal, Rob, and Richard Flacks. 2012. *Playing for Change: Music and Musicians in the Service of Social Movements*. Boulder: Paradigm Press.

Shapiro, Sophiline Cheam. 2008. "Cambodian Dance and the Individual Artist." In *Dance, Human Rights, and Social Justice: Dignity in Motion*, edited by Naomi Jackson and Toni Shapiro-Phim, 166–67. Lanham, MD: Scarecrow Press.

Shapiro. Sophiline Cheam. 2010. *The Lives of Giants* (Program Notes).

Shapiro, Toni. 1994. *Dance and the Spirit of Cambodia*. PhD diss., Cornell University.

Shapiro-Phim, Toni. 2002. "Dance, Music, and the Nature of Terror in Democratic Kampuchea." In *Annihilating Difference: The Anthropology of Genocide*, edited by Alexander Hinton, 179–93. Berkeley: University of California Press.

Shapiro-Phim, Toni. 2013. "Finding New Futures: Dancing Home." In *The Choreography of Resolution: Conflict, Movement, and Neuroscience*, edited by Michelle LeBaron, Carrie MacLeod, and Andrew Floyer Acland, 197–207. Chicago: American Bar Association.

Solnit, Rebecca. 2016. *Hope in the Dark.* 3rd ed. Chicago: Haymarket Books.

Thompson, James, Jenny Hughes, and Michael Balfour. 2008. *Performance in Place of War*. Chicago: University of Chicago Press.

Turino, Thomas. 2008. *Music as Social Life: The Politics of Participation.* Chicago: University of Chicago Press.

Varea, Roberto Gutiérrez. 2011. "Fire in the Memory." In *Acting Together: Performance and the Creative Transformation of Conflict*. Vol. I, 153–57. Oakland: New Village Press.

Zucker, Eve. 2013. *Forest of Struggle: Moralities of Remembrance in Upland Cambodia.* Honolulu: University of Hawai'i Press.

Part 2 | Empathy

5 | "You Can't Bake Bread without the Flour"

Empathy and Coexistence in Cambodia

Laura McGrew

Sam Nop was walking along a sandy rice paddy dike in the hot midday sun of Cambodia's Angkor Wat region, when he recognized a prison guard who had tortured him during the Khmer Rouge period—both were shocked to see each other.[1] When the Khmer Rouge ruled Cambodia between 1975 and 1979, more than a quarter of the population perished from overwork in the harsh labor camp environment; disease due to a complete absence of health care; starvation because of radical agricultural and economic policies; and execution, torture, and imprisonment resulting from purges of the educated, civil servants, and real and imagined enemies. A year had passed since the end of the Khmer Rouge regime, but Mr. Nop easily recognized the prison guard who had severely beaten him for picking up a discarded jackfruit seed. Mr. Nop remembered each and every one of the sixty prison guards and assumed all had blood on their hands—the guards could not refuse to carry out orders, or they would be killed. When the prison guard saw Mr. Nop, the guard's face turned white with fear but gradually regained color after they spoke for some time, and when Mr. Nop assured the guard that he did not blame him and was not going to seek revenge. After the guard apologized, Mr. Nop felt some relief and recognized that the guard would have been killed if he had not done what he was told. He felt empathy toward the former guard because it was not possible to refuse orders of Khmer Rouge leaders, and Mr. Nop saw the fear and the guilt that the guard carried around with him today. Mr. Nop also felt empathy for the ragged condition of the former guard in the present—life was difficult for everyone in Cambodia in 1979 in contrast to the guard's privileged position during the Khmer Rouge period.

The term empathy has entered the modern lexicon in the last decade, with a multitude of articles and references in academia and in the popular press, including notably an examination of the neuroscience of empathy.[2] In brief, empathy is defined as the ability of one person to move beyond sympathy or feeling sorry for "the other"[3] to step into their shoes and imagine what the other is experiencing and feeling, and then to communicate that back; the utility of empathy is its role in fostering coexistence and reconciliation, and ultimately, a peaceful society. In light of the various definitions of the processes and components of empathy found in the literature, in 2017 I sought out the views of a small sample of Cambodians working in the fields of dialogue facilitation, transitional justice, and other activities aimed toward recovery from mass violence. I also returned to research I conducted between 2006 and 2013 with victims, bystanders, and accused perpetrators, examining their opinions and feelings on empathy and its related concepts such as compassion, forgiveness, and mutual understanding. Do perpetrators, bystanders, and victim/survivors in Cambodia exhibit empathy toward each other in this post-conflict environment?

Based on my research and the literature, while the majority of victims have forgiven accused perpetrators of crimes committed during the Khmer Rouge period and shown empathy toward them, very few perpetrators and former Khmer Rouge cadre have expressed empathy toward their former victims. My research has shown, as has research by Angeliki Kanavou and Kosal Path (2017), that former Khmer Rouge more often focus on their *own* suffering and perceptions of heroism during and after the regime. Although empathy is an important building block of reconciliation, it is difficult to observe, thus researching empathy is notoriously problematic with few specific measures to study it. Nonetheless, the absence or presence of empathy is important to consider in the context of social recovery in the aftermath of mass violence.

Empathy is intricately linked to the other key concepts discussed in this volume, namely imagination and resilience. First, imagination is needed to understand what the "other" is feeling and step into their shoes. Second, coexistence (or the possibility of the ideal of reconciliation) is an underlying goal or condition desired after mass violence so that communities can live in peace. Healing, at least partially through the development of empathy, is one of the major processes needed to coexist peacefully. Third, resilience is also linked to empathy, in that people who develop empathy for others who have harmed them, or whom they have harmed, exhibit resilience and an improved ability to recover from mass violence.

Methodology

This chapter is based on my dissertation research conducted between 2006 and 2008 of a nonrandom convenience sample of more than 150 interviewees using a semi-structured questionnaire through which I examined a variety of research questions related to reconciliation.[4] The transcripts were analyzed using the NVIVO[5] computer program, classifying key words and examining theories based on the literature. In addition, I conducted 101 follow-up interviews with 120 people (individually and in small focus groups) in 2013 that provided additional data. For this chapter, in 2017, I conducted an additional ten interviews focusing specifically on empathy with Cambodian nongovernmental organization (NGO) staff persons working on dialogue and reconciliation programs with victims and perpetrators in Cambodia, as well as with one Buddhist monk and two self-identified Khmer Rouge victims.[6]

Background

History of Cambodia

By 1979, more than 1.7 million of Cambodia's population had perished under the draconian Khmer Rouge regime—out of 7 million in 1975 (Ciorciari and Chhang 2005, 250). The Khmer Rouge attempted to create an agrarian utopia modeled on the Chinese Cultural Revolution and in so doing targeted civil servants and those they considered intellectual "new people," idealizing the uneducated rural "old or base people." Although in the 1960s Cambodia under King Norodom Sihanouk had joined the non-aligned movement, war in Vietnam spilled over as the communist North Vietnamese ran portions of the infamous Ho Chi Minh Trail through eastern Cambodia and bombing campaigns by the United States killed tens of thousands. On April 17, 1975, Cambodia fell to the Khmer Rouge, resulting in "3 years, 8 months, and 20 days" of terror, mass population movements, torture, summary execution, starvation, overwork, and complete lack of social services (health care, education, etc.). Finally, in January 1979 Vietnamese troops entered Cambodia and pushed the Khmer Rouge to the Thai-Cambodian border, where a civil war (between the Eastern Bloc-supported People's Republic of Kampuchea and the Western Bloc-supported Non-Communist Resistance including the Khmer Rouge) ensued for a decade. The "Paris Peace Accords" in 1991 led to a UN mission

(United Nations Transitional Authority in Cambodia or UNTAC) from 1992–1993 where free elections, human rights education, refugee return, and other interventions created relative stability, though plagued by conflicts between the various Cambodian political factions.

Today, thirty years later, though the government is rife with corruption and human rights abuses abound, Cambodia remains largely at peace. The population is 98 percent Buddhist, and the government is a constitutional monarchy. Cambodia is primarily an agrarian society, with 80 percent of the population of sixteen million living in rural areas, and 49 percent of the population is under twenty-five years of age (*The World Factbook* 2019). While most non-Khmer Rouge at least initially returned to their home villages after the fall of the regime in 1979, or in 1993 after the UNTAC period, many Khmer Rouge gathered in Khmer Rouge strongholds that still exist around the country today. In these areas most of the residents are former Khmer Rouge, but their numbers have since been diluted with an influx of thousands who came seeking land and employment opportunities. While in urban areas people often do not know their neighbors' backgrounds, in rural villages everyone knows everyone—in communities all across Cambodia, victims, bystanders, and perpetrators (with all the fluid identities in between) are living side by side, in various states of coexistence.

Who Were the Perpetrators?

In this chapter, the terms "perpetrator" and "bystander" include former Khmer Rouge ("base" people, cadres, security personnel, or soldiers) who identify themselves as (former) Khmer Rouge and who have been accused by others of harming or killing others during the Khmer Rouge period. Some were accused of planning, some of ordering, and some of directly killing others. The Khmer Rouge leadership often transferred their cadre away from their home villages and placed them into leadership roles in other villages. Moving people from place to place was common practice across the country. But in some cases, lower-level perpetrators such as spies (*chhlop*), the henchmen who executed people or led them to their deaths, were kept in the same communities and were known by the victims. Mr. Pel, one of the key informants in my research, was in this situation, because as a *chhlop* he was responsible for bringing many victims to the prison or killing field to be executed. This "'intimate' crime leaves particularly deep marks, both individually and collectively, weakening the regulatory foundations of society" (Pouligny, Chesterman, and Schnabel 2007, 7).

Most of those within the Khmer Rouge movement, however, were also victims of the regime and its harsh conditions, having lost family members and friends through involuntary military service, hard work, and increasingly vicious internal purges. In addition to the killings and discrimination against the "new" people by the Khmer Rouge, there were also multiple internal purges, and most of the 15,000 people or more killed at the infamous Tuol Sleng Prison in Phnom Penh were Khmer Rouge cadre. While the focus of the trials for the Khmer Rouge leaders (the Extraordinary Chambers in the Courts of Cambodia or ECCC), as well as the focus of media reports and the international community, has been on the suffering of victim/survivors, gradually over time there has been increased attention to the (usually lesser) difficulties of the Khmer Rouge cadres and base people, including lower level perpetrators.

Trauma and Trust

Traumatic events that almost all Cambodians were subject to are events that "involve threats to lives or bodies; produce terror and feelings of helplessness; overwhelm an individual's or group's ability to cope or respond to the threat; lead to a sense of loss of control; and challenge a person's or group's sense that life is meaningful and orderly" (Yoder 2005, 10). Of course, the victim/survivors (new people and non-Khmer Rouge) experienced more trauma than those in more powerful positions including Khmer Rouge bystanders, cadre, and perpetrators. Layered on top of these specific traumatic events is the trauma caused by past and present structural violence that includes poverty and the lack of development, security, and human rights, especially in the rural areas.

After the terror, starvation, overwork, and instability of Cambodia's past, especially during the Khmer Rouge period, many Cambodians are plagued with health problems that include mental health disorders, diabetes, hypertension, and heart disease (Scully et al. 2010). The mental health disorders include major depression, anxiety disorder, post-traumatic stress disorder (PTSD), and conversion disorder (loss of specific sensory or motor functions without any organic cause) (Sonis et al. 2009; de Jong, Komproe, and van Ommeren 2003; van de Put and Eisenbruch 2002, 104).[7] Second generation effects have also been documented (Field, Muong, and Sochanvimean 2011; Kanavou, Path, and Doll 2010). However, the very concept of trauma and PTSD in non-Western countries has been debated, as these categories may not be sufficient to understand all the underlying cultural and psychological meanings (Beneduce 2007, 43;

Pouligny, Chesterman, and Schabel 2007, 6). For example, Cambodian psychiatrist Dr. Sotheara Chhim (2013) describes the conditions of *phey-khlach* (double fear), *dam-doeum-kor* (planting a kapok tree, meaning to remain mute), and a loss of togetherness as conditions beyond PTSD that better describe Cambodians' responses to trauma. These conditions are all obstacles to empathy and coexistence.

As the Khmer Rouge methodically broke family and community ties, asked people to report on or even kill others including family members, and conducted vicious purges, resultant trauma is pervasive and it is not surprising that mistrust is widespread (Zucker 2013; Eisenbruch 2007, 93). Fabienne Luco (2002), an anthropologist with extensive experience in Cambodia, observed that "at the slightest hurdle, mistrust comes running back" (87), and also emphasized the pressure in society to not draw attention to oneself, to avoid causing trouble, and the divisions between insiders and outsiders in the community (13–14). All of these factors (the aftereffects of trauma, lack of trust and togetherness, fear, and structural violence in today's society) combine to create challenges to reintegration of victims and perpetrators after mass violence and are obstacles to social recovery in Cambodia and in other post-conflict countries. One route to rebuilding society is the development of empathy between victims and perpetrators, albeit for differing reasons and in differing ways.

From Violent Conflict to Coexistence—Through Empathy

Both the acts of, and the trauma from, mass violence result in many harms and much suffering such as anger, depression, fear, hatred, and lack of trust. Healing from mass violence accordingly requires dealing with these strong emotions. Victims have often been dehumanized (which is integral to allowing perpetrators to justify their actions). To recover from mass violence, rehumanization and the development of empathy are important processes of healing.

What Is Empathy?

Several researchers in the field of neuroscience have mapped brain function in laboratory experiments, and some suggest that oxytocin, a chemical produced in the brain, increases our ability to feel empathy (Barraza and Zak 2009; Zak 2008, 91, 95). Emile Bruneau uses brain scans and psychological tests to study empathy to improve conflict intervention programs (for example, he found that short narratives exchanged between rival groups helped increase empathy), and to examine how empathy is suppressed during mass violence (Bruneau, Cikara, and Saxe 2015; Cikara, Bruneau, and Saxe 2011; Interlandi 2015). In spite of its rising popularity, empathy remains an elusive topic and is hard to measure (Interlandi 2015; Decety 2011, 35). There is even a backlash seen, for example, in Paul Bloom's book *Against Empathy*, where Bloom decries the more than 1,500 books on Amazon with "empathy" in the title or subtitle (Senior 2016).

Yet the development of empathy is described as a fundamental component of reconciliation, though there are some variations between definitions (Halpern and Weinstein 2004, 567; Huyse 2003, 20; and Schreiter 1992, 52–53). In one analysis, Jodi Halpern and Harvey Weinstein (2004) break down empathy to include three attributes: (1) the ability to individualize and resonate emotionally; (2) expressing curiosity about the "other's" perspective; and (3) developing the ability to tolerate ambiguity (571–72). Empathy can also be considered a distinct part of reconciliation: Luc Huyse (2003) described empathy as the third stage of reconciliation, the stages being first, replacing fear by nonviolent coexistence; second, building confidence and trust; and third, moving toward empathy (19–21). Theresa Wiseman's (1996) scheme of four components of empathy: (1) seeing the world as the other sees it; (2) being nonjudgmental; (3) understanding the other's feelings; and (4) communicating your understanding of the other's feelings is referenced widely by Brown and others.[8] Another aspect of empathy is related to gaining self-confidence, acknowledging humanity in the other, and distinguishing between a person and their actions (Huyse 2003, 20). "Empathy comes with the victims' willingness to listen to the reasons for the hatred of those who caused their pain and with the offenders' understanding of the anger and bitterness of those who suffered . . ." (Huyse 2003, 21). These definitions are similar in their focus on listening and understanding the other and somehow expressing understanding; it is through such processes that reconciliation may be achieved.

Empathy can be expressed in many ways—words, affect and expression, gestures, and actions: Jean Decety (2011) differentiates between a large range of affective, cognitive, and behavioral components of empathy (35). While empathy can be felt and expressed toward strangers, this chapter focuses on empathy between direct victims and perpetrators who experienced the trauma of the Khmer Rouge period, rather than between the Khmer Rouge senior leaders and their tens of thousands of victims.

Furthermore, I distinguish between empathy of victims toward perpetrators, of perpetrators toward victims, and the empathic listening demonstrated by Cambodian health and NGO workers toward their clients or beneficiaries.

The mind, heart, and emotions are all important aspects of empathy.[9] Ron Kraybill (1988) suggests the healing process involves a "unity of head and heart" (8). Similarly, Halpern and Weinstein (2004) suggest that reconciliation is a two-part process—intellectual (mind) and emotional (heart): "If reconciliation is not merely an intellectual but also an emotional process (*contritio cordis*), then a major role in making reconciliation between people possible, in generating a capacity for reconciliation, will be played by the education of attitudes, or what used to be known by the old-fashioned term 'cultivation of the heart'" (568). This observation can also be applied to the much more achievable condition of coexistence.

Perception is at the core of empathy—to empathize with others, you must see, feel, or perceive the condition of the other—including the feelings of the other. And on the path from violence to coexistence and reconciliation, changes in people's perceptions are essential to rehumanization and understanding: being able to show interest in "the other" and in their subjective interpretations is key (Halpern and Weinstein 2004, 565).

Closely related to empathy are the following terms:[10] compassion (sympathetic consciousness of others' distress together with a desire to alleviate it); sympathy (the act or capacity of entering into or sharing the feelings or interests of another); and pity (sympathetic sorrow for one suffering, distressed, or unhappy). Halpern and Weinstein (2004) describe the difference between sympathy and empathy as imagination: while both sympathy and empathy require "emotional resonance" and shared emotion, empathy goes a step further as perceptions are changed and individuals are imagined in a different way with real curiosity, and thereby breaking through stereotypes (268–69). Decety (2011) also notes that empathy can be generated from imagination (35).

While much research on individuals and communities after mass violence focuses on negative effects, Ervin Staub and Johanna Vollhardt (2008) have researched how experiences of, and psychological changes from, mass violence can "transform past suffering into altruism" such that such resilience after trauma can lead to empathy and altruism as positive "post-traumatic growth" outcomes (267–68). Burnet and Kahn (this volume) describe how narratives from courageous rescuers in Rwanda and elsewhere have served to model empathy and promote peaceful coexistence, again modeling positive change.

Dehumanization and Rehumanization

Dehumanization occurs when opponents see each other as less than human, as hated enemies, or even animals thereby allowing one group or individual to see the other as no longer sharing the same moral codes; it is characterized by a lack of empathy. Dehumanization arises out of group identity, essentially in-group favoritism and out-group exclusion or persecution (Halpern and Weinstein 2004, 566–67). More recent research indicates multiple factors that may work alone or in combination with dehumanization that can result in genocide and allow perpetrators to justify their violent behavior; these factors include in-group norms, peer pressure, coercion, opportunism, and obedience to authority. Research with Khmer Rouge cadre indicate their participation was based on vertical coercion (Williams 2018), and Kanavou and Path (2017) found that obedience to authority amongst Khmer Rouge cadre was a strong factor enabling their participation in violence; this tendency toward obedience persists to the present. Both perpetrators and victims may become dehumanized during periods of mass violence. The degree of dehumanization and the direct experience of dehumanizing practices an individual has experienced affects all future relationships. To understand recovery, one must understand the way dehumanization was created through the construction and deconstruction of the "enemy" (Theidon 2007, 103). The Khmer Rouge regime was notorious for using euphemisms (for example, to take for "education" or "re-education" meant to be killed), terrifying aphorisms ("to keep you is no gain, to destroy you is no loss"), and code words (to smash), all to signify death and killing in order to dehumanize the victims and to avoid dealing directly with atrocities. Cambodians today often repeat the Khmer Rouge slogans and euphemisms to describe the horror of the regime and their feelings in the past and present.

After people have been dehumanized, the process of rehumanization is a component of reconciliation whereby formerly opposing parties recognize each other's humanity and integrity, and thereby create bonds between them (Hicks 2008, 12–13). Halpern and Weinstein (2004) posit that processes of rehumanization, including the ability to see enemies as "real" people, are necessary after mass violence, and that these lead to empathy and eventually reconciliation—reconstruction of social ties and networks is a crucial aspect of rebuilding peace (562). Burnet and Kahn (this volume) also focus on the importance of recognizing a common humanity in all people as the core element driving courageous rescuer behavior, another example of empathy. All three processes (empathy, rehumanization, and coexistence) involve the development of being able to see the perspective of the other and all involve healing. Many respondents spoke about the Khmer Rouge regime's numerous methods of dehumanizing their victims, and though they remained disturbed by the memories, they expressed triumph in their ability to survive and thrive—especially with the dissolution of the Khmer Rouge movement and the ongoing trials against the leaders.

Empathy in Cambodia

Definitions of Empathy in Cambodia

Of the ten people I interviewed in 2017 specifically about empathy, five were confused about the meaning of the word but all were able to describe the concept. Indeed, there is no single word in the Cambodian language that defines empathy. Several also mentioned how difficult it was to measure, for example: "Empathy between victim and perpetrators? I have no concrete answer to that. . . . I do not have a practical actual observation of it" (IV# 4e). However, the NGO workers in the field of mental health and historical memory were clearer on the term than other interviewees—though when I opened my interviews with questions about empathy, those who had learned about empathic listening immediately thought of their own ability to empathize (and their need to limit it for their emotional well-being) rather than their observations of empathy demonstrated between victims and perpetrators. For example, this NGO fieldworker admitted his confusion but then went on to describe empathy quite clearly: "This word seems difficult, both the meaning and translation is difficult, as it seems like it is more internal, but we show it through action. . . . I am confused between sympathy and empathy, the words are similar, the meaning is also similar. . . . Empathy is like we understand people . . . and we use our feelings to understand their feelings, but mostly we show empathy through our actions or feelings" (IV# 3e). He also noted the importance of perceptions in the process of empathizing, as discussed above: "We also use our feelings, our perceptions, to understanding someone, if they are in a similar situation, or a different one" (IV# 3e).

There were several words in the Cambodian language (Khmer) used to define the words sympathy and empathy, but the mostly commonly used ones were: *anut* or *anut ahso* for sympathy (*anut* is also translated into English as pity) and *kar yol jchet* (directly translated as understanding the heart)[11] or *yok dung pi knyear* (directly translated as mutual understand-

ing) for empathy. Both Cambodian respondents and the scholarly literature at times have difficulty differentiating between sympathy and empathy. As one NGO worker who uses empathic listening in her work noted:
"*Yol jchet* is empathy. But sympathy? I can explain it in English but not in
Khmer" (IV# 4e). Several interviewees differentiated between sympathy
being negative and empathy being positive. For example, "Feeling *anut*
[sympathy or pity], you put yourself above, and you push them down.
When I cry, I don't want someone to *anut* me and look at me. If they listen
to me and say 'ohhhh, I feel worse, I feel vulnerable and like a victim. . . .'
Feeling *anut* doesn't help and doesn't teach people, but empathy does"
(IV# 4e). The Buddhist monk I interviewed on empathy brought Buddhist
teachings into his definition, promoting meditation to empathize with
others: "Only when we know our minds then we can know the minds of
others too, we can learn everything in us, we know ourselves and then we
know others" (IV# 5e).

There are various views on the sequencing of coexistence and reconciliation processes, which include expressions of empathy and sympathy,
among the 2017 interviewees as well as in the literature. However, all
sources agreed that empathy was a deeper, more complex concept than
sympathy and was a requirement for deep reconciliation. For example,
this NGO worker observed: "Empathy is the way we build up to have reconciliation in the final step, we have to go through empathy first. It is difficult to have reconciliation without empathy. If you don't show empathy,
your feelings are disconnected and it's not true reconciliation" (IV# 1e).
Another NGO worker noted: "Healing without empathy? I think not. It's
an entire process, you can't bake the bread without the flour" (IV# 4e).

As in the literature defining empathy discussed above, listening to "the
other," seeing different points of view (even if you do not agree with them),
and perceiving people in a new light are important first steps of the processes of empathy and reconciliation. My earlier interviewees supported
this definition, and this NGO interviewee who was involved in dialogue
programs (designed to improve community relations in villages of perpetrators and their direct victims) explained, "Empathy—is going beyond
[sympathy], it is deeper. We need to show empathy to people, especially
when we are working with victims and survivors; we must show them that
we are caring and respectful. We do this by listening carefully to their stories" (IV# 1e). Several chapters in this volume speak to the importance of
listening and storytelling (or narratives), including via the arts and traditions, in the processes of peaceful coexistence (see Burnet, Kahn, Llanos,
and Velasco).

This NGO respondent defined empathy in terms of the processes of active listening without judgment and rehumanization:

> Empathy is being able to understand the situation of the other, deeply, and the experience that the person is going through now, through active listening. It means to really listen to what is behind the words, instead of interjecting our own ideas, judgements, or perceptions. . . . As I learn more, and the other person feels secure and understood, this makes us feel as one, not divided. If everyone could exercise empathetic listening to conversations, we could humanize everyone, and it would be harder to commit violence—this is the core of the humanization of the others. (IV# 7e)

As mentioned above, empathy can be expressed in different ways: words, gestures, and actions. However, Staub and Vollhardt (2008) argue that true change and real empathy only occur when concrete actions are taken (270). Similarly, several Cambodian interviewees spoke about the importance of taking action to help others as part of empathy, as related to the difference between sympathy and empathy, such as this 2017 NGO worker interviewee:

> Empathy is more than sympathy which is the first step of the process; another step is empathy when you care, when you listen to the story of the survivors. With sympathy, you listen and respect their voice but empathy is beyond that—what can you do to make that situation change, to improve the situation that they are in now. For example, if those people have the status of victims, how can we work to support them to move out from victim to survivor. In this way empathy happens. . . . In Cambodian culture, and also in Asia generally, it is difficult to say "I'm sorry," but sometimes they take some action instead of using words. (IV# 1e)

Among traditionally conflict-avoiding Cambodians, verbal expressions of apology or accusations of misdoing are rare—thus gestures and actions are particularly important to express empathy and other emotions. I have written elsewhere (McGrew 2018) about accused former Khmer Rouge perpetrators' actions toward their communities after mass violence. Several accused perpetrators have become involved in religious practices—perhaps to atone for their bad deeds, to give back to society, to be accepted by their communities—or the most cynical view—to quickly make merit so they are reborn into the next life without the stains of their pasts as per Buddhist beliefs.

Although in theory the concepts of compassion (*karuna*) or loving kindness (*metta*) in the Buddhist canon should be familiar to Cambodians and are closely linked to sympathy and empathy, most of the ten 2017 interviewees did not produce these words when I asked them what empathy meant to them. However, in a 2008 interview the importance of tolerance and compassion was included in the definition of reconciliation provided by an accused perpetrator who is now a schoolteacher: "I think that it means that we negotiate with each other and we are not angry with each other anymore. Totally, we reconcile (*phsah phsaa*) in our heart and mind. We do not negotiate . . . using weapons, but we kill the anger of ourselves by developing tolerance (*khantei*)[12] for each other" (IV# 106).

The "heart" is often used as a metaphor for compassion and understanding (and by extension, empathy) in Cambodia, the development of which can be observed through people's actions. A UN/NGO worker living in a rural war-stricken area explained how the heart signifies compassion and understanding that are developed through listening and attention, another way of paying respect: "To know whether people have reconciled, firstly, we needed to look at their activities, as we could not necessarily recognize the heart of the people—we need to look at all the activities of reconciliation (*phsah phsaa knea*)" (IV # 103).

Victim-Perpetrator Relations—Victims' Empathy toward Perpetrators

In a review of the literature as well as research on more than one thousand respondents in the former Yugoslavia, Staub and Vollhardt (2008) concluded that understanding the history of perpetrators or their personal background can promote healing of victims (274). Similarly, my research found that victims' understanding of perpetrators' backgrounds can increase the possibility of empathic relations. For victims, their relationship (near or far neighbors, family, etc.) with the perpetrators is influenced by a variety of other factors such as their perceptions of the gravity of the offense, the age and motivation of the perpetrator, as well as degree of poverty or ignorance, and the behavior of perpetrators in the present. Both victims and perpetrators weigh these factors as they decide how to remember the past and frame the future (McGrew 2012). Yet there is no obligation for empathy, forgiveness, coexistence, or reconciliation, especially on the part of the victim: these decisions are entirely individual ones and if taken may serve to clear the mind and heart of suffering and to move on in life.

Communication and Relationship

In a 2017 interview, an NGO interviewee involved in a victim-perpetrator dialogue process observed the difficulties of measuring empathy, though noted that the quality of communication could yield clues:

> Empathy depends on the interaction or communication between them [victims and perpetrators], and the information flow between each other. In the work we did so far, it is still not clear if those people have empathy or not—it is difficult to measure. We can tell that at least the communication and relations have been reconnected among the parties, some social activities were reactivated or revitalized, so we can tell they are in the process of developing empathy. (IV# 1e)

The degree and quality of communication and relationships can change over time, especially when people are involved in an external dialogue process. This NGO interviewee felt that taking some kind of action as part of a process constituted empathy—and was thus also a way to observe or measure empathy across time:

> We heard from victims after they heard so many stories from the perpetrators, that the victims began to show their understanding of the situation of the perpetrator, and the perpetrator also showed understanding of the feeling of the victim after they lost their loved ones. So, this will lead them [the perpetrators] to do something to compensate for what they did in the past—they try to do something good now. Like joining the ceremony at the crime site, the site they used to kill people, and they do something at the site, a kind of action. This means they are in the process of having empathy and made progress. (IV# 1e)

Gravity of Offense

The gravity of the offense is an important factor in how the victims view the perpetrators and this affects how the reconciliation process proceeds. In general most of my respondents divided former Khmer Rouge into categories depending on the severity of the crimes they had committed and with how much cruelty—this resulted in a certain degree of guilt perceived: (1) serious—those who were very cruel and committed serious crimes, often killing large numbers of people; (2) moderate—those who committed crimes but only under orders or by those who were naively ignorant; (3) minor—those who tried to be kind and tried not to commit crimes. Many interviewees were aware of revenge killings in the immediate post-Khmer Rouge period, and few expressed remorse or empathy toward those (accused) perpetrators who were killed, as these were accused of the most serious and vicious crimes. On the other hand, those accused perpetrators classified in the third (minor) category were most often empathized with, depending on their motivation and other factors such as poverty, age, and ignorance.

Motivation

Perpetrators can also be categorized according to their motivation for committing offences. Was it because they were ordered to do so and, if so, were they afraid for their own lives? Did they take initiative and enjoy killing others? Did they do it for community gain or self-interest? Although only a handful of former Khmer Rouge have admitted any direct guilt at all; most former Khmer Rouge who were involved in the movement have claimed that they were under orders and living in fear of their lives (Williams 2018; Ea and Sim 2001). Khmer Rouge cadre and youth were often forced to kill others to demonstrate their loyalty to the revolution. Although research conducted by Stanley Milgram in 1964 has been questioned in more recent decades, his work showing that college students were remarkably susceptible to instructions from authority figures, including to commit torture (electric shocks), is often quoted to support overreliance on obedience as an explanation as to why perpetrators commit crimes (Williams 2018; Hinton 2004; Milgram 1974). The ability to resist inhumane orders, however, is less studied, and during the Khmer Rouge period resistance was usually met with immediate death.

Many respondents spoke of how "cruel" (*kach* or *sahav*) the perpetrators were; the perceived level of cruelty was closely related to assumptions about the motivation of the perpetrator, and if they acted by choice or not. Although my research did not specifically examine the motives of the perpetrators (few perpetrators admitted committing crimes at all much less speak about their motives), victims often interpreted motivations of former Khmer Rouge and could consider some motivations as mitigating factors (see below). Etcheson (2005) also noted that lower-level Khmer Rouge perpetrators were more easily accepted when victims could see they acted under coercion or due to ignorance (219).

In one community, a victim stated that he was living nearby former Khmer Rouge perpetrators who had done cruel things to him. At the same time, he was able to acknowledge that those former Khmer Rouge did not join by choice, so he was able to understand their involvement and express some empathy. In this narrative the victim, a farmer, was sitting next to a UN/NGO worker (who had also been victimized by the Khmer Rouge) and they openly discussed former Khmer Rouge perpetrators (and neighbors) one of whom had been sitting nearby before the interview started.

> UN/NGO WORKER: There are only the lower leaders around here; there are not any top leaders. These lower leaders had arrested and beat me, but later on, here [he pointed to a house near his house] we could not punish them because they were ordered from the top leaders. The top leaders ordered them to cut off the hands of the people who stole rice. Now, there are many cruel people in this village. I was beaten and tied up by them. If children stole rice, the spies (*chhlop*) arrested them, and beat some of them until they were unconscious. One man [a cruel perpetrator] lives to the south of my house.
>
> FARMER: . . . That man used to be the Khmer Rouge too. [He pointed to the place where someone had been sitting previously.]
>
> UN/NGO WORKER: At that time, everybody was Khmer Rouge because even if we did not want to be Khmer Rouge, we would die . . . if we were against them, we would be killed. (IV# 103)

As these victims understood that the motivation of the perpetrators was to avoid being killed and they would have been killed had they resisted, the victims were better able to develop empathy and live peacefully with their neighbors.

Poverty, Age, and Ignorance

Poverty, age, and ignorance were also important factors affecting victim-perpetrator relationships. Staub and Vollhardt (2008) suggest that understanding both the history of the specific perpetrator and the situation could assist victims in developing empathy (274). Many of my interviewees spoke with regret and anger about the Khmer Rouge regime's selection of ignorant uneducated people as local-level leaders. However, this tactic of selection used by the Khmer Rouge did not necessarily lead to anger against individual perpetrators; instead it became a mitigating factor for individuals' actions, reducing anger as they understood the predicaments of some perpetrators. For example, this respondent in a small group interview felt that an accused perpetrator's lack of education was a factor lessening the severity of his crimes: "He lives nearby, just two houses from here across the street. They [other villagers] have stopped saying anything bad against him. All those killers, they couldn't read at all, so it was easy to make them kill people. And it was the rule of Pol Pot to only choose people who never went to school to be leaders" (IV# 1).

Another mitigating factor is the age of the alleged perpetrator at the time of the past events. Many respondents still expressed resentment that their oppressors were often young people, which is not surprising given the great emphasis that is placed upon age, wisdom, and seniority in Cambodia's hierarchical social structure. Although they were angry at the individual young perpetrators, they were particularly incensed at the Khmer Rouge system that had appointed these young henchmen and had turned their social worlds upside down.

Perpetrators Do "Good Deeds" and Show Respect

When perpetrators exhibited changed behavior in the community by making amends or doing "good deeds" (described as visiting Buddhist temples and making merit by giving donations or by helping neighbors) and showing respect to others, the victims expressed more capacity to empathize with their situations during the Khmer Rouge period. Mr. Pel, the accused perpetrator mentioned above, was able to slowly reenter his community, first through an NGO dialogue program but then later by making donations and doing other "good deeds" at the Buddhist temple and the memorial for Khmer Rouge victims. Similarly, in the literature, the acts of offenders giving respect to former victims was an important part of reconciliation and restoring relationships (Huyse 2003, 24; Kriesberg 2001, 48; Rigby 2006, 8). The opening story in this chapter of Mr. Nop meeting his former torturer is an example of an offender paying respect to a victim by first showing fear, then followed by an apology, in order to restore some semblance of social order in the post-violence period.

Perpetrators Show Change of Heart

In one newly resettled area with large numbers of former Khmer Rouge, quotes from an elderly couple show the nuance of empathic relationships and the importance of changed behavior and changed hearts. The husband had been a Khmer Rouge cadre in the early "liberation" period (before 1975) but was then demoted and punished (for not agreeing to order monks to disrobe). The wife felt angry at the Khmer Rouge leader who had made her and her husband suffer. At the same time the couple could feel empathy for the leader and could understand that he was under orders, and they felt that in the post-Khmer Rouge period he had reformed, did good deeds, and had "changed his heart":

> WIFE: His house is over there, near here. I meet him when I am invited to a village ceremony. I never go to visit him on my own. But sometimes I meet him when I go to the pagoda. . . . Yes, I talk with him normally. I don't know what else to do because [his bad behavior against us] happened in the past.
>
> HUSBAND: I just talk with him normally because he was under their orders at that time but now he stopped his bad behavior a long time ago.
>
> WIFE: He changed his heart now. He does good things so I do good things back to him. (IV# 46)

Another victim recalled how one former Khmer Rouge cadre advised him how to behave so that he would not be killed and thus the victim felt open to listen to his perspective in the post-Khmer Rouge period:

> We don't blame them [former Khmer Rouge cadres] because some of them are victims too; they are not all bad people. Because when we lived in this village, they shared with me their views, and sometimes they talked to me and told me that I had to be careful. One said, "you have to wait until one day [the regime will be over] and you have to remain hopeful." He talked to me and told me that I should not rely on anybody, and that I should pay attention and respect *Angkar* [the authorities]. (IV# 132)

Even though this former Khmer Rouge cadre had committed crimes, the victim was able to feel empathy toward the cadre because of kindness showed during the Khmer Rouge period.

Mutual Empathy through Shared Suffering

A fundamental component of reconciliation (and rehumanization) is the ability of victim and perpetrator to live together and maintain an enduring relationship over time. Experience of shared suffering is one avenue for parties in conflict to develop empathy for each other—not however to equalize such suffering—as in most cases all parties to conflicts experienced hardship and trauma, but with wide variation in type and degree. Halpern and Weinstein (2004) describe the case of two women from warring sides in the former Yugoslavia who were seeking the remains of missing loved ones. Like the suffering shared by Cambodian victims and their former Khmer Rouge torturers, these women bonded over their shared mission—and their shared suffering (as also demonstrated by women survivors of violence in the Southern Cone, described by Llanos, this volume). Halpern and Weinstein argue that these interactions between the two women demonstrate shared values, with genuine respect for each other as moral agents (2004, 579). These examples of ongoing relationships relate closely to the concept of altruism and helping described by Staub and Vollhardt (2008), as action is needed to show the extent of the new perceptions and changed relationships. They suggest that people who have been exposed to violence and have been victims themselves are more likely to show empathy toward others (2008, 271–72, 275). Furthermore, Staub and Vollhardt concluded that victims showing greater empathy (in some studies only for those suffering similar violence) were more likely to help others (275–76). These dynamics may explain the shared suffering that seems to help Cambodian victims empathize with their former antagonists—even though their suffering was far from equivalent. This NGO worker brought up the concept of shared suffering: "Empathy is a process of mutual understanding—it is more about shared suffering, they come to understand each other. Yes, I killed all your relatives, but I would have been killed if I did not carry out my orders. You try to put yourself in their situation, but sometimes you cannot do so because the scale of suffering is so huge, but then time will help. This process is so important, if only they have a chance to meet and talk" (IV# 7e). These relationships I observed in Cambodia seem similar to those found by Halpern and Weinstein (2004): "The closest example of empathy comes from statements of survivors that reflect an understanding of the social pressure on members of the other group and occasional reflections of the experience of a common tragedy. 'Some of them are normal people who went through hell. They too had their own hell'" (571).

Another example of mutual empathy was observed by this NGO worker involved in a dialogue and healing project: "I think [the perpetrators] could feel empathy, somehow, they were able to understand and to

Fig. 5.1. Several NGOs conduct dialogue programs in Cambodia; here, the NGO Kdei Karuna holds a religious ceremony as part of a dialogue and healing project. (Used with permission from the NGO Kdei Karuna, http://www.kdei-karuna.org)

put themselves into the victim/survivor's situation. We also did the same [program] for torture survivors, though we didn't ask the same questions, we tried to help them understand what kind of pressure the former Khmer Rouge lived under. Some said they could not do anything, they received orders and if they didn't carry them out, they would have been killed also, and the survivors could see that" (IV# 2e).

A Buddhist monk who I interviewed in 2017 described mutual suffering in terms of compassion and common humanity, important components of empathy:

We should think of Maha Ghosananda[13], the formula that he used: "the suffering of Cambodia is deep," I add the phrase "suffering of humanity is the same, it is deep." Then his words continue—"from suffering, comes great compassion." However, we need to see the suffering; many people don't see it, and that is why they have no compassion. We must see, there is a lot of suffering, in ourselves and everywhere, more people than just ourselves suffer. If we see suffering, we develop great compassion, and great compassion makes a peaceful heart. . . . (IV #6e)

While shared suffering was relatively commonly acknowledged by victims, providing a basis for them to develop empathic feelings toward former Khmer Rouge and accused perpetrators, shared suffering expressed by accused perpetrators toward their victims was much rarer (not least because former Khmer Rouge are less accessible to researchers and the press, and are less likely to have developed trusting relationships with outsiders in whom they confide).

Perpetrators' Empathy Toward Victims

Rehumanization and the development of empathy are processes that are linked and overlapping. Among respondents in my 2008 research there were some expressions of empathy from victims toward perpetrators but none from perpetrators toward victims. The scarcity of statements of empathy from perpetrators toward their victims was probably at least partly due to the limited number of accused perpetrators I interviewed (only eight), but this lack of compassion from perpetrators toward victims has also been noted in the press about several notable accused perpetrators (Wright 2019; Mozingo 2012). In addition, Kanavou and Path (2017) found little empathy expressed toward victims by former Khmer Rouge cadre in direct interviews as well as in other sources. Although a few of former Tuol Sleng Prison Chief Duch's comments during his trial at the ECCC refer to an understanding of the plight of his former prisoners, ultimately his apologies and confessions were not fully recognized by his victims for various reasons. And while some of the prison guards at lower levels have expressed (usually half-hearted) remorse for their actions (claiming they were under orders), in rural Cambodia there have been few reports of empathy of perpetrators toward victims. Another important reason for the absence of expressions of empathy by perpetrators is related to the Cambodian cultural tendency to avoid the loss of face, and thus not to admit wrongdoing, as well as fear due to the ongoing trials for Khmer Rouge leaders. Once perpetrators acknowledge their victims have suffered, they are then on the slippery slope of acknowledging what they have done, and thus getting closer to confessing. This NGO worker had spoken with one of the former Khmer Rouge guards of the notorious Tuol Sleng Prison and expressed the difficulties of observing empathy, and the importance of the heart.

> I asked [the prison guard] this question, if he used to have empathetic feelings towards the victims because of the torture and the

killing, but he replied that he couldn't do anything, because he said if he did not kill, he would be killed—that's the answer that I heard from him. Thus, I don't have any conclusions about empathy towards victims during the Khmer Rouge regime. This argument that he could not do anything to help the victims is just an argument to reduce responsibility, I do not know what is in his heart. In fact, it depends on the direct victim themselves to observe; we as outsiders, we cannot know. (IV# 5e)

Perpetrators are undoubtedly also traumatized from physical and economic difficulties during the long years of war, loss of family members, and, at least for some, the violence they have inflicted upon others. Opening up their minds and memories to violent (and potentially morally repugnant) acts that they have committed in the past may be too painful to bear. They may also feel ashamed to have others know of heinous crimes they committed—especially their children and grandchildren. Finally, among my interviewees, the few accused perpetrators (or their family members and neighbors) have expressed fear of revenge attacks, and several respondents have described these attacks having taken place in the past.

Conclusion

In conclusion, rehumanization may occur through mutual understanding and the development of mutual respect and empathy—and these processes take time. For example, this victim respondent, a schoolteacher living in a war-affected community, described his journey toward coexistence and reconciliation: first, anger; next, observations about the perpetrator's behavior; and then, acting with empathy, compassion, tolerance, and ultimately forgiveness and letting go of the past. In the end, in this case, this ultimate forgiveness was dependent on the perpetrator's actions—he acted as a "good person" (did good deeds) and thanked the victims (showed respect).

Some spies (*chhlop*) were violent when they gave rice or food to the people. . . . There is one near here, but he could correct himself as a good person and has adapted to community life. Moreover, when the Khmer Rouge fled the country he did not follow them. The people forgave him. We did not remind him about the past even though we know about him being a spy. We told him that we tolerate each other as villagers in the same village because in the Khmer Rouge period, some people just followed the leaders—if they did not follow, they would face great difficulties. And then, he thanked us and held our hands. We would reassure him when we met each other in other ceremonies. When we came back at first, we had anger, but as we met each other every day, we had the idea that we could not be violent as he and the other Khmer Rouge were during that time. . . . We did not need to remind him or ourselves about this—if we still kept it in our minds, that problem would create new problems. (IV# 107)

This demonstration of healing, mutual understanding, and empathy provides a reason for hope in Cambodia. One accused perpetrator described earlier, Mr. Pel, had been living a lonely life in a constant state of fear, as a lone perpetrator among a community of victims. After an NGO dialogue project, many villagers expressed empathy toward him, understanding he was uneducated and would have been killed if he had not carried out his orders. At first, none of these victims had reached out to him, nor had he ever apologized. However, after a video dialogue program whereby victims and perpetrators listened to each other's stories on video first, then face to face, mutual understanding and empathy developed in the community. His good deeds in the community were interpreted as acts of contrition, allowing his direct victims to open their hearts to empathize with the accused perpetrator. Although he did not apologize clearly or speak of his deeds in the past directly, his good deeds were accepted as partial proxy measures though some direct victims were angry and frustrated at the lack of apology. Besides such NGO interventions, further hope for the future may lie with the passage of time, as memories fade further and Buddhist teachings of living in the present erode feelings of fear, anger, and pain. New research may also provide other avenues for healing, such as Kanavou and Path's (2017) research with Khmer Rouge cadre that "seeks to identify shifts from rule- and obedience-based behavior and thinking to genuine assessment of past collective and individual acts" (88). How can perpetrators begin to examine their acts in the past and develop more empathy toward their victims?

All this said, authentic, deep empathy (especially from perpetrators toward victims) seems to be relatively rare in Cambodia and elsewhere. In my 2008 research study, not unexpectedly, I found that none of the ten study areas had reached the idealized state of reconciliation, and only two showed some degree of moderate coexistence—elsewhere, victims and perpetrators were living entirely separate lives. Similarly, Halpern and Weinstein (2004), in their survey of 1,600 people from various sides of the conflict in Bosnia Herzegovina and Croatia, observed that while people from different groups were coexisting (working and living together), they found not a single demonstration of empathy with "a full-blown curiosity and emotional openness towards another's distinct perspective. . . . In our view, coexistence without empathy is both superficial and fragile. Just below the surface is mistrust, resentment, and even hatred" (570). In spite of Halpern and Weinstein's (2004) dismal view of Bosnia, my interviews in Cambodia indicate there is still hope for Cambodia's future social recovery exemplified by the story of Mr. Pel. Many NGOs are working on facilitating relationships, including empathy, as part of trauma healing and dialogue processes; and hope lies along these avenues, as expressed by this NGO worker: "I am personally really a fan of the empathy concept. I believe that the heart is at the core of humanization of the other. . . . I believe in the ability of humans to change, no matter how bad, they can change, and this leaves the door open for transformation. We live on one earth that we can share, and this is really the foundation of peace—empathy" (IV# 7e). Now almost forty years after the end of the Khmer Rouge period, and decades of peacebuilding interventions that have been grounded in local religious and traditions, lessons learned can be applied to other conflict and post-conflict settings. As the prevention of future violence is an ideal goal, one route may be to increase empathy between survivors of mass violence—many other pathways are described in this volume.

NOTES

1. All names are pseudonyms to protect the identity of interviewees. In addition, due to limited numbers of UN and NGO workers interviewed, they are identified as UN/NGO workers to protect their identities, except in the 2017 research on empathy when only NGO workers were interviewed. Tim Minea provided research assistance from 2006–17, with additional translation by Phann Chandara and Yim Mary in 2013.

2. See for example Brené Brown on empathy at the "Center for Building a Culture of Empathy" available at http://cultureofempathy.com/references/Experts/Brene-Brown.htm

3. The term "the other" is used to signify the victim or the perpetrator—the victim and "the other" perpetrator, or vice versa.

4. In addition, previous research I conducted in Cambodia in 1999 as an independent researcher provided the basis for later research see McGrew (2000).

5. See https://www.qsrinternational.com/nvivo/what-is-nvivo

6. Interviews are referenced by interview number (IV#): those conducted between 2006 and 2008 have numbers (e.g., IV# 4) while those conducted in 2017 have a number followed by "e" for interviews about empathy (e.g., IV# 4e).

7. Post-traumatic stress disorder (PTSD) developed from the 1980s as a model to understand suffering caused by a wide variety of traumatic events; it is characterized by the presence of three categories of symptoms—reexperiencing the traumatic event, hyperarousal and withdrawal, and numbing (Breslau 2004, 113, 115).

8. See for example Thieda 2014, *Psychology Today,* and Brené Brown's TEDxHouston talk in 2010: "The Power of Vulnerability" available at https://www.ted.com/talks/brene_brown_on_vulnerability

9. Burnet in this volume also describes the importance of "the heart" in the Rwandan context.

10. See https://www.merriam-webster.com/dictionary

11. Burnet's respondents in Rwanda define empathy in similar terms: "empathy is often expressed as 'having a good heart' and recognizing the humanity in other people" (this volume).

12. The meanings of the words for compassion (*karuna*) and tolerance (*khantei*) are similar.

13. Maha Ghosananda was a Cambodian monk with the title of Supreme Patriarch who was known as the father of the peace movement after the Khmer Rouge period.

REFERENCES

Barraza, Jorge A., and Paul J. Zak. 2009. "Empathy toward Strangers Triggers Oxytocin Release and Subsequent Generosity." *Annals of the New York Academy of Sciences* 1167: 182–89. http://www.nexthumanproject.com/references/Empathy_Towards_Strangers_Claremont.pdf

Beneduce, Roberto. 2007. "Contested Memories: Peacebuilding and Community Rehabilitation after Violence and Mass Crimes—a Medico-Anthropological Approach." In *After Mass Crime: Rebuilding States and Communities*, edited by Beatrice Pouligny, Simon Chesterman, and Albrecht Schnabel, 1–16. Tokyo: United Nations University Press.

Bloom, Paul. 2016. *Against Empathy: The Case for Rational Compassion.* New York: Harper Collins.

Breslau, Joshua. 2004. "Cultures of Trauma: Anthropological Views of Post-Traumatic Stress Disorder in International Health." *Culture, Medicine and Psychiatry* 28: 113–26.

Brown, Brené. 2010. "The Power of Vulnerability." TEDxHouston, June. https://www.ted.com/talks/brene_brown_on_vulnerability

Bruneau, Emile G., Mina Cikara, and Rebecca Saxe. 2015. "Minding the Gap: Narrative Descriptions about Mental States Attenuate Parochial Empathy." *PLoS ONE* 10, no. 10: e0140838. https://doi.org/10.1371/journal.pone.0140838

Chhim, Sotheara. 2013. "Baksbat (Broken Courage): A Trauma-Based Cultural Syndrome in Cambodia." *Medical Anthropology: Cross-Cultural Studies in Health and Illness* 32, no. 2: 160–73.

Cikara, Mina, Emile G. Bruneau, and Rebecca R. Saxe. 2011. "Us and Them: Intergroup Failures of Empathy." *Current Directions in Psychological Science* 20, no. 3: 149–53.

Ciorciari, John, and Youk Chhang. 2005. "Documenting the Crimes of Democratic Kampuchea." In *Bringing the Khmer Rouge to Justice: Prosecuting Mass Violence before the Cambodian Courts*, edited by Jaya Ramji and Beth Van Schaack, 221–306. Lewiston: Edwin Mellen Press.

de Jong, Joop T. V. M., Ivan H. Komproe, and Mark van Ommeren. 2003. "Common Mental Disorders in Post-conflict Settings." *Lancet* 361: 2128–30.

Decety, Jean. 2011. "The Neuroevolution of Empathy." *Annals of the New York Academy of Sciences*. Special Issue: Social Neuroscience: Gene, Environment, Brain, Body 1231: 35–45.

Ea, Meng-Try, and Sorya Sim. 2001. *Victims and Perpetrators? Testimony of Young Khmer Rouge Comrades*. Phnom Penh: Documentation Center of Cambodia.

Eisenbruch, Maurice. 2007. "The Uses and Abuses of Culture: Cultural Competence in Post-Mass-Crime Peacebuilding in Cambodia." In *After Mass Crime: Rebuilding States and Communities*, edited by Beatrice Pouligny, Simon Chesterman, and Albrecht Schnabel, 71–96. Tokyo: United Nations University Press.

Etcheson, Craig. 2005. "The Limits of Reconciliation in Cambodia's Communes." In *Roads to Reconciliation*, edited by Elin Skaar, Siri Gloppen, and Astri Suhrke, 201–24. Lanham: Lexington Books.

Field, Nigel P., Sophear Muong, and Vannavuth Sochanvimean. 2013. "Parental Styles in the Intergenerational Transmission of Trauma Stemming from the Khmer Rouge Regime in Cambodia." *American Journal of Orthopsychiatry* 83, no. 4: 483–94.

Halpern, Jodi, and Harvey M. Weinstein. 2004. "Rehumanizing the Other: Empathy and Reconciliation." *Human Rights Quarterly* 26: 561–83.

Hicks, Donna. 2008. "Reconciling with Dignity." Unpublished conference paper. "Developing Standards for Assistance to Victims of Terrorism," held March 10–11, at Tilburg, the Netherlands. European Forum for Restorative Justice: 1–24. http://www.euforumrj.org/readingroom/Terrorism/DHicks.pdf

Hinton, Alexander Laban. 2004. *Why Did They Kill? Cambodia in the Shadow of Genocide*. Berkeley: University of California Press.

Huyse, Lucien. 2003. "The Process of Reconciliation." In *Reconciliation after Violent Conflict: A Handbook*, edited by David Bloomfield, Teresa Barnes, and Lucien Huyse, 19–39. Stockholm: International Institute for Democracy and Electoral Assistance. http://www.idea.int/publications/reconciliation/upload/reconciliation_chap02.pdf

Interlandi, Jeneen. 2015. "The Brain's Empathy Gap: Can Mapping Neural Pathways Help Us Make Friends with Our Enemies?" *New York Times*, March 19. https://www.nytimes.com/2015/03/22/magazine/the-brains-empathy-gap.html?_r=1

Kanavou, Andrea Angeliki, and Kosal Path. 2017. "The Lingering Effects of Thought Reform: The Khmer Rouge S-21 Prison Personnel." *The Journal of Asian Studies* 76, no. 1: 87–105.

Kanavou, Angeliki, Kosal Path, and Kathleen Doll. 2016. "Breaking the Cycles of Repetition? The Cambodian Genocide Across Generations in Anglong Veng." In *Breaking Intergenerational Cycles of Repetition: A Global Dialogue on Historical Trauma and Memory*, edited by P. Gobodo-Madikizela. Opladen: Barbara Budrich.

Kraybill, Ron. 1988. "From Head to Heart: The Cycle of Reconciliation." *Conciliation Quarterly* 7, no. 4: 1–2, 8.

Kriesberg, Louis. 2001. "Changing Forms of Coexistence." In *Reconciliation, Justice, and Coexistence*, edited by Mohammed Abu-Nimer, 47–64. Oxford: Lexington Books.

Luco, Fabienne. 2002. *Between the Tiger and the Crocodile: An Anthropological Approach to the Traditional and New Practices of Local Conflict Resolution in Cambodia*. Phnom Penh: UNESCO.

McGrew, Laura. 2000. "Truth, Justice, Reconciliation and Peace: 20 Years after the Khmer Rouge." Unpublished report. Phnom Penh.

McGrew, Laura. 2012. "Pathways to Reconciliation in Cambodia." *Peace Review: A Journal of Social Justice* 23, no. 4: 514–21. http://www.tandfonline.com/doi/abs/10.1080/10402659.2011.625851

McGrew, Laura. 2018. "Changing Narratives of Victims and Perpetrators in Cambodia: Community Responses to Dialogue Interventions in the Presence of the Extraordinary Chambers in the Courts of Cambodia (ECCC)." In *Societies Emerging from Conflict: The Aftermath of Atrocity*, edited by Dennis Klein, 74–93. Newcastle upon Tyne: Cambridge Scholars.

Milgram, Stanley. 1974. *Obedience to Authority: An Experimental Review*. New York: Harper and Row.

Mozingo, Joe. 2010. "Coming to Terms with Sadism: An Orphan of the Killing Fields of the Khmer Rouge Struggles to Overcome His Anguish." *Los Angeles Times*, December 15. https://www.latimes.com/archives/la-xpm-2010-dec-15-la-me-bo-20101215-story.html

Pouligny, Beatrice, Simon Chesterman, and Albrecht Schnabel. 2007. "Introduction." In *After Mass Crime: Rebuilding States and Communities*, edited by Beatrice Pouligny, Simon Chesterman, and Albrecht Schnabel, 1–16. Tokyo: United Nations University Press.

Rigby, Andrew. 2006. "Twenty Observations on 'Post-Settlement' Reconciliation." Unpublished paper. Coventry: Coventry University.

Schreiter, Robert J. 1992. *Reconciliation: Mission & Ministry in a Changing Social Order*. 11th ed. Maryknoll: Orbis Books.

Scully, Mary F., Theanvy Kuoch, Richard A. Miller, Heang K. Tan, Lara L. Watkins, Rosanna C. Mey, and Poleak Sok. 2010. *Health and Well-being of Cambodians Living in the United States*. West Hartford, CT: Khmer Health Advocates.

Senior, Jennifer. 2016. "Against Empathy, or the Right Way to Feel Someone's Pain." *New York Times*, December 6. http://www.nytimes.com/2016/12/06/books/review-against-empathy-paul-bloom.html

Sonis, Jeffrey, James L. Gibson, Joop T. V. M. de Jong, Nigel Field, Sokhom Hean, and Ivan Komproe. 2009. "Probable Posttraumatic Stress Disorder and Disability in Cambodia Associations with Perceived Justice, Desire for Revenge, and Attitudes Toward the Khmer Rouge Trials." *Journal of the American Medical Association* 302, no. 5: 527–36.

Staub, Ervin, and Johanna Vollhardt. 2008. "Altruism Born of Suffering: The Roots of Caring and Helping After Victimization and Other Trauma." *American Journal of Orthopsychiatry* 78, no. 3: 267–80.

Theidon, Kimberly. 2007. "Intimate Enemies." In *After Mass Crime: Rebuilding States and Communities*, edited by Beatrice Pouligny, Simon Chesterman, and Albrecht Schnabel, 97–121. Tokyo: United Nations University Press.

Thieda, Kate. 2014. "Brené Brown on Empathy vs. Sympathy: Empathy Never Starts with the

Words, 'At least. . . .'" *Psychology Today*, August 12. https://www.psychologytoday.com/blog/partnering-in-mental-health/201408/bren-brown-empathy-vs-sympathy-0

van de Put, Willem, and Maurice Eisenbruch. 2002. "The Cambodian Experience." In *Trauma, War and Violence: Public Mental Health in Socio-Cultural Context*, edited by Joop de Jong, 93–155. New York: Kluwer Academic/Plenum.

Williams, Timothy. 2018. "Agency, Responsibility, and Culpability: The Complexity of Roles and Self-representations of Perpetrators." *Journal of Perpetrator Research* 2, no. 1: 39–64.

Wiseman, Theresa. 1996. "A Concept Analysis of Empathy." *Journal of Advanced Nursing* 23: 1162–67.

The World Factbook 2019. 2019. "People and Society: Cambodia." Washington, DC: Central Intelligence Agency. Accessed November 26, 2019. https://www.cia.gov/library/publications/the-world-factbook/geos/cb.html

Wright, George. 2019. "Nuon Chea: Cambodia's Unrepentant Perpetrator of Genocide." *BBC News*, August 6. https://www.bbc.com/news/world-asia-49234224

Yoder, Carolyn. 2005. *The Littlebook of Trauma Healing: When Violence Strikes and Community Security Is Threatened*. Intercourse, PA: Good Books.

Zak, Paul. 2008. "The Neurobiology of Trust." *Scientific American*, June.

Zucker, Eve M. 2013. *Forest of Struggle: Moralities of Remembrance in Upland Cambodia*. Honolulu: University of Hawai'i Press.

6 | Cultivating Empathy and Coexistence

Testimony about Rescue in the Rwandan Genocide

Jennie E. Burnet

A growing body of interdisciplinary literature on coexistence in the aftermath of mass atrocities places empathy at the heart of fostering better intergroup relations (see for example Bruneau and Saxe 2012; Halpern and Weinstein 2004; Hoffman 2000; Huyse 2003). Several of these studies demonstrate that sharing narratives—recounting them, having them be heard, and listening to them—is a key component of cultivating empathy and promoting peaceful coexistence (Bruneau and Saxe 2012; Huyse 2003; Schreiter 1992). As Huyse (2003, 21) writes, "empathy comes with victims' willingness to listen to the reasons for the hatred of those who caused their pain and with the offenders' understanding of the anger and bitterness of those who suffered." In research on the roles of Rwandan women in reconciliation, I found that grassroots women's organizations who used structured encounters of empathetic listening between genocide widows and women whose husbands were imprisoned for genocide crimes succeeded in working together and reducing conflict in their communities (Burnet 2012, 167–93). Llanos (this volume) reaches similar conclusions about women activists in the Southern Cone of South America.

More than twenty-five years after the 1994 genocide of Tutsi and massacres of those opposed to the genocide in Rwanda, the country still struggles with the long-term consequences of mass death and destruction.[1] Between April 6 and July 4, 1994, an estimated 800,000 Rwandans lost their lives in a state-sponsored genocide that targeted ethnic Tutsi (United Nations 1999).[2] In its aftermath, the post-genocide government, which was led by the Rwandan Patriotic Front (RPF) rebel group that came to power by stopping the genocide, sought to promote national unity and eliminate genocide ideology. To this end, public narratives about the genocide, its origins and causes, and its toll on victims formed the warp threads of the social fabric. During the annual period of national mourning (April 7–July 4), local radio and television stations broadcast news, testimony, music, and other programming about the genocide. These narratives speak extensively about perpetrators—what they did, how they killed—and victims and survivors—how they were killed, how they survived, what they suffered and continue to suffer. "Perpetrator" and "victim" often serve as metonyms for the ethnic labels, Hutu and Tutsi, which have been suppressed in public discourse in the interest of national unity (Burnet 2009).[3] A few stories about rescuers—people who risked their lives to save Tutsi and others targeted for killing—are also featured. These stories of rescue, however, are largely subsumed by the dominant narrative that focuses on perpetrators and victims.

In this chapter, I discuss the potential for testimony about ordinary rescuers to promote peaceful coexistence in Rwanda. By "ordinary rescuers" I mean Rwandans, of all ethnicities, who risked their lives to help save Tutsi during the genocide. Narratives about acts of rescue can help promote peaceful coexistence. First, these narratives model empathy. The vast majority of rescuers state that they were motivated by simple empathy for their fellow humans. Second, they offer opportunities for (Tutsi) genocide survivors, who directly experienced enormous harm, even evil, at the hands of their kin, neighbors, and countrymen, to see the good, or potential good, in their fellow Rwandans whether Hutu, Tutsi, or Twa. I begin by briefly summarizing some key theoretical insights about narratives, empathy, and coexistence. Then I examine the roles of testimony and silence in the aftermath of the genocide where narratives about rescue have been politicized and thus partially censured. Next, I describe the acts of rescue, motivations, and decision-making of rescuers in the Rwandan genocide. Three characteristics distinguished rescuers from others: empathy, courage, and a rejection of materialism. I conclude by reflecting on the connections between empathy, coexistence, and narratives about rescue.

In writing this chapter, I drew on 236 semistructured interviews and ethnographic observation in ten communities conducted in Rwanda in 2011, 2013, and 2014, as well as data collected in my earlier ethnographic research in Rwanda between 1997 and 2002.[4] The interviews consisted of open-ended questions and were conducted in Kinyarwanda, Swahili, Arabic, French, or English depending on the participants' preference. All research participants were offered anonymity.[5] When authorized by participants, the interviews were recorded, and handwritten or typed notes were taken for all interviews. In analyzing the interview data, themes were identified by looking for repetitions, similarities and differences, and indigenous typologies, as well as in vivo coding (Bernard and Ryan 2010, 69). I reserve the term "rescuer" for anyone who engaged in rescue who did not participate in the genocide whether by killing, raping, destroying property, or looting. I use the terms "rescuer behavior" and "acts of rescue" to describe actions taken to protect, evacuate, or otherwise assist Tutsi, regardless of whether the individual might also have participated in the genocide.

Peaceful Coexistence, Empathy, and Narratives

Once war has come to an end, outside interventions in the aftermath of mass atrocities often focus on peacebuilding. Within international institutions like the World Bank or United Nations agencies, peacebuilding most often boils down to state-building: strengthening and supporting state institutions to take over the task of running the government and managing internal conflict without violence (see for example United Nations Department of Peacekeeping Operations 2008). Peace studies scholars and practitioners have outlined bottom-up, grassroots approaches to promote peaceful coexistence in the aftermath of mass atrocities. Within this scholarship empathy and the use of narratives have been tied to coexistence.

Anthropologists who have focused on the local messiness of post-conflict reconstruction and transitional justice have offered salient critiques of these international peacebuilding frameworks. As Alexander Hinton has noted, the international community has privileged "a cluster of liberal normative goods, such as rule of law, peace, reconciliation, civil society, human rights, combating impunity, and justice" (Hinton 2010, 1). Elsewhere I have addressed the on-the-ground realities and inherently political nature of transitional justice, cohabitation, and so-called reconciliation in Rwanda (Burnet 2009, 2011, 2012). In this chapter, I focus on the longer-term dynamics of narratives about the country's difficult past and the potential for empathy to help build peaceful coexistence. This examination demonstrates that long-standing, local cultural traditions of "empathy" (*kugira umutima mwiza*, literally "to have a good heart") served as the foundation for acts of rescue during the 1994 genocide of Tutsi and have the potential to foster peaceful coexistence in the aftermath of mass violence.

What does coexistence mean? The peacebuilding literature has not come to full consensus on this question, but in general scholars and practitioners conceive of a continuum ranging from direct, violent conflict, war, or genocide on one end to durable peace on the other. Coexistence is generally conceived of as a midway point along this continuum. Weiner (1998) defines coexistence as "an accommodation between members of different communities or separate countries who live together without one collectivity trying to destroy or severely harm the other." Weiner's definition allows for competition and conflict, as long as they are pursued through "legitimate channels" (cited in Kriesberg 2001, 48). Applying this definition of coexistence to post-genocide Rwanda requires some adaptation of the concept because Hutu and Tutsi were not distinct communities (Burnet 2012, 41–73, 128–46). Thus I use the term "coexistence" to refer to the ad hoc accommodations made by Rwandans in the aftermath of the genocide (1994–2003) in order to live together without direct violence between ordinary citizens.

The peacebuilding literature sometimes distinguishes between coexistence and peaceful coexistence, a point further along the continuum toward a durable peace. Peaceful coexistence is often defined as a more robust or sustainable form of coexistence that goes beyond just living together without killing each other. Weiner (1998) identifies three elements to peaceful coexistence: (1) the parties formerly in conflict must accept that the other has the right to exist, (2) peaceful coexistence is a state in between open hostility or violence and reconciliation, and (3) peaceful coexistence has an ongoing dynamic that moves toward a durable peace. Yet again this conceptualization poses some problems for the Rwanda case. This perspective assumes that Hutu were on one side of the conflict and Tutsi on the other, whereas many Hutu, likely even a significant majority of them, were opposed to the genocide (see additional discussion below). Reconciliation is often identified as another stage along the continuum from open conflict to a durable peace. The peacebuilding literature defines reconciliation as the processes of rebuilding relationships between "parties that have experienced an oppressive relationship or a destructive conflict with each other" (Kriesberg 2001, 48).

The literature on peacebuilding generally agrees that empathy contributes to peaceful coexistence or reconciliation (see for example Halpern 2001; Halpern and Weinstein 2004; Hoffman 2000; Huyse 2003). Halpern and Weinstein (2004, 568) define empathy as "a process in which one person imagines the particular perspective of another person." Empathy differs from sympathy in three key ways. First of all, empathy requires "seeking the individual perspective of another" person rather than generalizing or stereotyping (Halpern and Weinstein 2004, 568). Second, it requires "genuine curiosity" about another person, their experiences, and their emotions (Halpern and Weinstein 2004, 568–69). Third, empathy requires "cognitive openness" and a tolerance for ambiguity (Halpern and Weinstein 2004, 569; Halpern 2001, 130–33, 143). Recognizing empathy can be a challenge as it can be expressed in many ways: through words, gestures, actions, facial expressions, or affect (DeCety 2011, 35; McGrew, this volume). Although empathy is recognized as a universal human emotion by neuroscientists (see for example DeCety 2011), it is expressed (and potentially experienced) differently in different cultures (Halpern and Weinstein 2004, 35). As discussed in more detail below, in Rwanda empathy is often expressed as "having a good heart" and recognizing the humanity in other people.

Recent research in social psychology and neuroscience demonstrates the roles of empathy and empathic listening to fostering better intergroup relations or reducing the salience of racial, ethnic, religious, sectarian, age, gender, sexual preference, or many other socially constructed categories of difference (see for example Bruneau and Saxe 2012, Monroe and Martinez 2009, Hoffman 2000, Huyse 2003). Empathy "increases tolerance and understanding" of differences associated with race, ethnicity, religion, age, disability, and sexual preference and thus reduces prejudice (Monroe and Martinez 2009, 148). Furthermore, "empathic involvement" with people from another social category can "shift attitudes towards members of that group," thus reducing the salience of the difference and reducing potential conflict (Monroe and Martinez 2009, 155). In addition, empathy relates in numerous ways to altruism, the motivation to rescue, and promoting peaceful coexistence.

Oliner and Oliner (1988) were the first researchers to identify empathy as a universal trait among rescuers during the Holocaust. In their study, they found that all Yad Vashem-certified rescuers stated that they were motivated by empathy. In a follow up study, Oliner (2002) connected empathy to altruism and demonstrated that Yad Vashem-certified rescuers from the Holocaust exhibited greater empathy toward Jews in particular and scored higher on measures of empathy in general. Numerous other researchers have found that empathy is critical to altruism and its motivation (e.g., Pessi 2009, 200; Seidler 1992; Monroe 1996; Cohen 1992; Jarymovicz 1992; Kohn 1990; Fogelman 1994). Several others have specifically highlighted empathy for or empathic involvement with victims or potential victims as shared features of rescuers during genocide (Fogelman

1994, Oliner and Oliner 1988, Monroe 1996, Staub 2003). Meyer (2009, 92–93) identifies "social or emotional closeness" to victims as a significant situational factor that increases a person's likelihood to stand up for the "non-material interests" and "integrity or welfare" of other people. Meyer defines social or emotional closeness as knowing someone personally or feeling a sense of belonging or solidarity "based on ethnicity, color, religion, or nationality or similar experiences" (Meyer 2009, 93).

Beyond the roles of empathy and empathic listening in fostering peaceful coexistence or reconciliation and in motivating rescuers, we might also ask whether coexistence can potentially help cultivate empathy. Can living next to each other in the absence of direct violence lead to empathy? My research in urban and rural Rwanda in the early years after the genocide suggests that coexistence, as opposed to peaceful coexistence, does not foster empathy. However, living together does form part of the foundation necessary for social encounters that create opportunities for empathic listening to occur (Burnet 2012, 167–93). In addition, people's basic human needs (water, food, clothing, and shelter) must also be met. In the remainder of this chapter, I explore the potential effects of testimony about rescuers during the Rwandan genocide to promote peaceful coexistence. Because community structure and social networks significantly shape individuals' behavior during mass atrocities (see for example Fujii 2011, McDoom 2014), these narratives can model a coalescence of empathy and peaceful coexistence.

Testimony and Silence in the Aftermath of the 1994 Genocide of Tutsi

Testimony itself can be a dangerous proposition in the aftermath of mass atrocities. After the 1994 genocide, rescue was a sensitive political issue in Rwanda. Many of the Tutsi who escaped death in the genocide, survived, at least in part, thanks to assistance from other people, whether for the entire period of their escape or just for certain fleeting moments. Immediately after the genocide, many survivors wanted to recognize the courageous individuals who had helped save their lives. Yet they found the political context made it too risky. As a national representative of the genocide survivor's association Ibuka explained, "There have been moments when it has been impossible to talk about rescuers during the genocide. Immediately after, many of us tried to [publicly] recognize the people who saved us, but we discovered it wasn't wise. The government didn't want to hear about it."[6] When I conducted research in Rwanda in the late 1990s, few people talked openly about the 1994 genocide (Burnet 2012, 79). While the reasons for their silence were numerous, principle among them was fear of attracting attention that could lead to accusations of genocide crimes.

Rescuers, in particular, remained silent for fear that their acts of rescue could be used to incriminate them for genocide crimes or that their testimony would incriminate family members or neighbors in genocide crimes. At the time, a single accusation meant imprisonment in terrible conditions with little hope of a trial or opportunity to be proven innocent. The country's justice system was at an impasse due to the massive number of accused genocide perpetrators and lack of infrastructure to investigate or prosecute them. One man explained,

> I tried to save someone. He stayed here in my house for weeks. He climbed over the rear wall [pointing to the compound wall behind the house]. We didn't know him. . . . I kept him here. . . . Then, we decided to flee. We could not bring him with us. I don't know what happened to him. . . . I do not say these things because people can misunderstand or twist my words to say that I am the one who had him killed.[7]

Despite its official policy of national unity, Rwandan government practices of national memory and genocide commemoration in the late 1990s and early 2000s politicized victimhood and globalized blame on Hutu (Burnet 2009, 80). Not only bystanders and rescuers faced intense scrutiny in the aftermath of the genocide. Survivors also discovered that the mere fact of their survival aroused suspicion for some RPF soldiers, in particular those whose entire family had been exterminated in the genocide, and for Tutsi who returned to Rwanda from the diaspora. Survivors sometimes faced stark accusations that they were complicit in or perpetrators of the genocide themselves.[8] This fear created obstacles to certain forms of coexistence.

In the late 1990s and early 2000s, the government exercised tight control over public representations of the genocide. The annual genocide commemoration ceremonies often included public recognition of people who had risked their lives to save Tutsi in the genocide. In most instances, a genocide survivor would give testimony and present the person who had helped them. The rescuer would then say a few words about why they had done what they had done. National Heroes Day recognized stories of rescue among other types of national heroes. For example, Felicité Niyitegeka, who saved scores of Tutsi in Gisenyi and died with others she refused to abandon, is among the national heroes.[9] Government-sponsored commemoration activities contained these narratives of rescue in official public discourse. This containment ensured that they did not create public heroes who could become potential political rivals of the RPF party or its candidates. Despite these limitations, these stories of rescue helped contribute to coexistence in that they modeled morally correct action and provided some public examples of "good Hutu."

Stories of rescuers promoted outside of official Rwandan government channels often faced government opposition. Internationally, perhaps the best-known rescuer is Paul Rusesabagina, the hotel manager who saved people at the *Hotel de Mille Collines*, as portrayed in the film *Hotel Rwanda*.[10] His story was first recounted by journalist Philip Gourevitch in his 1998 book, *We Wish to Inform You that Tomorrow We Will Be Killed with Our Families*. This story caught the attention of writer and director Terry George who then researched Rusesabagina's story and wrote and directed the film, which was released in 2004. In 2005, Rwandan journalists began a smear campaign against Rusesabagina.[11] The campaign begun by journalists was then taken up by politicians culminating in President Kagame condemning Rusesabagina by name during the 12th national genocide commemoration ceremony on April 6, 2006 (George 2006). Since then, the campaign against Rusesabagina has continued in the Rwandan and international media.[12] In 2014, the memoir of Edouard Kay-ihura, *Inside the Hotel Rwanda: The Surprising True Story . . . and Why It Matters Today*, recounted that Rusesabagina began demanding that refugees in the hotel pay for their food and rooms when he arrived and took over the hotel's management. The book jacket includes endorsements from important Rwandan government officials, General Romeo Dallaire, and others. Rusesabagina is but one example of a rescuer who gained public attention outside of Rwandan government channels and then found themselves the target of a smear campaign or other forms of social or political censure. These examples discouraged other rescuers as well as genocide survivors who wanted to recognize them from speaking publicly.

Between 2001 and 2011, Rwanda embarked on a mass experiment in transitional justice referred to as Gacaca or Gacaca courts. Based loosely on a customary conflict resolution mechanism, the Gacaca courts adjudicated more than one million cases of genocide crimes in grassroots courts staffed by ordinary citizens elected from the local population (Burnet 2008, 2010). In the midst of the Gacaca proceedings, the Rwandan government awarded the first Umurinzi Campaign Against Genocide medals recognizing those people who had resisted the 1994 genocide of Tutsi. In 2006, President Kagame awarded the Umurinzi medal to five Rwandan civilians in 2006 and sixteen Rwandan civilians in 2007 to recognize their courageous acts during the 1994 genocide (Republic of Rwanda 2016, 31–32). These official government awards set the stage for public dialogue about Rwandan civilians, especially Hutu and Twa, who had risked their lives to save people in the genocide.

Once the Gacaca courts completed their work in the late 2000s, public discourse opened slightly on the question of rescuers. In 2009, the national genocide survivors' association, Ibuka, launched a pilot research project to identify people it called "*indakemwa*," meaning "those who are morally beyond reproach." In the pilot study, Ibuka identified 372 people around the country who it has designated "presumed *indakemwa*" (Kayishema and Masabo 2010, 25). They were designated "presumed *indakemwa*" because no evidence surfaced to disqualify them during the study, but it potentially could in the future. The organization has not yet found funding to continue its research or to create a permanent process for identifying and verifying *indakemwa*.[13]

Shortly after Ibuka's pilot study, the Aegis Trust and the Kigali Genocide Memorial collaborated with PROOF: Media for Social Justice to create an exhibit about rescuers in 2010 (Kahn, this volume). The exhibit toured inside Rwanda as part of a program to promote coexistence and then was mounted as a special exhibit at the Kigali Genocide Memorial. I saw the exhibit myself in 2011. A few panels from the exhibit were then incorporated into the permanent exhibit of the Kigali Genocide Memorial Museum. The special exhibit and additions to the permanent exhibit formalized the inclusion of Hutu and Twa who were opposed to the genocide in the dominant national narrative about the 1994 genocide.

In 2017, President Kagame inaugurated the new Campaign Against Genocide Museum on the 30th anniversary of the Rwandan Patriotic Front's founding. The museum primarily tells the story of the RPF's military campaign to defeat the Rwandan army and government responsible for the genocide and drive them into exile between April 7 and July 14, 1994. The museum also recognizes Sister Félicité Niyitegeka who lost her life while helping Tutsi flee across the border to Congo at the Saint Pierre Pastoral Center in Gisenyi; Father Celestin Hakizimana who protected more than two thousand civilians in the Saint Paul Pastoral Center in Kigali until they could be rescued by the RPF; Sosthene Niyitegeka, an Adventist pastor and shopkeeper who organized the protection of more than one hundred people at his home near Ruhango in South Province; and several other Rwandan civilians who protected people during the 1994 genocide.

Acts of Rescue

As Ervin Staub (1993; 2003, 303) explained for the case of the Holocaust, the behaviors of perpetrators, bystanders, and heroic helpers are significantly shaped by the evolving context. In Rwanda, Hutu extremist propaganda had transformed social norms in the years leading up to the genocide, blaming Tutsi en masse for the ongoing civil war and economic problems of the country. Once the genocide began, the Hutu Power movement responsible for the genocide quickly mobilized the Interahamwe and Impuzamugambi militias to attack and kill Tutsi. Over the span of a few weeks, they attempted to engage the entire population in their genocidal project. "Once perpetrators begin to harm people, the resulting psychological changes make greater harm-doing probable" (Staub 2003, 325). This pressure to join in affects bystanders and rescuers alike. In Rwanda, local officials transformed everyday mechanisms for mobilizing the adult male population, like nightly security rounds and monthly communal labor (*umuganda*), into enforcement mechanisms for the genocide. Through these means, they initiated people who were initially reluctant to join in killing. First, they searched for people in hiding. Then, they became more likely to participate in mob violence; this, in turn, made it more likely for them to join in killing. Sometimes coercion was used to get people to comply. In this context, the simple act of refusing to participate can be viewed as a courageous act. As Meyer (2009, 93) notes, "violence is a major obstacle for courageous intervention" and the "inhibiting threshold is higher" the more severe the actual or perceived threat of violence.

Beyond refusing to participate, many people, including Hutu, Twa, and even Tutsi, helped people who were being targeted. They hid them in their homes, in stables, or elsewhere on their property. After learning about imminent attacks at public meetings, they warned people so that they could evade the mobs. They negotiated for the sparing of Tutsi lives by using money, cigarettes, beer, or other goods. They hid or protected children whose parents had been killed. They smuggled people across the border or gave them food, water, clothing, or other assistance. In some places where people sought protection, in churches, mosques, schools, or government buildings, they fought against attackers and died alongside

Tutsi. At a mosque in a rural community in eastern Rwanda, Muslims and Christians of all ethnicities sought refuge together (Viret 2011). When the Interahamwe militias attacked, they told Hutu refugees to leave. They refused to go and instead fought against the militiamen with their Tutsi neighbors (Viret 2011, 492). Most of them died.

Numerous external factors constrained the opportunity to rescue as well as the likelihood that these actions would be successful. Perhaps the most important of these were opportunity and proximity (Sémelin, Andrieu, and Gensburger 2008, 2011). In Rwanda, most people had the opportunity, even if fleeting, to provide assistance to someone targeted for killing. Hutu and Tutsi lived interspersed throughout most of the country. For example, Tutsi constituted 14–21 percent of the population in southern Rwanda (Guichaoua 2015, x). On the other hand, people had few opportunities to rescue in northwestern Rwanda where Tutsi were between less than 1 percent and 7 percent of the population in 1994 (Guichaoua 2015, x). Yet the lack of Tutsi in these regions did not prevent people from participating. Men in these communities were mobilized to go and attack Tutsi elsewhere.[14]

The border provided great opportunities for rescue although it was also used to trap Tutsi evading the death squads.[15] In the border town of Gisenyi, much of the border with Zaire was open scrubland or forest in 1994. Properties on the border became routes to evacuate people during the genocide. Traders who engaged in smuggling as part of their business had special knowledge of and access to these routes and used them to smuggle Tutsi across the border. Two *indakemwa* identified by Ibuka saved the lives of dozens of Tutsi in this way and requested no compensation for their assistance.[16] An old woman in Gisenyi smuggled Tutsi children across the border in broad daylight. She took the children one by one across the border telling the police and border guards that they were her grandchildren.[17] She crossed the border and left the children with relatives in Goma and then returned to Rwanda at a different border crossing. With these means, she saved the lives of more than seven Tutsi children whose parents had been killed in her neighborhood. She took these actions despite her daughter's objections.

In other communities, physical geography provided escape routes from massacre sites or gave people places to hide in banana plantations, forests, or marshes. In communities along the shores of Lake Kivu, the local population, who used boats for fishing and trade across the lake, evacuated Tutsi across the lake. Some they took to safety in Zaire, although it was a long and arduous trip. Others they took to Gisenyi, where they could find their own way to cross the border into Zaire. In Mugandamure in southern Rwanda, its history as a Swahili camp during colonialism made it easy for residents to erect roadblocks to close the neighborhood off to outsiders.[18] Residents then smuggled in Tutsi and hid them in their homes. On at least one occasion, a group of Interahamwe accompanied by soldiers forced their way into the neighborhood searching for specific people. These people were taken to a public square and killed. Nonetheless, the community succeeded in saving more than a hundred people.

Community structure and social networks significantly shaped individuals' behavior during the genocide (Fujii 2011, McDoom 2014). In two communities in western and southern Rwanda, a history of communal activities among Muslims encouraged individual acts of rescue and created social networks for organized efforts to rescue Tutsi. Strong cooperative culture and pro-social action, such as food sharing surrounding religious feasts, have been found to promote and maintain altruistic behavior in times of crisis (Pessi 2009, 201; Gintis 2003; Rushton 1982). During Muslim feast days, local Muslims included their non-Muslim neighbors in their celebrations and shared meat with them. In addition, the collective action to organize feasts created and reinforced social relationships and patterns of cooperation. These relationships and patterns made it more likely for Muslims in these communities to hide and protect Tutsi. On the other hand, in Gisenyi, Muslims were closely tied to the political elites who became the primary architects of the genocide. Virtually all Muslim men we interviewed in Gisenyi town said that they were members of the MRND political party in 1994, whereas Muslim men elsewhere in Rwanda indicated that they had not joined any party because Islam forbid it. Muslims in Gisenyi, particularly young men, faced enormous social pressure to join in the violence (as illustrated below in Ali's story).

Having a Good Heart: Empathy and Rescue

Beyond simple opportunity, rescuers drew on an internal moral compass that guided their decisions. In interviews, genocide survivors and rescuers themselves described rescuers as people "who have a good heart" (*bafite umutima mwiza*), a Kinyarwanda phrase that encompasses a person's mind, character, and spirit. As one Muslim woman who at the age of twenty-one saved several Tutsi lives explained: "The reason why some people saved people while others didn't . . . it went with the person's heart;

the one who had a beastly heart didn't save the person but, the one who had a merciful heart which understood that a human being is a human being, saved that person."[19] In Rwandan conceptions of the self and of the function of the body, the mind is not perceived as being attached to the head or the brain. Thoughts and feelings emanate from the heart. Thus the word heart (*umutima*) in Kinyarwanda is synonymous with the word conscience in English. In chapter 5 of this volume, McGrew describes the ways in which Western philosophy and the literature on peacebuilding describe empathy as involving both head and heart. Empathy and reconciliation involve both emotional and intellectual processes and to succeed require a "unity of head and heart" (Kraybill 1988, 8 [cited in Fisher 2001, 34]; Halpern and Weinstein 2004). In essence, Rwandans conceive of heart and mind as unified and indistinguishable except for when a person uses their cunning to intentionally deceive others.

The most common way interviewees explained why some people risked their lives to save others was to say they had "a good heart," "a merciful heart," or saw Tutsi and others being targeted as "innocent" of any crime or as "humans." A female genocide survivor, who was only nine years old in 1994, explained:

> People rescued victims from personal compassion. In general terms people who got involved in the violence were mostly motivated by material possessions they could get from the victims. They perceived the victims' death as an opportunity to get access to their things/property. On the positive side, there were people who were not interested in the victims' material possessions and preferred to rescue them because they were also convinced that the victims were innocent.[20]

In essence, they explained that these people had empathy for others. As McGrew demonstrates in the case of Cambodia (this volume), empathy is an inoculation against dehumanization, which is a necessary component of genocide. People who can empathize still see others as humans who are worthy of compassion.

Rescuers required enormous courage in addition to empathy and "having a good heart." A female genocide survivor who was fifteen years old in 1994 explained that having a good heart was not enough, "It requires courage for people to help others despite the risk. There is also a good heart, but it is courage."[21] In short, the moral compulsion to help their kin, neighbors, or coworkers was only the starting point. To succeed in rescuing people, those with the desire to help had to have the courage to disobey orders from local officials, stand up to armed militiamen and soldiers, or negotiate calmly and cleverly with irrational, often inebriated, Interahamwe.

These internal moral orientations—having a good heart, being courageous, and eschewing material possessions—were the most frequently cited among interviewees who talked about rescuers' motivations. While any of these human impulses could be based on religious belief, Rwandans distinguished between these general moral orientations based on an understanding of a common humanity from explicit religious faith and practice. Empathy in rescue often draws on preexisting moral tenets, as Kahn discusses in chapter 7 of this book. Because the major religions in Rwanda, including Christianity and Islam, forbid murder, people assume that religion should have discouraged participation in the genocide. Nonetheless, people of all faiths, and even the clergy and religious leaders, were among the perpetrators.[22] People of all faiths were also among the victims. Unlike many other instances of communal violence or genocide, such as the Holocaust in Europe or the civil wars in Northern Ireland, Sri Lanka, or Bosnia-Herzegovina, religion did not serve as "an ascriptive identifier to single out" individuals to kill in the 1994 genocide in Rwanda (Longman 2009, 306). Christian churches became key massacre sites as ethnic Tutsi and others targeted in the genocide gathered there seeking sanctuary from the killing. Mosques rarely became massacre sites, because the imams closed the mosques during the genocide and instructed Muslims to pray at home.[23]

Religion featured prominently in some explanations of rescuer behavior and the distinctions between people who joined the genocide and those who refused to participate. Both Muslim and Christian rescuers depicted a fear of God as part of their motivation for trying to help Tutsi, or characterized their actions as purely being an instrument of God's will. As one Muslim rescuer explained, "Our religion, Islam, doesn't allow people to spill our neighbors' blood. We looked and we only saw brothers here. You could not think about killing this person, because he was a brother, someone who would have rescued you too, if you needed help."[24] Another Muslim rescuer attributed his acts of rescue to God saying, "It was not me who protected them, it was Allah."[25] In response to being asked why he saved people, a Catholic man said, because of "God and my Christian belief."[26] A Pentecostal man who was a FAR soldier in the Rwandan army explained,

I was a soldier inside Rwanda. I was a Christian from ADEPR. Following my beliefs and how I saw other religions, the true believer
didn't participate in the genocide. I mean the true faith is not about
religion. Whether it is a Muslim, a Catholic, an Adventist, and my
fellow Pentecost, those who were true believers never got involved.
I am among those who rescued people, and among those who did
not participate.[27]

In this rescuer's testimony, the theme of empathy is revealed through his
conception of all religions as being equal in terms of prohibiting murder.
"True believers never got involved." All the more remarkable in his story
is the courage he demonstrated by refusing to participate in the genocide.
The vast majority of FAR soldiers found themselves implicated in the
genocide because they complied with orders from superior officers that
involved participating in genocide (Des Forges 1999, 208–11). Some FAR
soldiers found the means to avoid involving themselves in the genocide by
focusing solely on actions related to ensuring security for civilians or to
fighting the RPF rebels. However, if their commanding officer actively
enforced the genocide policy, they risked being executed on the spot (Des
Forges 1999, 210).

Coexistence, Testimony, and Rescue

The empathy, courage, and humanity demonstrated by those who rescued
during the genocide have had many long-term impacts on the people they
saved. As discussed earlier in this chapter, many genocide survivors who
were rescued have had an ongoing desire to recognize the people who
saved them by telling their stories. Many survivors have maintained ongoing friendships or kin-like relationships with their rescuers. A genocide
survivor in Gisenyi took me to meet the old woman who had smuggled
him across the border to Goma in broad daylight when he was fourteen
years old. She then carried across his surviving siblings and many other
children from the neighborhood. Although neither she nor her family
knew her exact age when I met her in 2013, she was probably in her mid-
to late eighties. Given her age, she had trouble remembering the details of
what she had done in 1994. She even struggled to have a coherent conversation. The man she had rescued when he was still a boy regularly visited
her, bringing her favorite drink of banana beer and new clothing when she
needed it. He told me that he treated her as if she were his grandmother

who had perished in the genocide. Another survivor we interviewed, a woman, spoke for nearly four hours straight to give us her eyewitness testimony of Felicité Niyitegeka's courageous acts. Repeatedly during the interview, she exhorted us to tell Felicité's story so that people would know of the good deeds she had done and the sacrifice she had made. Clearly genocide survivors who were helped by Hutu or Twa during the genocide recognized that not all of them were perpetrators or heartless bystanders. As Zucker, Mieth, and Shapiro-Phim (this volume) explore in detail, these experiences allow them to imagine a past and a future where at least some Hutu and Twa are good. They thus tended to be more open to trust Rwandans from all backgrounds and not only survivors likes themselves.

Yet simply sharing narratives of diverse points of view is not enough. People must also receive feedback on the empirical truth (or lack thereof) of their testimony as well as the potential emotional impact of their testimony on others. In Rwanda, these types of conversations have taken place at the grassroots level in churches, mosques, and civil society organizations. As Velasco (this volume) relates for Colombia, grassroots organizations provide marginalized people with opportunities to participate in the processes of memory construction dominated by state institutions. In addition, the government has focused on national unity and reconciliation and documentation and commemoration of the genocide (as discussed above). These programs have an impact on the ways people understand their experiences, their past, and the potential impact of their testimony on others.

The story of Ali, both a genocide survivor and a perpetrator, illustrates some important effects of narratives about genocide and about the past on coexistence in the present and the potential for reconciliation in the future. Ali was twenty years old at the time of the genocide, born to a Hutu father and Tutsi mother. He lived in Gisenyi town, a region dominated by extremist Hutu Power political parties, in a neighborhood overrun by Interahamwe. Due to his mixed ethnic heritage and his youth, Ali was harassed and faced intense pressure to participate. A Muslim, Ali explained how he became involved in the genocide: "Those who survived, in my mother's family, sought refuge at our home. They were able to survive, and they are still there."[28] Beyond the harassment he faced from Interahamwe in the streets or in his own home, Ali's father advised him to go on security patrols as a way to protect himself and also the family. Ali clarified:

[my father] told me, "Get up and be with them, do not kill if they do. Just go with them and sit where they sit, to show them that you're with them. If they keep on saying that you are an accomplice [meaning an accomplice of the RPF rebels] they will kill you as well." So . . . I would go with them. . . . Sometimes when they came to wake me up, [my father] would give me money they called "flash-light fees" to buy batteries for the flashlights they would use at night. That was money they bought alcohol with . . . he would give them like 5,000 francs to buy me a night off.[29]

At the time of the genocide, both Ali and his family understood his actions as a way to avoid participating in the genocide while giving the appearance of compliance to local officials and Interahamwe militias.

When I first interviewed him in 2011, Ali insisted that he had not participated in the genocide. He claimed that he confessed to genocide crimes as a way to get out of prison. He repeatedly said that he had done "nothing wrong" in 1994. In 2013, he understood his actions in a new light. As he explained:

> I was accused and put in prison. . . . Then, I listened to what the Government came to teach us in prison about admitting crimes. I told them, "Given that I didn't kill anyone, what shall I confess to?" But because I listened to what they taught us, I finally understood that genocide crimes are not only about getting a machete and killing. Genocide is a collective crime. Some people were accomplices. Others contributed to the planning and did the deed itself. But even the fact that you were standing all three together made the one who was killing confident because he knew that he was with you. That made the one you had gone to kill weaker and kept him from defending himself. What might he have done if there had been one killer? But because we were three, it made the killer strong.[30]

Over time Ali had come to understand his actions in 1994 in a new way. He came to see the moral wrong in what he had done even if it had seemed a logical, least wrong choice that minimized threats to his family or himself. The evolution in Ali's thinking illustrates the influence of national narratives and state-building practices to promote reconciliation. These efforts compel perpetrators and bystanders to accept their legal and moral complicity in the genocide. Some, such as Ali, eventually see their actions in a new light. Others pretend to go along as a way to move forward in their lives.

Genocide survivors who were not helped by others during the genocide understandably tend to have very negative views of their fellow Rwandans. They are often distrusting and relatively closed to new relationships. They often assume the worst about people. Nonetheless, hearing stories of rescue, especially those told by other survivors, opens up new possibilities and ways of seeing others. An interpreter who assisted during several interviews with *indakemwa* explained how the stories gave her new hope. A genocide survivor herself, she had received no assistance during the genocide from her Hutu neighbors or strangers. She and her family saved themselves. After several interviews with *indakemwa* and the survivors they had helped, the interpreter said, "Thank you for involving me in this research. I didn't know of stories like this. Knowing that people could sacrifice so much to try to save a Tutsi. It brings a good feeling in my heart."[31]

Sharing the stories about rescuers with genocide survivors and Tutsi who were not in Rwanda during the genocide or who were born after the genocide can help them recognize the good in "the other" category that has become demonized through the experiences of violence during the genocide, their recollections after the genocide, and their exposure to evidence of atrocities in the aftermath through courts, media coverage, discovery of remains, and so on. As Kahn relates (this volume), stories of rescue can help society members envision a new future and rediscover empathy. Rescuers' stories can help restore some hope and the potential to trust others. In the aftermath, sharing stories with people in the social categories associated with perpetrators or bystanders can allow them to see themselves and their own actions in a new light. It can also provide role models that allow them to imagine themselves acting in a different or new way. Empathy is thus a component of lasting, sustainable peace as McGrew (this volume) shows in the case of Cambodia.

Beyond modeling empathy or restoring hope to survivors, sharing the stories of rescue during mass atrocities can help foster peaceful coexistence in other ways. As Gordon describes (this volume), peaceful coexistence requires the equitable distribution of narratives so that many points of view can be heard while still accounting for empirical facts. In Somaliland, the emergence of a new national identity required the detoxification of "identity markers of 'victim' and 'perpetrator'" (Gordon, this volume). In Rwanda, genocide survivors were the only ones who could give testimony publicly in the early years after the genocide. This situation impeded peaceful coexistence by publicly erasing the wrongs suffered by Hutu victims of the genocide or those suffered by Rwandans of all ethnicities at the hands of the RPF forces or the new government (Burnet 2012). While testimony from genocide survivors in Rwanda (and elsewhere) deserves a special place in public discourse, ignoring the harm suffered by others risks creating resentments that fuel genocide denial or minimize the genocide as "only war."

In the first ten years after the Rwandan genocide, many projects that became peacebuilding or reconciliation projects did not start with these intentions. In my earlier work, I looked at several of these in different parts of the country. They began by addressing people's basic needs, often beginning with genocide survivors and then evolving to consider other people facing similar difficulties. Then they organically grew into peacebuilding or reconciliation activities. Essential to most of the projects that were successful in generating peaceful coexistence was a redistribution of narratives. For example, in a Roman Catholic parish in southern Rwanda, a grassroots women's cooperative brought together genocide widows, widows "from life" (meaning widows whose husbands had died of natural causes or at the hands of the RPF), and women whose husbands were in prison accused of genocide crimes. At first, these three different categories of women could not meet or talk together. When they did, they competed over whose suffering was the greatest. The parish priest who brought the women together created a method whereby a single woman recounted her experiences without interruption from the others. After she spoke, he asked the women who were listening to silently reflect on ways in which the witness's experiences and suffering were similar to their own. Then he led the women in prayer. Through this process, the women learned how to listen to each other and many of them (re)discovered empathy. This process of creating spaces where people could speak about what had happened to them and be heard by others was common to several other grassroots reconciliation initiatives I have observed. This dual process of speaking and being heard was the key to helping individuals find a way forward and building new relationships.

Given that Hutu and Twa who attempted to rescue Tutsi in the genocide remained vulnerable to being accused of or implicated in mass atrocities, the public space for cultivating empathy was occluded. The lack of public testimony about rescue—whether heroic, morally pure rescue, or the morally ambiguous rescue in the grey zone—allows for the ongoing demonization of certain categories of Rwandans as presumed perpetrators. It is important to recognize the good, no matter how fleeting, that occurred amidst the evil of genocide. It is important to combat the impression that all Hutu or Twa were perpetrators or bystanders. While our data cannot precisely measure the numbers of people who saved or helped

Tutsi, our data do demonstrate that rescuer behavior was widespread. Testimonies about rescuers can help contribute to peacebuilding and peaceful coexistence, but we have to be sensitive to what is possible at any given moment in time.

NOTES

1. How to label the mass killings and genocide that occurred in Rwandan in 1994 is highly politicized. In earlier writings, I used terms like "Rwandan genocide," "1994 genocide and massacres," or "genocide and massacres" following terminology in Kinyarwanda *itsembabwoko n'itsembatsemba* (genocide and massacres) preferred by the government between 1997 and 2002 when the bulk of my fieldwork was completed (Burnet 2012, 20–21). In the mid-2000s, the government changed to prefer *jenoside* (genocide) or *jenoside ya 1994* (1994 genocide) in place of *itsembabwoko n'itsembatsemba* (Waldorf 2009, 104–5). This formulation avoided mention of ethnicity, which was repressed from public discourse in the interest of national reconciliation (Waldorf 2009, 104–5). In 2008, the government introduced the more precise term "jenoside yakorewe abaTutsi muri 1994" (literally, "genocide that carried away the Tutsis in 1994") in a revision of the 2003 constitution (Republic of Rwanda 2008). The change was intended to clarify who, precisely, was the target of the genocide. Yet this language shift erased the Hutu and Twa victims of the genocide who were killed because of their party affiliation, refusal to participate in the genocide, or actions taken to help Tutsi escape. Despite this drawback, I use "genocide of Tutsi" to reflect the internal shift in language and to acknowledge the genocide's primary targets.

2. Estimates of how many people died in the 1994 genocide range from 500,000 (Des Forges 1999, 15) to one million (MINALOC 2004, 21). For more on the numbers of dead and their politicization, see Scott Straus (2006, 51).

3. The social categories "Hutu," "Tutsi," and "Twa" predate the colonial era in Rwanda, but their meanings and significance have changed dramatically over time. They are not marked by differences in language, culture, religion, or territory in recorded history. During European colonialism, they were racialized and began to operate in ways analogous to race categories elsewhere in the world (for additional explanation, see Burnet 2012, 14–16).

4. Some interviews cited were conducted by coinvestigator and anthropologist Hager El Hadidi. This research was supported by the University of Louisville Research Foundation and Department of Anthropology and the National Science Foundation under Grant Nos. 1230062 and 1550655. Any opinions, findings, and conclusions or recommendations expressed in this material are those of the author and do not necessarily reflect the views of the National Science Foundation.

5. In line with human subjects protocols, all interviewee names and names mentioned in interview data are pseudonyms unless otherwise noted.

6. Interview with Ibuka national representative by author, Kigali, Rwanda, 2013,

7. Interview by author, Kigali, Rwanda, 2011.

8. Interviews by the author, multiple locations in Rwanda, 1997, 1998, 1999, 2000, 2001. See also video testimony in the National Genocide Memorial Museum in Kigali.

9. Niyitegeka's name has not been changed since her story is well known. Because she is dead, there was no need to render accounts of her deeds anonymous.

10. Rusesabagina's name has not been changed since his case is well known and only public sources were cited.

11. The film's director, Terry George, defended the version of events recounted in the film and explained the timeline of the smear campaign against Rusesabagina in a *Washington Post* opinion editorial in May 2006. "Smearing a Hero," by Terry George, *Washington Post* website, published May 10, 2006, accessed February 18, 2017, at http://www.washingtonpost.com/wp-dyn/content/article/2006/05/09/AR2006050901242.html

12. See for example, "Hotel Rwanda—Without the Hollywood Ending," by Linda Melvern, *The Guardian* website, published November 17, 2011, accessed February 24, 2017, at https://www.theguardian.com/commentisfree/2011/nov/17/hotel-rwanda-hollywood-ending

13. Interviews by author, Rwanda, 2014–2016.

14. Interview by author, Kayove district, West province, Rwanda, 2013.

15. See for example the patrols and massacres of Tutsi along the Akanyaru River at Rwanda's southern border with Burundi (Des Forges 1999, 287–89).

16. Interviews by author and Hager El Hadidi, Gisenyi, Rwanda, 2013.

17. Interview by author, Gisenyi, Rwanda, 2013.

18. Interviews by author and by El Hadidi, Mugandamure, Rwanda, 2013.

19. Interview by author, Nkora, Rwanda, October 2013.

20. Interview by El Hadidi, Nkora, Rwanda, October 2013.

21. Interview by El Hadidi, Biryogo, Rwanda, November 2013.

22. Muslims comprised less than 2 percent of the population at the time according to government statistics (Longman 2009, 4). While some people have claimed that Muslims resisted participating in the genocide or did not kill other Muslims (Longman 2009, 196), data from our research show that Muslims did participate in the genocide, even killing other Muslims.

23. Interviews by author and El Hadidi, various locations, Rwanda, 2013.

24. Interview by author, Mugandamure, Rwanda, July 2013.

25. Interview by El Hadidi, Gisenyi, Rwanda, October 2013.

26. Interview by El Hadidi, Gisenyi, Rwanda, November 2013.

27. Interview by El Hadidi, Nyanza, Rwanda, August 2013.

28. Interview by author, Gisenyi, Rwanda, October 2013.

29. Interview by author, Gisenyi, Rwanda, October 2013.

30. Interview by author, Gisenyi, Rwanda, October 2013.

31. Personal communication to author, Kigali, Rwanda, April 2014.

REFERENCES

Andrieu, Claire. 2011. "Conclusion: Rescue, A Notion Revisited." In *Resisting Genocide: The Multiple Forms of Rescue*, edited by Jacques Sémelin, Claire Andrieu, and Sarah Gensburger, 495–506. New York: Columbia University Press.

Bernard, H. Russell, and Gery W. Ryan. 2010. *Analyzing Qualitative Data: Systematic Approaches*. Los Angeles: SAGE Publications.

Bruneau, Emile G., and Rebecca Saxe. 2012. "The Power of Being Heard: The Benefits of

'Perspective-Giving' in the Context of Intergroup Conflict." *Journal of Experimental Social Psychology* 48, no. 4: 855–66.

Burnet, Jennie E. 2008. "The Injustice of Local Justice: Truth, Reconciliation, and Revenge in Rwanda." *Genocide Studies and Prevention* 3, no. 2: 173–93.

Burnet, Jennie E. 2009. "Whose Genocide? Whose Truth? Representations of Victim and Perpetrator in Rwanda." In *Genocide: Truth, Memory and Representation*, edited by Alex Laban Hinton and Kevin O'Neill, 80–110. Durham: Duke University Press.

Burnet, Jennie E. 2010. "(In)justice: Truth, Reconciliation, and Revenge in Rwanda's Gacaca." In *Transitional Justice: Global Mechanisms and Local Realities after Genocide and Mass Violence*, edited by Alexander Laban Hinton, 95–118. New Brunswick, NJ: Rutgers University Press.

Burnet, Jennie E. 2012. *Genocide Lives in Us: Women, Memory, and Silence in Rwanda*. Madison: University of Wisconsin Press.

Cohen, Ronald. 1992. "Altruism and the Evolution of Civil Society." In *Embracing the Other: Philosophical, Psychological, and Historical Perspectives on Altruism*, edited by Pearl M. Oliner, Samuel P. Oliner, Lawrence Baron, Lawrence A. Blum, Dennis L. Krebs, and M. Zuzanna Smolenska, 104–30. New York and London: New York University Press.

DeCety, Jean. 2011. "The Neuroevolution of Empathy: Neuroevolution of Empathy and Concern." *Annals of the New York Academy of Sciences* 1231, no. 1: 35–45.

Des Forges, Alison Liebhafsky, Human Rights Watch (Organization), and Fédération internationale des droits de l'homme. 1999. *"Leave none to tell the story": Genocide in Rwanda*. New York and Paris: Human Rights Watch and International Federation of Human Rights.

Fisher, Ronald J. 2001. "Social-Psychological Processes in Interactive Conflict Analysis and Reconciliation." In *Reconciliation, Justice, and Coexistence: Theory and Practice*, edited by Mohammed Abu-Nimer, 25–46. New York: Lexington Books.

Fogelman, Eva. 1994. *Conscience & Courage: Rescuers of Jews during the Holocaust*. New York: Anchor Books.

Fujii, Lee Ann. 2011. "Rescuers and Killer-Rescuers During the Rwandan Genocide: Rethinking Standard Categories of Analysis." In *Resisting Genocide: The Multiple Forms of Rescue*, edited by Jacques Sémelin, Claire Andrieu, and Sarah Gensburger, 145–57. New York: Columbia University Press.

George, Terry. 2006. "Smearing a Hero." *Washington Post*, May 9. Accessed February 18, 2017. http://www.washingtonpost.com/wpdyn/content/article/2006/05/09/AR2006050901242.html

Gintis, H. 2003. "Solving the Puzzle of Prosociality." *Rationality and Society* 15, no. 15: 155–87.

Gourevitch, Philip. 1998. *We Wish to Inform You That Tomorrow We Will Be Killed with Our Families: Stories from Rwanda*. New York: Farrar, Straus & Giroux.

Guichaoua, André. 2015. *From War to Genocide: Criminal Politics in Rwanda, 1990–1994*. Translated by Don E. Webster. Madison: University of Wisconsin Press.

Halpern, Jodi. 2001. *From Detached Concern to Empathy: Humanizing Medical Practice*. New York: Oxford University Press.

Halpern, Jodi, and Harvey M. Weinstein. 2004. "Rehumanizing the Other: Empathy and Reconciliation." *Human Rights Quarterly* 26, no. 3: 561–83.

Hinton, Alexander Laban. 2010. *Transitional Justice: Global Mechanisms and Local Realities after Genocide and Mass Violence*. New Brunswick, NJ: Rutgers University Press.

Hoffman, Martin L. 2000. *Empathy and Moral Development: Implications for Caring and Justice*. Cambridge: Cambridge University Press.

Huyse, Lucien. 2003. "The Process of Reconciliation." In *Reconciliation after Violent Conflict: A Handbook*, edited by David Bloomfield, Terri Barnes, Lucien Huyse, and International Institute for Democracy and Electoral Assistance, 19–33. Handbook Series. Stockholm: International IDEA.

Jarymowicz, Maria. 1992. "Self, We, and Other(s): Schemata, Distinctiveness, and Altruism." In *Embracing the Other: Philosophical, Psychological, and Historical Perspectives on Altruism*, edited by Pearl M. Oliner, Samuel P. Oliner, Lawrence Baron, Lawrence A. Blum, Dennis L. Krebs, and M. Zuzanna Smolenska, 194–212. New York and London: New York University Press.

Kayihura, Edouard, and Kerry Zukus. 2014. *Inside the Hotel Rwanda: The Surprising True Story . . . and Why it Matters Today*. Dallas: BenBella Books.

Kayishema, Jean-Marie, and Francois Masabo. 2010. *Les Justes Rwandais "Indakemwa."* Kigali, Rwanda: Ibuka.

Kohn, Alfie. 1990. *The Brighter Side of Human Nature: Altruism and Empathy in Everyday Life*. New York: Basic Books.

Kraybill, Ronald S. 1988. "From Head to Heart: The Cycle of Reconciliation." *Mennonite Conciliation Quarterly* 7, no. 4.

Kriesberg, Louis. 2001. "Changing Forms of Coexistence." In *Reconciliation, Justice, and Coexistence: Theory & Practice*, edited by Mohammed Abu-Nimer, 47–64. Lanham, MD: Lexington Books.

Longman, Timothy Paul. 2009. *Christianity and Genocide in Rwanda*. Cambridge: Cambridge University Press.

McDoom, Omar Shahabudin. 2014. "Antisocial Capital: A Profile of Rwandan Genocide Perpetrators' Social Networks." *Journal of Conflict Resolution* 58, no. 5: 865–93. https://doi.org/10.1177/0022002713484282

Meyer, Gerd. 2009. "Taking Risks for Others: Social Courage as a Public Virtue." In *On Behalf of Others: The Psychology of Care in a Global World*, edited by Sarah Scuzzarello, Catarina Kinnvall, and Kristen Renwick Monroe, 82–105. Oxford: Oxford University Press.

Ministry of Local Government, Communal Development, and Social Affairs (MINALOC). 2004. *Denombrement des victimes du génocide*. Kigali, Rwanda.

Monroe, Kristen R. 1996. *The Heart of Altruism: Perceptions of a Common Humanity*. Princeton: Princeton University Press.

Monroe, Kristen R., and Maria Luisa Martinez. 2009. "Empathy, Prejudice, and Fostering Tolerance." In *On Behalf of Others: The Psychology of Care in a Global World*, edited by Sarah Scuzzarello, Catarina Kinnvall, and Kristen Renwick Monroe, 147–62. Oxford: Oxford University Press.

Oliner, Pearl M., Samuel P. Oliner, L. Baron, L. A. Blum, D. L. Krebs, and M. Z. Smolenska. 1992. *Embracing the Other: Philosophical, Psychological, and Historical Perspectives on Altruism*. New York: New York University Press.

Oliner, Samuel P. 2002. "Extraordinary Acts of Ordinary People: Faces of Heroism and Altruism." In *Altruism and Altruistic Love: Science, Philosophy, and Religion in Dialogue*, edited by Stephen G. Post, Lynn G. Underwood, Jeffrey P. Schloss, and William B. Hurlbut, 123–39. Oxford: Oxford University Press.

Oliner, Samuel P., and Pearl M. Oliner. 1988. *The Altruistic Personality: Rescuers of Jews in Nazi Europe*. New York: Free Press.

Pessi, Anne B. 2009. "Spirit of Altruism? On the Role of the Finnish Church as a Promoter of Altruism of Individuals and of Society." In *On Behalf of Others: The Psychology of Care in a Global World*, edited by Sarah Scuzzarello, Catarina Kinnvall, and Kristen Renwick Monroe, 147–62. Oxford: Oxford University Press.

Republic of Rwanda. 2008. "Amendment of 13/8/2008 of the Constitution of the Republic of Rwanda of 4 June 2003 as Amended to Date." *Official Gazette of the Republic of Rwanda*, Special of August 13.

Republic of Rwanda. 2016. *Urutonde Rw'abanyarwanda N'Abanyamahanga Bahawe Imidali N'Impeta By'Ishimwe*. Kigali, Rwanda: Chancellery for Heroes, National Orders and Decorations of Honour (Cheno).

Rushton, J. P. 1982. "Altruism and Society—A Social Learning Perspective." *Ethics* 92, no. 3: 425–46.

Schreiter, Robert J. 1992. *Reconciliation: Mission and Ministry in a Changing Social Order*. Maryknoll, NY: Orbis Books.

Seidler, Victor J. 1992. "Rescue, Righteousness, and Morality." In *Embracing the Other*, edited by Pearl M. Oliner, Samuel P. Oliner, Lawrence Baron, Lawrence A. Blum, Dennis L. Krebs, and M. Zuzanna Smolenska, 48–66. New York: New York University Press.

Sémelin, Jacques, Claire Andrieu, and Sarah Gensburger. 2008. *La résistance aux génocides*. Paris: Les Presses des SciencesPo.

Sémelin, Jacques, Claire Andrieu, and Sarah Gensburger. 2011. *Resisting Genocide: The Multiple Forms of Rescue*. Translated by Emma Bentley and Cynthia Schoch. New York: Columbia University Press.

Staub, Ervin. 1993. "The Psychology of Bystanders, Perpetrators, and Heroic Helpers." *International Journal of Intercultural Relations* 17 (January): 315–41.

Staub, Ervin. 2003. *The Psychology of Good and Evil: Why Children, Adults, and Groups Help and Harm Others*. Cambridge: Cambridge University Press.

Straus, Scott. 2006. *The Order of Genocide: Race, Power, and War in Rwanda*. Ithaca: Cornell University Press.

United Nations. 1999. *Report of the Independent Inquiry into Actions of the United Nations during the 1994 Genocide in Rwanda*.

United Nations Department of Peacekeeping Operations. 2008. "United Nations Peacekeeping Operations: Principles and Guidelines." Approved by Jean-Marie Guéhenno, USG/DPKO. January 18, 2008. https://www.un.org/ruleoflaw/files/Capstone_Doctrine_ENG.pdf

Viret, Emmanuel. 2011. "Social Cohesion and State of Exception: The Muslims of Mabare during the Genocide in Rwanda." In *Resisting Genocide: The Multiple Forms of Rescue*, edited by Jacques Sémelin, Claire Andrieu, and Sarah Gensburger, 481–94. New York: Columbia University Press.

Waldorf, Lars. 2009. "Revisiting Hotel Rwanda: Genocide Ideology, Reconciliation, and Rescuers." *Journal of Genocide Research* 11, no. 1: 101–25.

Weiner, Eugene. 1998. *The Handbook of Interethnic Coexistence*. New York: Continuum.

7 | The Rescuers

The Role of Testimony as a
Peacebuilding Tool to Create Empathy

Leora Kahn

"When there is peace a machete can cut hair."
—Kinyarwanda proverb

"The neighbor before the house and the companion before the road."
—Arabic proverb

Rescuers' testimonies document the presence of rescue behavior during genocide or mass violence and promote insight into the conditions that support prosocial behavior in the face of communal violence. It is critical to have a better understanding of these extraordinary acts of altruism and empathy by ordinary people as the global community continues to grapple with how to respond to mass violence. Highlighting the value of the rescuer behavior and rescuers' testimonies in post-conflict societies and providing civil society with role models can establish a pathway to coexistence. Rescuer narratives enable citizens to imagine themselves as rescuers instead of as perpetrators or bystanders (see also Burnet, this volume). My purpose in studying rescuers' testimonies is not to investigate the individual psychology of rescuers. Nor is it to suggest that rescuers occupy a higher plane of morality than everyone else. Rather, my aim is more of a sociological inquiry—that is, to explore the cultural and societal conditions that promote rescue behavior and use it to promote peacebuilding through education.

PROOF: Media for Social Justice is a human rights nonprofit that uses visual storytelling to tell the stories of courageous people who have lived through human rights violations. Working with local partners and international organizations like NATO; TRIAL International, a Swiss NGO that works against impunity; and the United Nations, PROOF produces exhibits that travel worldwide. Through my work as founder and executive director of PROOF I have collected and researched the testimonies of rescuers in Sri Lanka, Bosnia, Rwanda, Cambodia, and Iraq. These testimonies are stories of people who risked their lives to save the "other": Hutus who rescued Tutsis during the Rwandan genocide; Serbs and Croats who saved each other during the Bosnian genocide; Buddhists, Muslims, and Christians who crossed religious lines to save one another in Sri Lanka; Khmer Rouge and villagers who became rescuers during the reign of Pol Pot in Cambodia; and Shiites and Sunnis who rescued each other and who cooperated to rescue others fleeing from ISIS in Iraq. I have been studying and documenting these rescuers over a decade, recording their stories, photographing them, and then developing traveling exhibits about moral courage based on their testimonies. Rescuers are significant in that they disrupt the narrative that holds that everyone in the identified perpetrator group is indeed a perpetrator, and in some cases they can potentially act to interrupt mass violence if/when there is another occurrence. This interruption can be the tool that is necessary for peacebuilding.

In this chapter I share and analyze rescuers in three separate case studies: Bosnia, Rwanda, and Iraq.

Background

On April 6, 2011, the US State Department held a commemoration of the 60th anniversary of the 1951 Convention Related to the Status of Refugees. In preparation for this event, the State Department contacted the Yale Genocide Studies Program where I working as a visiting fellow at the time. They were interested in the rescuer testimonies that I had collected, as they were preparing to honor those who had the courage to stand up against those in power to rescue the "other" in contexts of mass violence. In addition to recognizing them for their courage, they also acknowledged their role as peacebuilders in the aftermaths of mass violence. The intention was to present the courageous people who rescued others as role models and to suggest that the flow of refugees fleeing violent situations may be curbed if more individuals took it upon themselves to rescue others in these contexts, such as those being honored. Several rescuers were recognized at the commemoration, including Captain Mbaye Diagne, a

Fig. 7.1. Josephine Dusabimana

UN Senegalese peacekeeper stationed in Rwanda in 1994 who saved six hundred Rwandans before he was killed by a stray mortar shell, and Josephine Dusabimana, a Hutu who rescued Tutsis by hiding them in her home and then bringing them to safety by canoeing across Lake Kiva to the Congo at night. Hillary Clinton, then acting U.S. secretary of state, speaking at the event said of Josephine, "Heroes such as Josephine have inspired Rwandans to build a different kind of society today. And Josephine, I salute and thank you for your example of such great courage and reconciliation."

In her speech Clinton noted the extraordinary courage of the rescuers and reminded the audience that these individuals never forgot their common humanity with those deemed as "others"; that rather than stand by when atrocities were taking place they chose to "act on behalf of those who are in jeopardy."

One of those people who acted on behalf of those in jeopardy was a Rwandan Hutu named Christine. Recognizing a stranger as not the "other" but as someone in a desperate situation, Christine, together with her three daughters, hid a Tutsi family in her barn. Explaining her decision she said:

> I went to the gate and opened the door and saw a group of people standing there. I was scared and praying inside, but I heard God's

voice within me saying, don't be afraid. After opening the gate, they walked in the yard. It was dark and a man said to me, "We are going to put a huge burden on your shoulders. Are you ready to take it? If not, let us know so we can continue on our way." I replied to that man, "I am ready to die with you." I hid them in the barn next to my house. (personal communication, Christine)

One might ask: why would the US State Department want to honor *rescuers* during a *refugee* day? One explanation is that rescuers can serve as role models for others. Their actions during times of violence and crisis demonstrate what it means to have a moral compass. If more people acted as upstanders in times of mass violence, then others are likely to follow. If there are fewer killings, there would be fewer refugees—that is, fewer people fleeing conflict zones and troubled areas where there are mass killings. My definition of an upstander is a person who speaks or acts in support of an individual and who intervenes on behalf of a person being attacked. The testimonies of rescuers convey these ideals and demonstrate peacebuilding by treating "others" as fellow human beings.

What common traits unite people who fight against genocide when it is occurring? How do these people think about themselves, those they save, and their own behavior that differs from those around them that have committed violence? How do they maintain cultural norms when others have forgotten or discarded them? And, most importantly, can we teach moral behavior to young people before the next conflict begins by using testimonies as a tool for peacebuilding? While these questions can't be answered at this point in time, I will try to offer some preliminary findings that emerge from my fieldwork, a portion of which is detailed in the following three case studies.

Bosnia and Herzegovina (BIH)

Borivoje and Ljubinka Lelek, Serbian husband and wife, lived with their Muslim neighbors without any problems in the former Yugoslavia. But in 1991, Bosnia and Herzegovina declared independence, igniting a four-year civil war. The Bosnian population was multiethnic, composed of Muslim Bosniaks (44 percent), Orthodox Serbs (31 percent), and Catholic Croats (17 percent). In April 1992, the Bosnian Serbs attacked the city of Sarajevo, which was ethnically mixed at the time. This siege lasted for almost two years. Beyond Sarajevo, nationalist Croat and Serb forces were carrying

Fig. 7.2. Borivoje and Ljubinka Lelek

out ethnic cleansing attacks across the country. By the end of the war in 1995, according to the US Holocaust Memorial Museum in Washington, DC, an estimated one hundred thousand people were killed, 80 percent of whom were Bosniaks.

In July 1995, Bosnian Serb forces killed as many as eight thousand Bosniak men and boys from the town of Srebrenica (US Holocaust Memorial Museum website at https://www.ushmm.org/confront-genocide/cases/bosnia-herzegovina). While this war was raging, the Leleks lived peacefully with their Muslim neighbors in adjoining villages near Rogatica in the Republika Srpska. Serb and Muslim neighbors had an agreement that if one or the other's army came, they would safeguard each other.

> We never had any kind of conflicts or situations in which we argued. We always had a nice time together. We helped each other. So, the war surprised us, and we thought that there would be an agreement and that everything would be stopped. In my family, some of my cousins helped their Muslim neighbors during the war, and some didn't. We helped anyone from our neighborhood who came to us.

We helped them go to the free territory so they could get to Muslim territory. The risk was enormous, but we had to do it. Now, everything is the same as it was: we didn't have problems before the war, and we don't have any now. We have nothing against our neighbors, and they have nothing against us. Never. If everybody thought like our neighbors and we did, we would never have war—there would never be a reason for one to start. (personal communication, Lelek)

This testimony challenges the common assumption that different groups have historically hated one another. The Leleks' testimonies show that such assumptions represent a homogenization of history and group identity. Theirs is a memory of sharing between them and their Muslim neighbors. *Their memory is not historical, it is communal.* In other words, rather than holding onto memories of past insults or grievances, they held shared memories of their joys and sorrows together, because of the closeness and proximity of their villages.

Martha Minow and Nancy L. Rosenblum's (2002) important work on the role of memory shows how and when forgetting can be fatal. Communally held memories can help prevent atrocities (Minow and Rosenblum 2002). Longstanding and bitter enmity between religious and ethnic groups is not a foregone conclusion or unalterable eventuality. A lot depends on community traditions of social interaction, commerce, and municipal cooperation—in other words, customs. As Mr. Lelek told me in his testimony, his Serb family attended their Muslim neighbors' celebrations, weddings, births, and other communal celebrations as they did his. Why would this custom change with the onslaught of conflict? Why should larger regional tensions disrupt their lifelong relationships? The Leleks live in Republika Srpska, which is governed by a very nationalist and right-wing part of Bosnia and Herzegovina. They were part of the minority in their area that clung to the memory of communal harmony between them and their Muslim neighbors. The community didn't "buy into" collective memories of past hurts and past violence. The memories they chose to invoke were not the memories imposed upon them from outside political forces but of their own community (see also Shapiro-Phim and Zucker, this vol.).

The history of the three ethnic groups is a complicated one. Religion has been a major factor of conflict in all three groups. The Serbs are Orthodox Christians who lived in Bosnia during almost four centuries of Ottoman Turkish occupation. The Croats are Catholics who were part of the Austro-Hungarian Empire. The first Yugoslav state (1918–41) was under a

Serbian king and army and a Serb-dominated political system. During World War II the Croats sided with the Nazis. More than a million Serbs and Jews died.

Gil Eyal's (2007) work on collective memory is interesting in this context. He suggests that "a sense of a crisis of memory, and the diagnosis of too much or too little memory, are generated not by the universal nature of human memory but by a historically specific *will to memory*, a constellation of discourses and practices within which memory is entrusted with a certain goal and function, and is invested, routinely, as an institutional matter, with certain hopes and fears as to what it can do" (16). The Leleks "willed" themselves to remember the positive memories. They had to manage real fears combined with their hope that they would not get caught as they helped their neighbors and friends flee to safety. This action—preserving and accessing memories of weddings, celebrations, and warm friendship—enabled them to rescue despite the prevailing ideologies and risks that such an act implies.

In 2011, PROOF opened an exhibit highlighting the testimonies and photos of rescuers from Bosnia such as the Leleks that included representation of all ethnic groups—Croatians, Serbs, Muslims, and Jews. Each of the individuals featured in the exhibit had saved "the other" during conflict. The exhibit, organized in conjunction with NATO, the city of Sarajevo, and the US embassy, was pitched as a peacebuilding project showcasing role models from all of the ethnic groups and promoting a more peaceful coexistence.

After I spent two years collecting testimonies and photographing the Bosnian rescuers, an exhibit of the work opened at the BBI Center, a public square in Sarajevo, in 2011. The goals of the exhibit and the conference were stated as follows:

> This exhibit is designed to raise awareness for the need to stand up to the injustices that are still happening in the world around us, and to contribute to the understanding of peace. We hope these provocative stories will inspire the viewer to think about the courageous choices that can be made every day and become "rescuers" in your own communities wherever injustice exists.

Figure 7.3 shows the diversity of the audience who came to view the photos and read the testimonies. The diverse crowd that attended the exhibit represented the population of Sarajevo (Bosnia and Herzegovina Demographics Profile 2018–Index Mundi). Their reactions were positive.

Fig. 7.3. Sarajevo, Bosnia, outdoor exhibit

Most were surprised by the concept that there had been rescuers from other groups helping each other. Others commented that they knew of people that had participated in rescue. But notably all were intrigued and interested in the ideas of helping or rescuing others.

Along with the exhibit, a conference for high school and college students was organized. The conference, like the exhibit, was titled "Picturing Moral Courage." More than 150 students from all over the Balkans—Macedonia, Serbia, Croatia, and Bosnia—attended the conference. The students listened to talks by Erwin Staub, social psychologist; Steven Smith, a scholar of the Shoah; and James Smith, of the Aegis Trust. Personal stories of rescuers were told. The embassy sponsored a Bosnian youth panel entitled "Youth Speak Out" where students shared their views on peace and reconciliation. These students were being trained to be future leaders by the United States Embassy. The embassy was thereby reinforcing the role of young people as peacebuilders in their society. This multiethnic group had worked together to build relationships despite the ethnic barriers that had developed since the war.

The exhibit, "*The Rescuers: Picturing Moral Courage*," has subsequently traveled throughout the Balkans. It has been shown in eighteen venues in Bosnia including Mostar, Banjaukia, and other small towns. As "*The Rescuers*" traveled around the Balkans, more than four hundred high school and college students participated in accompanying workshops. Sabina

Čehajić-Clancy, a social psychologist at the Sarajevo School of Science and Technology, conducted a study of participants who attended the workshops, the results of which were published with her coauthor Michał Bilewicz. The study included seventy-five (forty-six females, twenty-nine males with a median age of 20.09) from five different cities or towns across BIH. These seventy-five students completed evaluation surveys before and after viewing the exhibition and films and participating in workshops. The same questionnaire was given to be completed before and after the workshop. Čehajić-Clancy, asked students to respond to statements such as: "I am ready to forgive other groups things that they have done during the war," "I could never forgive the committed crimes" (reverse coded), and "My group should never forgive other groups their misdeeds" (reverse coded).

The reliability of the results was good both before the intervention (a = .78) and after the intervention (a = .83). Čehajić-Clancy said, "Belief in reconciliation was measured with three items which were created for the purpose of this study." These included: "I doubt that we will ever be able to live together in peace" (reverse coded), "I believe that we can cooperate together," and "I believe that we can build a country together." The reliability was a = .66 before the intervention and a = .72 after the intervention (Čehajić-Clancy and Bilewicz 2017, 292). Preliminary results of these evaluations revealed that, after participating in the program, 75 percent were willing to forgive the out-group for their previous misdeeds, and there was a marked increase in participants' belief in the possibility of reconciliation. As one of the first experimental studies of its kind, it is an important indicator of how, through presenting positive, moral exemplars, sustainable reconciliation is possible (2017, 292).

Rwanda

Augustin Kagmaore is a Hutu farmer who lives near Lake Kivu. Kagmaore was a rescuer during the 1994 genocide in Rwanda where more than 800,000 Tutsis and moderate Hutus were murdered by militia and Rwandan government forces. The killings lasted one hundred days. Kagmaore was one of thirty people who were interviewed for this peacebuilding project. In 1994, he and his children managed to rescue more than twenty people fleeing from the genocide. His testimony described how and why he did it. The most telling portion of his testimony is when he talks about his motives:

Young people need to learn and start to do what is good like it used to be in the culture. They must learn how to look after others and stop being cowards. Killing people . . . you kill a person, you don't eat them . . . you throw them in the street where they rot. What good does that do you? Nothing. Yes, nothing. But for me, I see the advantages of saving them. We talk . . . if I have a wedding, they'll be the ones to bring the wine. How about you who killed them? Are you going to go in the bush where you threw their bodies and tell them to get you wine for your wedding? No that's impossible. So, people must have the culture and the mind of doing what is good. (personal communication, Kagmaore)

The interesting part of this testimony is that it shows that his belief in cultural norms supports acts of moral courage. He says about bringing wine, going to a wedding: how can you do that if you have killed someone? In other words, a person who would do such a thing would be an outcast. He considers this a problem when the genocide is over: how are they going to look into someone's dead eyes and bring them wine?

In his testimony he tells about a woman who "came to my home and asked to be let in. I asked her where she had been since the beginning of the assaults and she said she was hiding in a Hutu neighbor's house. I hid her and others in small forest of bee trees that killers wouldn't dare enter. So they would hide in the forest and spend the night among bees. It is true cowardice to not do anything for someone dying right in your sight." What Augustin is saying is that there's no excuse for not acting.

Julius Adekunle, a scholar of African studies, asserts that in the past all groups in Rwanda lived together peacefully, and local customs dictated mutual respect for one another (Adekunle 2007, 8). Augustin talks about himself as rescuer, as a potential peacebuilder, who can help youth participate in the preservation of local customs. These customs are expressions of the moral foundation of society. Rescuers' testimonies illustrate and bolster this point. They speak to the role of customs in maintaining the social fabric and in promoting the kinds of interdependence and social bonds that ideally serve to check the outbreak of mass violence.

Augustin maintained his family customs by asserting his traditional role within the Rwandan family. He dictated what the family should do in a situation of rescuing. In the testimony, he states that his children were all involved in the rescue of the Tutsi—they brought them to the Congo for safety, as their father told them to do. Augustin's testimony stands out not only because he rescued but also because he had thought about the future,

Fig. 7.4. Augustin Kagmaore

and how his actions might be instructional in preventing irreversible actions on the part of future generations.

I turn now to an additional testimony from Rwanda, that of Joseph Habineza. Joseph was fifty-four years old at the time of the interview and living in the Karongi district of Rwanda where he had rescued.

> After the first attack on the village of Kabuga, people began to flee, and I invited a group of around fifty people to come into my house out of the rain. It was mostly strangers squeezed into the small house and overflowing into the backyard, but I couldn't let them stay out in the rain.
>
> I managed to escape the soldiers looking for me and found some money I had saved up to pay for the children refugees at my house to escape through Lake Kivu into neighboring Congo. There they were met by Inkotanyi rebels and were safe. At that point, people realized that it was up to us to protect ourselves. Killings were escalating and this made it clear to us that it was genocide.
>
> A young man came to my house and after seeing the number of people, he immediately ran to alert the militias that I had given refuge to the whole group. They damaged a water pipe that ran to

my house, thinking that if we were deprived of water we would have to go to a neighbor's house and they would have us trapped. After days of fending off the militia's attacks, they brought a truck full of soldiers with heavy machine guns. Someone threw a grenade inside the house while I was out, destroying the entire left half and killing many refugees in the blast. When I returned to see the damage, the militias at the gate arrested me. They wanted to get into the house but I stopped them. They smashed my knee with an axe and I fell down. I looked at the horrible wound and saw my leg only hanging on to the muscles. They raised a machete to break my back, but I moved, getting a painful but not deadly cut. I was struggling on the ground using my last force, so they smashed my face with a club. Finally, four girls saw me and took me to the hospital where my leg was amputated." (personal communication, Habineza)

I asked Joseph what led him to act so bravely and why he was the only one to do so in his small village, where all of his neighbors went to the same Pentecostal church as him. Joseph explained:

Throughout my life I had known Tutsi people and they had never done anything wrong to me; we used to help each other and got along very well. I felt that I had to do something to help them during those horrible times of genocide. Before the genocide, I was a religious person, but so many people had lost their faith, otherwise so many lives would have been spared. Animosity had taken over and that is why we lost so many lives. If more people had chosen to save at least a few others, we would have made a big difference. Unfortunately, in our village, no one else had the courage to help the people in need. It was as if they had all become militias, even the people that used to appear to be true Christians." (personal communication, Habineza)

Joseph says that people used to be Christians, meaning that there should have been some moral fiber in their actions. He is implying that by "appearing to be Christians," going to church every Sunday, they are really hypocrites because true Christians would have followed the Bible and not kill their neighbor and fellow church mates. In Joseph's community it was customary to attend church every week and pray together. Instead of praying together, his neighbors who he attended church with regularly attempted to kill him. At the time of the interview, Joseph was scared to talk to us, and we had to bring him to our hotel to hear his testimony. In Joseph's view, "Animosity had taken over and that is why we lost so many lives." His explanation of why no other members of his community helped the Tutsis was that they "lacked courage," which might mean that they were too frightened to participate.

Both of these rescuers, Joseph and Augustin, stood up against their own communities and risk to their families to save the so-called enemy. They had known and lived with Tutsis, and neither their memories nor their everyday customs were changed because the Rwandan government told them to kill or declared Tutsis as "cockroaches," and not Rwandan citizens.

Alison Des Forges of Human Rights Watch reported that "church authorities left the way clear for officials, politicians, and propagandists to assert that the slaughter actually met with God's favor" (Des Forge 1999, 246). There is a long history in Rwanda that supports this accusation. Since the country gained independence from Belgium, the hierarchy of the roles of the ethnic groups changed, and so did the leadership of the church. The Tutsis, once the elite and dominant class, were now subjected to the Hutus' power. The Tutsi church leaders were replaced by Hutus, with Tutsis relegated to minor church roles. These heads of the churches were sympathetic to the genocide because it allowed them to retain their power in the church. This also meant that they supported the anti-Tutsi government message and maintained their allegiance to the Hutu-led government. Many church employees and lay leaders became members of the militias so they could defend the country from "the Tutsi menace" (246). Rwandan Christians came to believe that killing Tutsis was consistent with well-established church practice (Longman 2001, 163–86).

The Rwandan rescuers and their testimonies were featured in an exhibit I created in 2010, sixteen years after the genocide. The strategy was to use the testimonies and portraits of the rescuers to provide prosocial role models, showing people who had displayed empathy toward the "other." The exhibit was thereby also meant as a tool for coexistence. The rescuers represent Hutus who did not kill but who had stood up, demonstrating importantly to young Rwandans that not all Hutus were killers.

The teachers at the museum were trained in a workshop by the Karuana Center for Peacebuilding to use the testimonies and photos to teach the students about the exhibit as it traveled to schools and community centers. The goal of the training was to prepare the education staff of the Gisozi Memorial Museum to maximize the use of the traveling exhibit on rescuers as a peacebuilding tool to encourage community dialogue and classroom discussion on standing up against intolerance, thereby creating a culture of empathy. During the workshop the trainers used examples of moral courage in order to inspire young Rwandans to think about what it would mean today to counter early signs of prejudice so that ethnic tension and dehumanization never again progress to the point of mass killings. The participants analyzed their own responses to the exhibit and imagined the range of responses others might have, both Hutu and Tutsi, survivors, perpetrators, and bystanders, young and old. The participants were asked to address the phenomenon of rescue in other genocides or episodes of mass violence; how intolerance can lead to dehumanization and, eventually, killing; what it takes to move from mere coexistence to a more fully inclusive, tolerant society; how identity becomes wounded during communal violence and what it takes to heal; and specific strategies for using the exhibit to stimulate positive discussion and dialogue on building a culture of tolerance with community groups and in schools.

The educators were very engaged and clearly felt the exhibit had tremendous potential as a peacebuilding tool. They thought it would be helpful to bring the rescuers to schools, as the exhibit tours, so that students could ask direct questions and better understand what enabled rescuers to act differently. Much time was spent thinking about how to relate these unusually courageous acts that occurred under extreme circumstances and carried great personal risk to the students' everyday experiences. Students could be led to observe the small ways that they and their peers are either pulled into expressions of intolerance or do nothing to intervene. How does this kind of peer pressure operate in their schools? How as young people can they contribute to building a culture where mass violence will never happen again?

Iraq

In May 2015 I attended a conference in Erbil, Iraq, on "Women's Resistance to Extremism and Terrorism & Their Struggle for Rights, Peace & Security." The purpose of the trip was to meet with people who might have access to rescuer stories, as well as hear anyone who might be testifying at the conference. The collection of these stories would be delivered to Yale's Genocide Studies Program, for the purpose of expanding their archive of rescuers testimonies that are used as a teaching resource. An additional purpose of the trip was to provide local organizations with materials to help prevent future violence. I hired a local photographer and interpreter to photograph the rescuers we interviewed.[1] In Iraq, as in other conflict affected areas around the world where accounts of atrocities abound, there are also many stories of ordinary heroes who risked their lives to save members of "enemy groups," as well as "bright spots" of community members working to bridge divides, often on their own initiative. Under this objective, our goal was to widely promulgate positive stories of interfaith and interethnic rescue and collaboration. Our proposal was to collect testimonies in a manner that would be culturally sensitive, safe, and unlikely to create any kind of backlash, providing an essential counterpoint to rising antiminority rhetoric. Given the conflict in Iraq is still active, it remains dangerous for a team to go and do these types of interviews. For this reason, this case study is not as developed as some of the others where the conflict was further in the past.

Our project began with two women we met, one Sunni and one Shiite. Together these women saved Shiite army soldiers who were fleeing from ISIS (Islamic State of Iraq and Syria) in 2014. During 2013, more than 8,800 people were killed by ISIS, most of them civilians, according to UN reports. *The Guardian* stated that "Iraqi officials reported that two divisions of Iraqi soldiers—roughly 30,000 men—simply turned and ran in the face of the assault by an insurgent force of just 800 fighters. ISIS extremists roamed freely on Wednesday through the streets of Mosul, openly surprised at the ease with which they took Iraq's second largest city after three days of sporadic fighting" (Chulov, Hawramy, and Ackerman 2014). Aliya Khalaf Salih was an Iraqi woman who lived in a small village outside Mosul. Her son had been one of the soldiers who had fled from ISIS. He had come to her to ask her to help six of his friends from the Iraqi army.

Aliya said:

> These are the things that I do all my life. I am surprised that people are now making a big deal about these six boys, because all my life I have been doing this. It's natural for me, and when I see someone who needs help, I would take off my dress and give it to her, and whatever money I have I would give it to her; it's natural for me. (personal communication, Aliya)

Aliya saved these young men with the help of her family. They hired taxies and then drove them across the border to Kurdistan, where they went through various ISIS checkpoints and where she delivered them to her friend Ameera at the Kurdistan border. Aliya's testimony serves as an example of someone who took huge risks—not only to herself but to her

Fig. 7.5. Aliya Khalaf Salih and Ameera

six daughters and daughters-in-law, endangering all their lives as well as the lives of the taxi drivers who drove them. This is another case of a family working together to rescue others, similar to the other cases that have been discussed.

Aliya and her friend Ameera also agreed to be interviewed for my research. Both of these women had given a presentation to the two hundred people at the conference, sharing their powerful testimonies and acknowledging that it is important for all to know that a Shiite and a Sunni could, and did, work together to make a difference by saving lives. Aliya testified that what she had done was not out of the ordinary for her. She has always cared for people or done whatever is necessary to help people throughout her life. She posits that this should be no different now.

Aliya explained, "This is what you do as a person, a human being. Why wouldn't you do it?" These Iraqi women, like Albert Camus's protagonist Dr. Bernard Rieux in *The Plague*, knowingly risk their lives because they continue to remember what life is supposed to be regardless of the consequences. ISIS was their plague, but they managed to retain their moral and cultural values.

Conclusion

Much has been written about the role of historical memory as a vehicle for revenge. For example, Mahmood Mamdani's *When Victims Become Killers: Colonialism, Nativism, and the Genocide in Rwanda* (2001) explains the tensions of postcolonial Rwanda through the lens of the colonialist history, viewing conflicts between Hutus and Tutsis as the outcome of colonialist-driven construction of differences between the ethnic groups. By contrast, relatively little has been written on societal memory in the form of prosocial customs and how it informs rescue behavior. Rescuers' testimonies provide the evidential basis for asserting the peacebuilding potential of rescue narratives. These narratives complicate history by reminding us of the possibility of opposing the tide of mass violence and by providing younger generations with positive role models and local heroes.

Erwin Staub (1993) states:

> we can expect individuals, groups, and nations to act early along a continuum of destruction, when the danger to themselves is limited, and the potential exists for inhibiting the evolution of increasing destructiveness. This will only happen if people—children, adults, whole societies—develop an awareness of their common humanity with other people, as well as of the psychological processes in themselves that turn them against others. Institutions and modes of functioning can develop that embody a shared humanity and make exclusion from the moral realm more difficult. (318)

Rescue stories, in particular, provide much needed narratives of independent thinking, compassion, empathy, and moral courage. They provide essential models for social renewal and can be used by community groups and schools to develop a social ethic of empathy, one that promotes inclusive, cooperative relations between identity groups and eschews violence.

Rescuer testimonies document and promote prosocial behavior and effectively challenge assumptions about the hegemony of historical memory in perpetuating intergroup conflict and strife. Their narratives show that historical memory and old grudges need not—and don't always—trump empathy. The testimonies of upstanders demonstrate the possibility of resisting the tremendous pressure during mass violence to abandon empathy and succumb to hate-filled group-think and prejudice. In doing so, these testimonies provide youth of post-conflict societies with local heroes and role models who, more than abstract texts preaching morality and good behavior, show how empathy, dignity, and cultural memory can serve the aims of peace and coexistence.

NOTE

1. The forum was organized by Iraqi al-Amal Association in collaboration with a number of governmental and nongovernmental agencies. I was invited by the Karuna Center for Peacebuilding, based in Amherst, Massachusetts, which had submitted a proposal to the US State Department for a peacebuilding project targeting the different sects in the region.

REFERENCES

Adekunle, Julius O. 2007. *Culture and Customs of Rwanda.* Westport, CT: Greenwood Press.

Bosnia and Herzegovina Demographics Profile. 2018. Accessed November 15, 2019. https://www.indexmundi.com/bosnia_and_herzegovina/demographics_profile.html

Čehajić-Clancy, Sabina, and MichaÅ Bilewicz. 2017. "Fostering Reconciliation through Historical Moral Exemplars in a Postconflict Society." *Peace and Conflict: Journal of Peace Psychology* 23, no. 3: 288–96.

Chulov, Martin, Fazel Hawramy, and Spencer Ackerman. 2014. "Iraq Army Capitulates to ISIS Militants in Four Cities." *Guardian*, June 11. https://www.theguardian.com/world/2014/jun/11/mosul-isis-gunmen-middle-east-states

Des Forges, Alison. 1999. *Leave None to Tell the Story: Genocide in Rwanda.* New York and London: Human Rights Watch.

Desjarlais, Robert, and Arthur Kleinman. 1994. "Violence and Demoralization in the New World Disorder." *Anthropology Today* 10, no. 5: 9–12.

Edwards, Julie Biando, and Stephan P. Edwards. 2008. "Culture and the New Iraq: The Iraq National Library and Archive, 'Imagined Community,' and the Future of the Iraqi Nation." *Libraries & the Cultural Record* 43, no. 3: 327–42.

Eyal, Gil. 2004. "Identity and Trauma: Two Forms of the Will to Memory." *History and Memory* 16, no. 1: 5–36.

Greitemeyer, Tobias. 2011. "Effects of Prosocial Media on Social Behavior." *Current Directions in Psychological Science* 20, no. 4: 28–38.

Kaplan, Robert Balkan. 1993. *Ghosts: A Journey Through History.* New York: St. Martin's Press.

Longman, Timothy. 2017. *Memory and Justice in Post-Genocide Rwanda.* Cambridge: Cambridge University Press.

Mamdani, Mahmood. 2002. *When Victims Become Killers: Colonialism, Nativism, and the Genocide in Rwanda.* Princeton: Princeton University Press.

Minow, Martha, and Nancy L. Rosenblum. 2002. *Breaking the Cycles of Hatred: Memory, Law, and Repair.* Princeton: Princeton University Press.

Nawas, Hiam. 2017. "Holding Arab Culture Accountable." *Washington Institute for Near East Policy*. May 5.

Staub, Ervin. 2003. *The Psychology of Good and Evil: Why Children, Adults, and Groups Help and Harm Others*. Cambridge: Cambridge University Press.

United States Holocaust Memorial Museum. 2013. "Bosnia and Herzegovina, 1992–1995." Accessed November 15, 2019. https://www.ushmm.org/confront-genocide/cases/bosnia-herzegovina

Wahlin, Willhemina, and Leora Kahn. 2015. "Difficult Exhibitions in Difficult Sites: An Investigation of Exhibition Design Practice for the Rescuers in Bosnia and Herzegovina." *Design Journal* 18, no. 4: 535–54.

Part 3 | Resilience

8 | Women's Survival and Memory Narratives in the Southern Cone

Resilience and Gender Justice

Bernardita Llanos

An ever-increasing number of testimonies, documentaries, films, and photographic collections denouncing human rights violations has emerged after the return to democracy in Argentina (1984), Chile (1990), and Uruguay (1986) to the present day that has resulted in what can be considered an alternative memory archive of the countless abuses that took place against political foes during the past dictatorships in the Southern Cone. In these wide-ranging cultural productions, survivors of torture and abuses and their children have become storytellers and witnesses who confront the past and today's neoliberal societies with questions about justice, truth, and memory. The various Truth and Reconciliation Commission reports in the three countries[1] have also generated an abundance of testimonies from the victims, their relatives, and the perpetrators that have given rise to public outrage, social mobilization, and political activism, as well as a myriad of plays, novels, and documentaries that reflect on the dictatorships and their aftermath, presenting new outlooks on what the future may hold.

We can find similarities in other countries that have suffered violence in the way testimonies and audiovisual materials serve to shape narratives of survival and memory and the need for inclusion. As documentarian Ricardo Velasco shows in this volume, his film *After the Crossfire: Memories of Violence and Displacement* (2014) underscores the fate of displaced populations in Colombia due to eruption of violence. The film focuses on a coastal Afro-Colombian population, historically marginalized by the state, relocated in the Chocó region in Bahía Solano.[2] The escalation of violence against displaced communities mostly of Afro-Colombian and indigenous descent has given rise to an ethno-territorial movement that is one of the most significant democratic developments in the country, as Velasco's chapter states. New forms of leadership and governance have developed in these communities despite ongoing harassment and death threats to their leaders by paramilitary groups hired by transnational extractive businesses and narcotraffickers. The number of activists killed has escalated to three hundred since 2016 when the peace accords were signed, raising serious questions about the progress made in the peace process.[3]

The "memory turn" in Latin America, as Michael Lazzara argues, has undergone different debates within each specific country, giving rise to the first, second, and currently third stages of development in the Southern Cone (Lazzara 2017, 11). In this way, we can see that the concern with memory and a recent violent past shows specific time frames that also may underscore different issues and perspectives as memory narratives evolve in time.

In the cultural landscape of the Southern Cone, women survivors' accounts represent a crucial archive to learn not only about the political and gender violence that women endured in secret detention centers administered by the dictatorships; they are also—perhaps more significantly for this article—a testimony of individual and group resilience, progressive politics, and a reservoir of knowledge. The strength survivors have developed throughout the years is a vital source of hope and belief in the power of women to bring about social and political change. The stories analyzed in this article show us a path to self- and social transformation where gender is a key component to understand women's survival and contribution in societies that have had a violent historical period.

Historical Context

Examining past atrocities committed by agents of the state and civil servants who worked for the dictatorships in Argentina, Chile, and Uruguay shows how modern authoritarianism conceived the nation as a war place where political enemies needed to be brutally crushed. Women who were political and social activists in left-wing organizations faired especially badly in what was a warfare state. As militants they were targeted, humiliated, and sexually degraded while being illegally detained, tortured, and killed. The violence they endured was part of a gendered policy that cut through political repression and was specifically designed for females involved in progressive politics and social organizing—militants, high-ranking leaders in student organizations, unions, and political parties. The dictatorial agenda was meant to strip women of their rights as citizens and human beings. Another notable goal was to deter females in the larger society from ever participating in the political life of the country for years to come. The military used terror tactics, corporal and sexual punishment of political prisoners, and disappearance (or "murder without a body," which became their signature) to show its power over a cowed and fear-stricken population. In the meantime, the military ran free in military gear or undercover through streets in cities under curfew. They perse-cuted, kidnapped, and got rid of their political opponents in illegal prisons without leaving records of their actions.

The hiding and destruction of culpatory evidence as well as the corpses has been an ongoing topic in documentaries focusing on Latin American dictatorships. The films by exiled and internationally renowned Chilean director Patricio Guzmán have been emblematic in pondering on this vio-lent past through an ethical lens that underscores the absence of human rights, trauma, and the fate of the disappeared and their relatives.[4] In this same vein, documentarians in Argentina such as David Blaustein and Andrés di Tella have represented the struggles of former *Montonero* mili-tants as well as the fight of the *Madres* and *Abuelas* of Plaza de Mayo to know what happened to their children and grandchildren during the state repression. These visual productions have served to keep both social and historical memory alive and the struggle for truth and justice as an ongo-ing and relevant political and cultural issue to reckon with today (Llanos 2016, 248).

Agents of the dictatorial state and their civil officials resorted to vio-lence for political ends with the help of abundant local and international resources, as Marc Cooper's book *Pinochet and Me* (2001) reveals and as the detailed scholarly studies on the Southern Cone by Steven Stern (2010), Michael Lazzara (2017), Francesca Lessa (2013), and Gabriela Fried (2017) among others show. The Cold War situation laid the ideological foundations for the rise of Latin American authoritarian governments and set the stage for the fight against communism, allying right-wing parties with the armed forces against leftist organizations. Military coups in Argentina, Chile, and Uruguay took anticommunism as a mission in the region aided by the United States government and the CIA covert (finan-cial, ideological, and military) involvement directed toward destabilizing the countries' democratically elected governments. Anticommunist propaganda and a huge influx of funding from the United States were used to plan the coups with the armed forces and their civil sympathizers, preparing the ground to establish the dictatorships. Historian Peter Kornbluh in his now famous book *The Pinochet File* (2003) examines thirty years of declassified documents on Chile showing the United States complicity in the military coup and the atrocities that took place. The film *Missing* (1982) by Costa Gravas was one of the first to portray this complicity and the toll paid by Chileans and US citizens who supported Allende's democratic path to Socialism.

During the Southern Cone dictatorships, surveillance, censorship, persecution, unlawful imprisonment, and ultimately the annihilation of political opponents on the left were the new norm, as the cases of Guatemala and other Central American nations had shown in the previous decades. The Cold War framework shaped hemispheric and national political conflicts that reached a governability crisis in which the ruling classes and the right, backed by the American government, called the armed forces to take control in their respective countries.

In this context, traditional and discriminatory gender norms cut across hierarchical structures and institutions that modeled their ideals according to a military image of men whose training and discipline allowed them to sacrifice for the country in order to save it from the cancer of communism. In this metaphorical language, the nation was a pure and healthy body that had been infected with cancerous cells representing leftist militants and guerrilla leaders. The dictatorship's call was to rid the country of subversives and terrorists in a dirty war that would restore Western and Christian values. This hegemonic position is clearly expressed by Argentine Jorge Rafael Videla's[5] definition of a terrorist: "Un terrorista no es solo alguien con un revólver o una bomba, sino también aquel que propaga ideas contrarias a la civilización occidental y cristiana" ("A terrorist is not only someone with a gun or a bomb but also who propagates ideas contrary to Western and Christian civilization") (Feitlowitz 2015, 63). The internal enemy defied not only a political understanding of society but a cultural one that went against the very foundation of the Argentine nation. The same was true with the Chilean and Uruguayan military leaderships. They developed a narrative where terrorists were barbarians who wanted to destroy civilized society. The dictatorial state instrumentalized this narrative by using illegal and secret methods to kidnap, detain, torture, and rape political prisoners. However, the dictatorships intentionally kept these abuses out of the public eye and committed atrocities with impunity.

For instance, Jorge Rafael Videla deliberately hid these arrests and deaths in secrecy in clandestine centers. State terrorism victims in Argentina were buried in mass graves or dropped from airplanes into the ocean or the Rio de la Plata, while others disappeared, totaling 30,000 according to most estimates. Between 1973 and 1990 Pinochet used very similar tactics in Chile to get rid of 3,065 citizens and tortured 40,000 according to official figures of the National Institute of Human Rights (Instituto Nacional de Derechos Humanos) and the international press.[6] In Uruguay, Juan Bordaberry's governments—in 1971–1973, and later in his civil-military dictatorship (1973–1976)—were responsible for the disappearance of 210 Uruguayans and 380,000 exiles (14 percent of the entire population).[7]

The military's nationalist discourse saw soldiers and their supporters fighting for the nation and its return to a pristine state for which perpetual warfare was required. The past was cleansed of all political activities and references that were considered to have corrupted the fatherland. Politics became a dirty word that was stigmatized in the new national vocabulary. Marguerite Feitlowitz calls the linguistic regime of the dictatorship "the lexicon of terror," a discursive formation that allowed for the criminalization and demonization of the disappeared (2015, 63–66). In her book *A Lexicon of Terror: Argentina and the Legacies of Torture*, Feitlowitz underscores the military language used by state leaders such as Jorge Rafael Videla and Emilio Massera who naturalized the notion that their enemies were not humans (2015, 63–66).

In this plotline women were seen as wives and mothers, reproductive agents who had the role of securing the needs of their husbands and children in the home. This was the way to serve the nation, performing their God-given role. From there on the mother as citizen exercised her power in the private sphere. Any other identity was foreclosed and brutally extirpated from the public sphere, now surveilled and monitored for potential transgressors. Women's clothing and behaviors were drastically changed to conform to dictatorial codes and protocols. Females, adults and girls, could only wear skirts and those who persisted in wearing pants got them cut off by any given soldier while walking the streets. Young men got their hair and beards cut off so that they would resemble the soldier-like citizen the dictatorship wanted to propagate in the younger male generation.

The link between gender and violence in this authoritarian context shows that sexual torture was especially directed toward women and used as a system to reeducate them politically while imposing unconditional obedience through fear and pain. How these brutal dictatorships operated in the Southern Cone with prisoners in secret detention centers has been particularly noteworthy in the accounts of women survivors, ethnic minorities, and the second and even third generations who grew up after the arrival of democracy. The children and grandchildren of the disappeared have also told their own stories about state terrorism in documentaries that chronicle their experiences. In the case of Argentina, one of the most outrageous human rights violations was the theft of five hundred babies born to mothers who were political prisoners in captivity before being disappeared. The children were given up in illegal adoptions to army officers and their supporters. Through the relentless work of the organization *Abuelas* of Plaza de Mayo, 130 have been recovered and their identities restituted. Many of these recovered children, today young adults, belong to the human rights organization Hijos por la Identidad y la Justicia Contra el Olvido y el Silencio (HIJOS, or Children for Identity and Justice Against Forgetting and Silence). The group was founded in 1995 and has reinvigorated the struggle for justice, memory, and truth in the younger Argentine generation. HIJOS is known for its innovative practices such as *escraches* (public shaming) of former torturers and military personnel together with other discursive and political interventions (Bravo 2012).[8] Through national *Encuentros* (public gatherings) and workshops held in Cordoba and other cities in the provinces the daughters and sons of the disappeared became a collective. Many had been living in exile, whereas others were raised by relatives in Argentina without knowing much about the violent national and family past. It was precisely the need to learn more about state terrorism, their own origins, and what happened to their parents that led them to look for others with similar stories. Interviews, testimonies, and reportages reveal that these youth found brothers and sisters in HIJOS while organizing to struggle for the right to identity, memory, and justice. Today they join other activist groups in condemning the sentence reduction and release from jail of hundreds of torturers that was made possible by a government campaign "to downplay the abuses of the military" and the ruling of the Supreme Court of Argentina in 2017 (Goni 2017).

Women Survivors' Stories

Testimonies and stories of women activists whose political involvement in the 1970s defied long-standing patriarchal norms of gender and female roles in general reveal that they became direct victims of the cruel and "macho subjects," as cultural critic Jean Franco calls them in her book *Cruel*

Modernity (2013). These violent macho men worked for the secret police either as state agents or civil servants helping to operate the clandestine prisons and overseeing interrogation methods, torture sessions, and ultimately the murder of their fellow citizens. They used extreme cruelty, as Franco writes, to assert their gender identity and omnipotent power. These trained torturers enforced programmatic as well as personal forms of abuse to humiliate and destroy militants because they were guaranteed impunity in the secret concentration camps spread throughout Argentina, Chile, and Uruguay. Operation Condor (*Plan Cóndor* in Spanish) epitomized a planned intelligence operation and a concerted regional effort of the dictatorships in Argentina, Bolivia, Brazil, Chile, Paraguay, and Uruguay in which they shared information, surveillance reports, kidnappings, illegal imprisonments, and transportation of political prisoners from one country to another. The CIA backed these efforts that according to estimates left 500,000 victims, of which 400,000 were kidnapped, 50,000 killed, and 30,000 disappeared between 1973 and 1978 (Tynnila 2017).[9]

In the Southern Cone countries, female militants were doubly punished during state terror campaigns for becoming politicized and stepping out of the private domain where they were supposed to belong by God's design. In this way gender introduced a differential, as sociologists together with feminists and law scholars have pointed out. They argue that the extent and repertoire of gendered human rights violations reveal that women activists were chastised from the very start of the dictatorships. They were punished not only to inflict damage over the regime's political male opponents but also, and more importantly for my argument, to erase any sense of agency and freedom—in particular, the belief that they were sexually free and emancipated. Women's access to higher education and labor and their participation in left wing parties in the previous decade came to an abrupt and violent halt. Many of the militants on the more radical left were college students or members of Catholic base groups close to Liberation Theology that made social justice their goal. They were deeply aware of the social and economic disparities in their countries and wanted to end them to build a more just society.

In this article, I argue that women's memory accounts are expressions of an active memory and resilience that revisits the past to imagine and demand a democratic society where gender justice and women's rights are legally recognized and socially respected. Recognition and empathy for another human being's vulnerability and suffering and the development of resilience to overcome experiences of violence and abuse become central elements that shape women's survival and their memories. Furthermore, the meaning these women give these past events today is crucial if they are to have a sense of purpose and hopefulness to pass on to others. As social scientists claim resilience is related to a set of beliefs and habits of mind in which individuals believe they have agency and that there is a meaning to life, so what they do matters. Andrew Zolli finds that the ability to bounce back and show resilience after traumatic events is related to how strong people's belief systems are in helping them learn from their experiences (2012). Feminist collectives and organizations of female survivors of political prisons in collaboration with human rights organizations have created women's support groups, where listening and sharing experiences have been central to going beyond individual trauma and moving forward. Through the analysis of testimonies and documentaries we can trace the emergence of a narrative of hope and empowerment in which women's solidarity groups lead the way to regaining a voice and an activist identity for themselves and other women. Their demands in a postdictatorial and democratic context show the challenges women have had to face to publicly denounce rape and sexual torture as terror tactics of past dictatorships. As Fried (2017) claims, gender played a differential role in the dictatorship in Uruguay. The case of the survivor's collective of the more than sixty women who were political prisoners in 1985 at the Penal Punta Rieles has had a significant impact in making public the fate of women prisoners and their resilience to survive, organize, and denounce the crimes collectively. Their testimonies in 2010–2011 allowed the emergence of the first stories about sexual abuse in the dictatorship's prisons. The testimony of senior female survivors in the TV program *Esta boca es mía* ("This Is My Mouth") in August 2011 shocked Uruguayan society that did not know, pretended not to know, or simply did not want to know that sexual torture along with other forms of sexualized violence had taken place in all detention centers. Watching two older survivors speak on a popular TV program about the sexual abuses they suffered, keeping their poise and dignity while giving testimony, had a strong impact. A couple of months later, twenty-nine women survivors of Punta Rieles formalized their complaint to a court in Montevideo with the support of psychologists and human rights organization as Fried (2017, 156–57) shows.

Legally recognizing sexual abuse as torture has been a major struggle for former political prisoners in Argentina, Chile, and Uruguay. The difficult and oftentimes excruciating process of remembering buried experiences of humiliation and sexual torture and sharing silenced events has contributed to revisiting the past and reclaiming identity, the female body, and women's rights. This process has unfolded within women's groups in which support and empathy have strengthened individual and group resilience to pushback. The next step in reclaiming citizenship has been for women to come out and publicly denounce the crimes committed by the state in a fight that has been won by individuals and groups of women survivors in Argentina (the first case in 2010 in La Plata) and in Uruguay (by the group of twenty-eight women survivors in 2011).

In Chile, however, sexual torture remains absent as a legal category despite the existence of a collection of testimonies in the last Truth and Reconciliation Commission, also called "Valech II Report" (2010–2011), which is paradoxically considered classified information for the next fifty years. As in the case of Argentina and Uruguay, in Chile we also see women's mobilization and organizations across social lines to campaign and march in the streets to demand justice and more specifically gender justice. Academics and legal experts have also been crucial in making visible the crimes committed against women by the dictatorship, thus pressuring the state for due justice. In Chile after years of keeping silent and feeling ashamed, four former political prisoners filed a complaint of sexual torture in the Supreme Court in 2014 accusing the state and their torturers of brutal forms of sexual abuse and debasement. They also demanded that the penal code be reformed to include torture and sexual violence in their political nature as crimes against humanity.[10]

Gender justice is an area that is slowly gaining traction in the Southern Cone as a significant field that is inextricably linked to human and women's rights. Both sets of rights were systematically violated during the dictatorships of Argentina, Chile, and Uruguay. The progress made in the legal realm within international human rights law after Yugoslavia's civil war in the 1990s brought about a change of paradigm in the way sexual abuse was understood. The fact that Argentina and Uruguay had progressive governments, Nestor Kishner's government (2003–2007) and his wife Cristina Fernández's (2007–2015) in Argentina, and José Mujica's (2010–2015) in Uruguay, respectively, had an impact in how gender justice was understood and applied in the context of human rights violations committed by state terrorism. The shift to considering rape and sexual abuses as crimes against humanity established the legal recognition of rape as a form of gender and sexual torture that targets particularly women. In this way, rape conducted as a routine in warfare became legally categorized and penalized as a cruel war crime that may take place within a nation or among nations. These changes in international human rights law resulted in important developments in Argentina, such as the truth trials involving past crimes committed by the military, the cases of the children taken from their political prisoner parents, and the unconstitutionality of the amnesty laws (Lessa 2013, 69). As Lessa notes, the Argentine judiciary became more receptive to international law arguments and principles in the post–Cold War context where the international community had become more concerned with human rights and justice (2013, 69).

The female survivor of political and sexual violence is the protagonist of these stories of survival and solidarity. Throughout the decades her representation has shifted from the condemned outcast and betrayer of political commitment and party comrades in order to survive in the 1980s and 1990s, to a social and feminist activist today who participates in human rights and women's collectives and protests for women's rights. Here I distinguish between the sexual violence against women in wars as part of the victors' spoils and the subsequent objectification of females from what took place in Argentina, Chile, and Uruguay where women were selectively targeted, persecuted, and sexually abused and tortured because they were militants.

As the documentaries *The Shoah* (dir. Claude Lanzman, 1985) and *The Act of Killing* (dir. Joshua Opperheimer, 2012) show, the way torturers and killers deal with past crimes varies a great deal, from denial to outright justification to having haunting dreams of the slaughtered victims. In the case of torturers in Argentina, Chile, and Uruguay, the intimate relationship they had with their prisoners adds another layer to this form of crime (alongside kidnapping, illegal detention, brutal interrogation and torture methods, isolation, and so on), involving sexual torture and a sadomasochist power relation. The distinctness of sexual torture is that it presents theoretical and legal challenges that are akin to incest and domestic violence, confronting us with the process of chipping away identity that the victim undergoes in the relationship with the abuser. In survivors' testimonies, documentaries, and fictional accounts, the torture scenes show a perverse theater with established patriarchal protocols, gender scripts, and roles directed by the torturer.

Gender and Human Rights

Feminist legal scholars and social scientists have been key in arguing the cause of women's rights and human rights in war and genocide contexts by identifying the significance of rape as a programmatic measure to humiliate women alongside a myriad of coercive means of intimidation and outright torture. In fact, Carole Sheffield calls this sexual terrorism, since it is "the system by which males frighten and, by frightening, control and dominate women"; she goes further to assert that "the right of men to control the female body is a cornerstone of patriarchy" (2007, 111). In her interpretation, the taproot of patriarchy is the masculine/warrior ideal where masculinity "must include not only a proclivity for violence but also all those characteristics claimed by warriors: aggression, control, emotional reserve, rationality, sexual potency, etc." (2007, 113). This description of maleness comes very close to the military's ideal conduct and value system. In contrast, survivors' accounts contest male narratives of heroism and political consensus sponsored by neoliberalism today alongside the legacy of a compulsory maternity embodied in the mother-citizen of the dictatorship, as Catherine O'Rourke argues (2012, 139). The cultural gendered images demand that women comply with a patriarchal protocol that has been widely questioned by young feminist activists in Argentina and Chile in the demands for free, safe, and legal abortions alongside the condemnation of violence against women.

In her work *Intimate Enemies: Violence and Reconciliation in Perú* (2012), Kimberly Theidon sheds light on gender dynamics during the civil war and postwar Peruvian society by showing that male power and sexual abuse are imbedded in the cultural fabric where political violence and genocide take place. She also argues for the need of truth commissions and citizens in general to pay attention to rape and male sexual behavior in war contexts to advance women's rights. As Theidon shows, warfare exacerbates a masculinist ideology that endorses the imposition of force and harm to those deemed enemies. Evidence of this is found in women's memory accounts and testimonies as well as indigenous sectors and other minorities persecuted by the authoritarian state.

In the military's ideology, female militants had stepped out of their natural role and identity. Instead of following their womanly responsibilities, they had claimed a political identity and even gender independence. Almost all political prisoners were sexualized and insulted by the torturers. The insult "slut" cuts across testimonies, literary and visual representations, revealing a sexist core that reflected violence and rage. In this same line, Ana Longoni argues that the figure of the *puta* (slut in Spanish) in the Argentine imaginary strongly associates women with treason (2007). She explains that the condition of prostitution is only attributed to women and associated with sexual submission and betrayal. Thus, women political prisoners were not only physically tortured, but were also slandered as promiscuous by their own husbands, their political comrades, and the military (Longoni 2007, 150). The former MIR (Movement of the

Revolutionary Left) militant Maria Isabel relates that there were special ways to torture and mistreat women to establish from the beginning that they were not compliant with their feminine role and were considered "sluts," sexually available to any man. She states that the torturers "repeated that you were a slut in each torture . . . that you had gotten there because a guy had seduced you and you were dumb and a slut for having gotten into that situation . . . the mistreatment was for being a woman who had gotten involved in something that was not her business because politics was a male thing and you should be at home as a good wife and mother having kids, this was a big difference and we saw it right away . . . they mandated that you assume the classic feminine role" (*Rescatar*, 80).[11]

Torture and sexism worked in tandem to reduce activists to submission and to debase them. Miriam Lewin and Olga Wornat in *Putas y guerrilleras* (2014) stamp in the title of their book the sexist insult ("slut") to vindicate their political activism and gender identities against the sexual and verbal abuse they suffered, denouncing the sexual crimes committed in the detention camps by the Argentine dictatorship. Their survival stories were silenced longer than those of other survivors since they feared being called betrayers and collaborators with the genocide perpetrated by the government. Furthermore, it also took survivors' collectives and organizations a long time to understand that they were victims of the circumstances rather than free agents, as Wornat asserts (2014, 120).

In addition, the events they witnessed and experienced happened a long time ago (three to four decades in some cases depending on when they were made public), to be used as evidence in court or as elements in the reconstruction of a traumatic past history, thus rendering many women silent and crimes against gender and sexuality invisible. Rape and sexual abuse as torture were unspoken for many years by the "reappeared" (*reaparecidas*), as survivors in general were called. Many felt ashamed and guilty for having lived or were made to feel this way by others despite the fact that there was no direct relationship between survival and cooperation with the demands the torturers made in the torture chamber (Lewin and Wornat 2013, 28). All prisoners were condemned to death: they all bear the piercing pain of the *picana* (electric prod), suffocation through waterboarding, and the terror of dying by firing squad (in fact many of the disappeared were killed in this way). As Lewin and Wornat argue, kidnapped and detained activists did not know what they had to do or avoid doing to survive even for a couple of days (2013, 29).

In a context of fear and complete uncertainty, the general explanation outside the detention camps was that women survivors were alive because they had sex with their captors, and that they were not victims but rather had chosen to give in to the torturers' pressure. They were accused of betraying their mandate as women, that of society, and that of the organization they participated in. Lewin and Wornat say that they were seen as independent agents, free to choose in the concentration camps where they were held (2013, 30 and 31). As a response they denounce the gender regime and cultural values imposed on women's sexuality that were illegally imprisoned: "they supposed that we as women had the power to resist sexual violence, the advances of the repressors and that we could preserve the 'altar' of our unpolluted bodies. . . . Women had a treasure to keep, a purity to safeguard, a mandate to obey. They had convinced us that it was like that" (Lewin and Wornat 2013, 31). Women survivors' bodies were confiscated, and they did not have the ability to escape from the abuses and degrading treatment of the military who had defeated them and kept them in complete subservience (370).

Many years after keeping silent and not acknowledging their pain, survivors in general have started rethinking and understanding what actually was at play in the detention centers. Through a long process of self-examination and group sharing, they have come to realize how their rights as women were abused and how they were raped because of their gender, on the one hand, and their politics, on the other. Survivors have also asserted that they want to leave a legacy about their activism and commitment for social change and justice to the next generations. Barbara Sutton in her interviews of former activists in Argentina shows how strong and resilient they are today keeping their commitment for social justice by participating in numerous organizations. Their stories, however, have not been heard as much as other women's narratives who are more gender normative, such as the *Madres* and *Abuelas* of Plaza de Mayo as Sutton notes (2015, 10 and 16). Former political prisoners transgressed cultural and gender norms and want to share their experiences and memories—of survival, resilience, and commitment with a utopia—so that they can pass on the baton (2015, 11, 12, and 16). In spite of the fact that in the Southern Cone dictatorships and postdictatorship societies the term "rescuer behavior" is not used to refer to the behavior of political prisoners as it is in a context of mass violence (i.e., Rwanda, Sierra Leone, Iraq in this volume), this category shares many of the actions that women practiced while being held prisoners. Protecting one another, providing material and emotional assistance, supporting the needy, hiding information to help another fellow prisoner, and making efforts to save others are all part of the behavioral pattern and ethics that shape survivors' accounts. These experiences have sustained them through the pain suffered and impact how they live and who they are today. Ultimately, it is these moments of good that form the foundation of individual and collective resilience, providing a fertile ground for social coexistence after violent political periods.

As one Argentine survivor puts it, "We were prisoners, even more, we were disappeared, out of the world. They had all the power over us, the survivors" (Lewin and Wornat, 371). In spite of being alive they felt wiped out from the face of the earth. In this frightening situation the support and solidarity of fellow prisoners create an affective network to withstand torture, fear, and the threat of death.

Nubia Becker, a Chilean survivor, reiterates in her testimony *Una mujer en Villa Grimaldi* (1986 [2011]) the same condition of being a disappeared, using the term to underscore illegal imprisonment in secret centers. Only the captors knew where prisoners were held. Becker says that the cells were like dog cages where prisoners were held captive after being beaten, insulted, and tortured in what resembled a living hell. Instead of humans they turned them into "bleeding rags" who were unable to speak (2011, 56, 71, and 74). Becker reveals the fact that in the capital city of Santiago there were a lot of detention centers where rape was used as a means of torture and intimidation, places such as La Venda Sexy ("The Sexy Blindfold"), La Venda of Calle Londres ("The Blindfold of Londres St."), La Venda of Calle Domingo Cañas ("The Blindfold of Domingo Cañas St.") (76), all of them located in residential neighborhoods or downtown.

Chilean documentarian Gloria Camiruaga in her film *La Venda* (2000, "The Blindfold") tackles precisely this issue and presents eleven survivors of political and sexual torture of the deadly La Venda Sexy. The women share a fractured narration of the past where trauma and resilience are key. This is a pioneering work based on testimonials that offer a topography of Chile's clandestine prisons and their programmatic use of sexual violence as torture against women. It also shows survivors telling their stories directly to the camera while denouncing the crimes committed by the state. Each woman experienced extreme physical and psychological pain and humiliation, but each also shows courage, inner strength, and resilience. This is a seminal visual work that identifies the state crimes and the impact they had on the survivors who were able to provide an account of what happened to them at the hands of the repressors, and on the ongoing process of reconstituting psychically and politically. The group of survivors meets for tea, as they normally do, to share their experiences and memories in front of the camera. What is distinct about these survivors is that they are college educated and professionals who became politicized in the late 1960s. In hindsight they say that they never expected what happened to them during the Pinochet dictatorship. Their personal stories follow a similar plot line describing what they were doing before the coup d'état of 1973 and what happened after: all eleven were kidnapped by the secret police and put in clandestine prisons for days or weeks, sometimes months and even years. Part of the routine in these centers was to keep female prisoners naked and blindfolded while being beaten and sexually abused. Interrogation sessions and electric shocks were experienced by all of the survivors alongside a range of sexual crimes. Resilience infuses activism, as demonstrated by the attempts today to recuperate the house where La Venda Sexy was located as a memory site. Former political prisoners, human rights organizations, and feminist collectives have recently put a plaque on the sidewalk that tells what took place there.

Empathy is another salient trait in these stories where resilience and solidarity combine to make survivors mentally and emotionally strong. For instance, one survivor named Gladys Díaz pointedly describes that it was "an act of love" toward a suffering prisoner, who had been horrendously beaten with chains and his flesh opened and raw, that made her want his life to end quickly. This was the only way to stop his pain. The ability to blur the line between self and other, feeling what the other is feeling is related to empathy, an affective interpersonal skill essential for social attachments, as Jean Decety asserts (2011, 1). Acts of compassion and care in horrific conditions are also underscored as expressions of humanity in the face of daily threats and terror, as the massacres in Rwanda and Cambodia also attest in this volume. Artistic expressions, storytelling, testimonies, and documentaries all serve to provide an aesthetic and ethical frame to give meaning to extreme and atrocious experiences.

As the documentary *La Venda* shows, many survivors were exiled for years and returned to Chile in the late 1980s and early 1990s, feeling uprooted and estranged in their country of origin. Many testified to the truth commissions and some met their torturers in court. Gladys Díaz retells meeting military official Miguel Krassnoff, her cold and brutal torturer. She notes that like other prisoners, she had made him larger than life by turning him into an all-powerful god who had their lives in his hands. In the documentary, she recognizes that Krassnoff was totally different to what she had imagined, to the point that she had given him a completely different physical appearance. What is significant about this realization is that being free to testify changed her self-perception from powerless and small to strong and confident. Meeting Krassnoff for the first time in a judicial trial made her feel empowered. Furthermore, Díaz had the opportunity to look him straight in the eye and speak up against his crimes. Ultimately, she saw him for what he was: a military criminal. Díaz's resilience can be seen here in the reframing of her torture experience and the ways she has examined and changed her own life narrative.

The Argentine documentary film *Campo de Batalla, cuerpo de mujer* ("Battleground, Female Body"), directed by Fernando Alvarez in 2014, does something that resembles the documentary *La Venda* a decade later. It presents eighteen women survivors who tell their experiences of sexual violence in the prison camps. The film also reiterates the gendered and sexual nature of violence inflicted on women militants while underscoring their survival and resistance. The survivors' struggles culminate in a trial for human rights violations against the perpetrators. Resilience and gender are again highlighted as individual and collective traits that allow women not only to make sense of past atrocities but also to shape their present identity and outlook toward the future. They all agree that coexistence with their perpetrators is hard, and that a democratic and strong legal system is fundamental in Argentina so that this never happens again. The support of human rights groups, women's collectives and feminist groups, and the judicial systems here all combined to help build a network of resilience geared toward women's rights activism. Through years of feminist work and struggle with patriarchal institutions and the law, democratic coexistence became possible.

In the testimonial book she coauthored, *Ese infierno. Conversaciones con cinco mujeres sobrevivientes de la ESMA* (2001, "That Inferno. Conversations with Five Women Survivors from the ESMA"), Miriam Lewin describes the sexual violence she experienced in the torture chamber of one of Argentina's largest extermination centers in Buenos Aires, the ESMA:[12] "There were screams, insults and one of the guys pulled my blindfold. I was naked and tied. He neared his penis while the rest of them threatened me: We will take you one by one, bitch" (2013, 68). Lewin's clarity and resilience are key in her accounts of the past in which she retells the brutal and sexualized treatment of prisoners like herself and also how they survived and resisted. Her experiences have reached a wide audience through televised testimonies, online interviews, and printed publications that have helped educate about the past and further women's fight for gender and reproductive rights in Argentina.

As Cath Collins, Katherine Hite, and Alfredo Joignant argue, in Latin America and particularly in Chile, "elite-level silences seem mostly to hamper rather than to lead society's effort to come to terms with the past"

(2013, 22). Voicing the pain around this past and fighting for due justice are needed in order to come to terms with "difficult historical memories" and human rights violations as a country (Collins 2013, 22–23). In my view, this is precisely what women's memory accounts do by voicing painful past experiences while also highlighting the ways to persist individually and as a gender group in the present. In this sense, giving voice to their stories fosters a connection between a traumatic past and the present, underscoring the importance of relationships with other women to rebuild identity and a still divided society.

In the early 1990s, former MIR militant, Chilean Marcia Alejandra Merino, in her testimony *Mi Verdad: más allá del horror yo acuso* (1993, "My truth: Beyond Horror I Accuse") provides a catalogue of the horror of sexual abuses endured by women prisoners to break them. The impact that torture and coercion had on her completely changed and estranged Merino from her past. It distanced her from former militants and friends while making her keenly aware of her wrongs and ethical void. Her previous life and identity became vacated, leaving her with a sense of being dead. She was detained in La Venda of Calle Domingo Cañas in Santiago, which she visits for the first time during the filming of the documentary *La Flaca Alejandra. Vida y muerte de una mujer chilena* (1994), directed by Carmen Castillo, also a former MIR militant. This is a powerful tour-de-force film where Merino's experiences as a left-wing militant, political prisoner, and agent of the military's secret police take center stage. Merino's testimony, together with *El infierno* (1993; *The Inferno. A Story of Terror and Survival in Chile*, 1994) by Luz Arce, are emblematic texts that confess the "wrongs" committed by these two female militants turned collaborators. Both ask for forgiveness while calling out the brutal torture and rapes that dramatically changed their identities and ideologies. Interestingly, both testimonies received little attention by the general public when they came out, probably due to the need of the Transitional Concertación government to move on by reconciling and forgetting past atrocities. Both women were at the mercy of their captors and in subservient positions in which self-determination and choice were extremely limited, if not outright impossible. Any choices they made were under intimidation and daily violence, which according to the new views on human rights internationally, cannot be considered free acts.

Along these lines is Ana Forcinito's argument on coercive settings and sexual violence in the context of state terrorism prisons (2017). She notes the way narratives of romance and honor make the victim guilty instead of acknowledging the impossibility of consent under these conditions.

The alibi of honor only reinforces masculinity and denies that coercion and violation have taken place. Until 1999, rape in Argentina was considered a crime against female honesty. Only after the change in the definition of rape that took place that same year, the crime became one against physical integrity (Forcinito 2017, 188–89). Without women's pushback and their political and feminist activism this crucial modification in the law would not have been possible.

Chilean writer Fátima Sime in her novel *Carne de perra* (2009, "Bitch's Body") represents the experience of captivity, torture, and sexual abuse of a former militant from a gender perspective, providing a new take on what sexual torture means for female sexuality and subjectivity. The most interesting innovation in her nuanced treatment of the figure of the captive turned collaborator is her use of a gender lens that allows the exploration of larger social issues related to justice, and more pointedly the need for gender justice and women's rights. The novel also problematizes the sexual and affective relationship between a victim and her torturer, deploying a critique of the Stockholm Syndrome framework and the romantic plot. Sime shows that under captivity and violence against women there can be no consensual sexual relationship and that decision-making for the victim is structurally bound to subordination and fear. The critic Ksenija Bilbija in the interpretation of the novel states that it is only through the protagonist's confrontation with the past that she can overcome the wounds and heal. For Maria Rosa, like other victims of state terrorism, the past is relived in the present and only reconstructing the traumatic events and narrating her own story can she break free from her powerful torturer (Bilbija 2017, 99–100).

The patriarchal system that rules social relationships and power in the three Southern Cone countries examined here shows its starkest and cruel face in the detention centers, as we have seen. As Carole Sheffield argues, "violence against women is power expressed sexually" (Sheffield 2007, 128). The crime scenes underscore the connection between power and gender in the camps and urban prison centers, where torturers used their authority to dictate what female political prisoners had to do for them or an entire group of soldiers or agents. They exercised their authority by verbally and sexually abusing women, using rape as a form of torture. At the opposite end were the group of women prisoners who embraced the recently tortured, as Maria Isabel, a former MIR militant, remembers: "a group of women held you, after the torture, they held you in a way that made you feel that you were in a different space than the one you had been in minutes before" (Pizarro and Santos 2016, 79). This support is key for the formation of women's solidarity groups during the transitional governments and beyond. Empathy and other solidarity practices in which survivors engaged during their detention are resources that later enabled the symbolization of trauma in their accounts, building a community of women survivors and in some cases denouncing the victimizers. In her book *Surviving State Terror*, Barbara Sutton asserts that "the memory of embodied survival" and resistance that oral testimonies by survivors reveal shows "small acts" of good and connection to other human beings at the center, reminding us that agency can take multiple shapes and does not need to be grandiose or monumental (2018, 177). In these memories of survival, small changes, as Sutton writes, have a cumulative impact that shape "minimal stories that also make history" (2018, 177–78). Sutton posits an intriguing question about the transgressive quality of the "feminizing" aspects of captivity in Latin American secret prisons that Franco identified early on in analyzing the cultural text (2013, 178). In fact, they both conclude that this feminization allowed for survival and resistance.

In this way, former political prisoners and political activists contribute today to the making of cultural memory in postdictatorial societies still struggling to come to terms with a violent past. These former militants and survivors have joined the public conversation late, but they are key players for democracy to move forward in "the process of addressing the legacy of past violence and rebuilding the broken relationships it has caused" (Bloomfield, Barnes, and Huyse 2003, 4–5).

Women's narratives of survival are key in order to understand the extent of patriarchal state violence and the ways that gender was structural to the torture script "beyond the perpetuation of evident forms of sexual violence," as Sutton demonstrates (2018, 240). These stories present a subjectivity that acknowledges, remembers, and learns from that shattering past to build the present and envision the future. They also speak of bonds of empathy and solidarity born in the midst of terror and pain. We can trace the emergence of a narrative of hope and empowerment, opening a new phase in memory narratives where gender rights are weighed in the experience of political violence and sexual torture. Collectives of women survivors and human rights organizations have fought to make the demands for human rights and gender justice heard in the courts and on the streets. They have engaged in what feminist legal scholar Catherine MacKinnon calls "butterfly politics," showing the "crucial dimensions of legal political activism, strategic choice of moments of initiation, dynamics of intervention and blow back and its anticipation and the collaborative effects of collective recursion" (2017, 2). Writers of literature, testimonies, and documentarians have also shared similar concerns about truth, justice, and memory, contributing to this wave for gender rights.

While progress toward gender justice has been made in Argentina and Uruguay, Chile still lags behind. As the legal context reveals, women survivors in Chile have not received due justice for the sexual crimes they suffered. Though it has not been a key part of the current political debate on violence against women, the crime for sexual torture has to be categorized and incorporated into the law. However, in contrast to the Chilean judiciary system, literature, written and visual testimonies as well as documentaries, have been at the forefront in representing these experiences and advancing women's rights as human rights.

In 2010, a survivor in Argentina won her case in the first trial for sexual torture against the dictatorship in a courthouse in La Plata. In Uruguay, a landmark collective trial for sexual torture against women was won in 2011. Both cultural scenarios reveal that the judiciary systems in these countries have changed to expand the meaning of sexual torture as a crime against humanity that is imprescriptible. It is my hope that Chile will follow suit, advancing women's gender rights and human rights as its neighbors.

Paying attention to state violence and violence against women through a gender lens is not only important but crucial today in Latin America and the rest of the world, especially since we live in a time where violence is glorified, macho masculinity is exalted, and white supremacy and heteropatriarchal ideals are gaining legitimacy. These survivors' stories "carry memories of social change and valuable political perspectives," as Sutton says (2018, 253), to point us in a different direction: a more humane one. I believe they offer the seeds for the future, for building a better and more just society. Empathy and resilience are crucial aspects in these memory narratives that connect self and other through survival and resistance to extreme forms of abuse and pain. Reflecting back on them empowers not only survivors but also their listeners and viewers. From them we can learn new modes of gender kinship and solidarity that reframe democratic discourse and practices after a violent past. The stories provide a path for more peaceful forms of coexistence where the voices and agency of women acquire new meaning and are valued.

NOTES

1. The three countries have had varying numbers of Truth Commission Reports, Argentina (*Nunca Más* 1984, *Never Again*), Chile (Comisión de Verdad y Reconciliación

1990, Valech I 2005 and Valech II 2010–2011), and Uruguay (Comisión Investigadora sobre la Situación de Personas Desaparecidas y Hechos que la Motivaron 1985, Investigative Commission for the Situation of Disappeared Persons and the Facts that Motivated it). Chile's Commissions are an international exception in that they have kept the testimonies classified and made them available only to the courts. Argentina and Uruguay, on the other hand, have given public access to the information in the commissions' reports. For more info consult: https://www.camara.cl/pdf.aspx?prmTIPO=DOCUME NTOCOMUNICACIONCUENTA&prmID=14005

2. http://www.afterthecrossfire.com/

3. https://es.globalvoices.org/2018/09/27/con-el-proceso-de-paz-de-colombia-estancado-aumentan-las-cifras-de-activistas-asesinados/

4. His notable *The Battle of Chile* (1973–76), *Chile: The Obstinate Memory* (1997), *The Pinochet Case* (2001), as well as his two more recent films, *Nostalgia for the Light* (2010) and *The Pearl Button* (2015), speak about the painful memories of this violent past and the ways the dictatorship in Chile violated human rights, leaving Chileans still today split about that past and what took place.

5. Jorge Rafael Videla was head of the Argentine military Junta that overthrew President Isabel Perón with a coup d'état. He was the senior commander in the army and a dictator from 1976 to 1981. He died in prison in 2003 and was sentenced to fifty years for crimes against humanity and children's abductions during the dirty war campaign he directed. His equivalent in Uruguay was the civil dictator Juan Bordaberry, who supported by a military coup governed the country from 1973 to 1976 until he was ousted from power by the military. He also died in prison in 2011, sentenced to thirty years for violating the constitution by participating in the coup.

6. However, this last figure was disputed by the Relatives of the Disappeared (*Agrupación de Familiares de Detenidos Desaparecidos*), a human rights organization that claimed that 22,000 denunciations were rejected by the commission. See: https://elpais.com/diario/2011/08/20/internacional/1313791208_850215.html

7. See: https://journals.openedition.org/nuevomundo/67888

8. See https://www.researchgate.net/publication/317468017_HIJOS_in_Argentina_The_Emergence_of_Practices_and_Discourses_in_the_Struggle_for_Memory_Truth_and_Justice

9. https://blogs.helsinki.fi/temashispanicos/?p=160

10. The Penal Code in Chile dates to 1874 and does not consider sexual violence and sexual torture as major crimes. See https://www.clarin.com/mundo/Denuncian-torturas-sexuales-dictadura-chilena_0_BJCUX5w5DXe.html. This complaint took place during Michelle Bachelet's government whose gender and human rights agenda made women's rights a priority; however, Bachelet was not able to include a gender perspective in the law.

11. All translations are mine unless noted.

12. ESMA stood for Escuela de Mecánica de la Marina (Mechanical Navy School). Today it is a memorial museum that was inaugurated in 2004 by Néstor Kischner's government.

REFERENCES

Actis, Manu, Cristina Inés Aldini, and Miriam Lewin. 2001. *Ese Infierno. Conversaciones con cinco mujeres sobrevivientes de la ESMA*. Buenos Aires: Sudamericana.

Alvarez, Fernando. 2014. *Campo de Batalla, cuerpo de mujer* (documentary).

Arce, Luz. 1993. *El infierno*. Santiago: Tajamar Editores.

Becker, Nubia. 1986. *Una mujer en Villa Grimaldi*. Santiago: Pehuén.

Bilbija, Ksenija. 2017. "El síndrome de Estocolmo: ajustes de cuenta y otros saldos literarios en la ficción posdictatorial chilena." In *Poner el cuerpo: rescatar y visibilizar las marcas sexuales y de género en los archivos dictatoriales del Cono Sur*, edited by Ksenija Bilbija, Ana Forcinito, and Bernardita Llanos, 85–105. Santiago: Cuarto Propio.

Bloomfield, David, Teresa Barnes, and Lucien Huyse, eds. 2003. *Reconciliation After Violent Conflict. A Handbook*. Sweden: International IDEA.

Bravo, Nazareno. 2012. "HIJOS in Argentina: The Emergence of Practices and Discourses in the Struggle for Memory, Truth and Justice." Accessed November 11, 2018. https://www.researchgate.net/publication/317468017

Camiruaga, Gloria. 2000. *La Venda* (documentary).

Castillo, Carmen. 1993. *La Flaca Alejandra. Vida y muerte de una mujer chilena* (documentary).

Centro de Derechos Humanos UDP. 2016. Accessed April 17, 2017. http://www.derechoshumanos.udp.cl/derechoshumanos/index.php/informe-anual?layout=edit&id=191

Collins, Cath, Katherine Hite, and Alfredo Joignant, eds. 2013. *The Politics of Memory in Chile. From Pinochet to Bachelet*. Boulder and London: University of Rochester.

"Con el proceso de paz de Colombia estancado, aumentan las cifras de activistas asesinados." Accessed November 12, 2018. https://es.globalvoices.org/2018/09/27/con-el-proceso-de-paz-de-colombia-estancado-aumentan-las-cifras-de-activistas-asesinados

Decety, Jean. 2011. "The Neuroevolution of Empathy." *Annals of the New York Academy of Sciences*. Special Issue: *Social Neuroscience: Gene, Environment, Brain, Body* 1231, no. 1: 35–45.

Feitlowitz, Marguerite. 2015. *El lexicón del terror*. Buenos Aires: Prometeo Libros.

Franco, Jean. 2013. *Cruel Modernity*. Durham: Duke University Press.

Fried, Gabriela. 2017. "Las reglas de la casa: violencia sexual como instrumento de violencia de estado en los centros de tortura (1972–1982) en Uruguay." In *Poner el cuerpo: rescatar y visibilizar las marcas sexuales y de género en los archivos dictatoriales del Cono Sur*, edited by Ksenija Bilbija, Ana Forcinito, and Bernardita Llanos, 147–70. Santiago: Cuarto Propio.

Goni, Uki. 2017. "Fury in Argentina over Ruling That Could See Human Rights Abusers Walk Free." *Guardian*, May 4. https://www.theguardian.com/world/2017/may/04/argentina-supreme-court-human-rights

Informe Anual sobre Derechos Humanos en Chile 2016 (UDP). 2016. Cap. 1 Verdad, Justicia, Reparación y Memoria, November, 19–79. Accessed April 17, 2017. http://www.derechoshumanos.udp.cl/derechoshumanos/images/InformeAnual/2016/Collinsyotros_verdadyjusticia.pdf. http://www.desaparecidos.org/uru/eng.html

Instituto Nacional de Derechos Humanos. n.d. Accessed April 17, 2017. http://www.indh.cl/resena-institucional/historia

Kornbluh, Peter. 2003. *The Pinochet File: The Declassified Dossier on Atrocity and Accountability*. New York: The New Press.

Lazzara, Michael. 2017. "The Memory Turn." In *New Approaches to Latin American Studies: Culture and Power*, edited by Juan Poblete, 14–31. New York: Routledge.

Lessa, Francesca. 2013. *Memory and Transitional Justice in Argentina and Uruguay: Against Impunity*. New York: Palgrave Macmillan.

Lewin, Miriam, and Olga Wornat. 2014. *Putas y guerrilleras. Crímenes sexuales en los centros clandestinos de detención. La perversión de los represores y la controversia en la militancia. Las historias silenciadas. El debate pendiente*. Buenos Aires: Planeta.

Llanos, Bernardita. 2016. "Caught Off Guard at the Crossroad of Ideology and Affect: Documentary Films by the Daughters of Revolutionaries." In *Latin American Documentary Film in the New Millennium*, edited by Maria Guadalupe Arenillas and Michael Lazzara, 243–58. New York: Palgrave.

Longoni, Ana. 2007. *Traiciones. La figura del traidor en los relatos acerca de los sobrevivientes de la represión*. Buenos Aires: Norma.

MacKinnon, Catharine A. 2017. *Butterfly Politics*. Cambridge and London: The Belknap Press of Harvard University Press.

Merino, Marcia Alejandra. 1993. *Mi verdad: Más allá del horror, yo acuso*. Santiago: A.T.G.

Museo de la memoria y de los Derechos Humanos. n.d. Accessed April 17, 2017. http://ww3.museodelamemoria.cl

O'Rourke, Catherine. 2012. "Transitioning to What? Transitional Justice and Gendered Citizen in Chile and Colombia." In *Gender in Transitional Justice*, edited by Susanne Buckley-Zistel and Ruth Stanley, 136–60. New York and London: Palgrave Macmillan.

Pizarro, Carolina, and Santos, José, eds. 2016. *Revisitar la catástrofe. Prisión política en el Chile dictatorial*. Santiago: Pehuén.

Sheffield, Carole J. 2007. "Sexual Terrorism." In *Gender Violence. Interdisciplinary Perspectives*, edited by Laura L. O'Toole, Jessica R. Schiffman, and Margie L. Kiter Edwards, 111–29. New York and London: New York University Press.

Sime, Fátima. 2009. *Carne de perra*. Santiago: LOM.

Stern, Steven. 2010. *Reckoning with Pinochet. The Memory Question in Democratic Chile 1989–2006*. Durham: Duke University Press.

Sutton, Barbara. 2015. "Terror, testimonio, y transmisión: Voces de mujeres sobrevivientes de centros clandestinos de detención en Argentina (1976–1983)." *Mora* 21, no. 1: 5–23.

Sutton, Barbara. 2018. *Surviving State Terror. Women's Testimonies of Repression and Resistance in Argentina*. New York: New York University Press.

Theidon, Kimberly. 2012. *Intimate Enemies. Violence and Reconciliation in Peru*. Philadelphia: University of Pennsylvania Press.

Tynnila, Suvi M. 2017. "Operación Cóndor." Accessed November 11, 2018. https://blogs.helsinki.fi/temashispanicos/?p=160

Velasco, Ricardo. 2014. *After the Crossfire: Memories of Violence and Memory*. Accessed November 12, 2018. http://www.afterthecrossfire.com/

Zolli, Andrew. 2012. "'Resilience' Looks at How Systems Bounce Back." Accessed August 20, 2017. http://www.npr.org/2012/07/27/157489677

9 | Toward Resilient Cultural Initiatives of Memory and Reconciliation among Rural Displaced Populations in Transitional Colombia

Ricardo A. Velasco

In this chapter I discuss three border crossing cultural initiatives of memory developed by state and civil society actors in the context of Colombia's current transitional justice conjuncture. I focus on the potential of these initiatives for promoting peace and reconciliation among forcibly displaced communities living in isolated border regions at the limits of national sovereignty. I situate the practices described in relation to a transitional justice process in which the creation of a culture of peace and the promotion of initiatives aimed at dignifying the victims of the armed conflict is of central importance. The chapter explores the links between culture, peaceful coexistence, resilience, and collective agency by analyzing cultural processes being developed in the border region between Panama and Colombia. These initiatives are discussed in contrast to institutional platforms designed to include displaced populations living in exile into the process of national reconciliation.

In the approach I propose, I use the term reconciliation following the category in transitional justice discourse, to stress how the initiatives I discuss relate or contribute to a specific historic conjuncture in Colombia. I use coexistence as a broader category in relation to the central theme of the volume, to refer not only to peaceful living among communities affected by violence but also to where victims and actors belonging to armed groups need to come to terms with the violent past of a nation that has endured more than sixty years of internal conflict. I link coexistence to symbolic processes of memory construction that foster a culture of inclusion and participation and are in this way shaping the imaginary of a post-conflict nation. This articulation is similar to that proposed by Llanos in this volume, who analyzes memory accounts by women in Latin America's postdictatorial Southern Cone. For Llanos, memory narratives become expressions of agency and resilience "that revisit the past to imagine and demand a democratic society where gender justice and women's rights are legally recognized and socially respected." Within the context I discuss, I argue that sustainable memory and reconciliation initiatives need to go beyond institutional models and technology-centered approaches and promote cultural processes from the grassroots level that activate participation in memory construction and foster inclusion and resilience through civic engagement around local community problems. This becomes increasingly relevant in areas with weak institutional presence or among peoples who have become stateless after forced migration. I articulate my argument about the crucial importance of these types of initiatives to counteract institutional centralization and what I term "structural amnesia," a term that helps illuminate the links between violence and state abandonment.

The chapter also puts forward a transnational approach, bringing to light how a microscale flow of ideas, resources, processes of cultural activism, and social actors is able to produce border crossing practices of memory. I use the notion of "border crossing" in relation to the concept of "transnational memory," which, as de Cesari and Rigney (2014) have rightly observed, makes possible an analytical focus on the flow of memories and the material presence of borders. But beyond geopolitical borders, the approach also considers technological barriers as borders as well as the symbolic borders being crossed in the process of creating sustainable peaceful coexistence. It is this transgression of symbolic barriers that has made possible the formation of transnational solidarities among social actors belonging to a broad range of sociocultural spheres, including vulnerable ethnic minorities in the condition of forced displacement.

How are cultural initiatives of memory construction helping communities affected by violence to become resilient and reengage in social and civic life? How are these processes contributing to reconciliation efforts beyond national borders? To answer these questions, I first elaborate the historical and political context of the transitional justice conjuncture in Colombia to illuminate the relation I propose between memory, reconciliation, and culture. I discuss some of the limitations of institutional models, particularly with respect to communities that have migrated outside Colombia but are still entitled to their rights to truth, justice, and reparation. Second, I discuss civil society initiatives developed in Jaqué, Panama, and Juradó, Colombia, including my practice with documentary filmmaking to explore the possibilities of activist research and audiovisual testimony for resilient memory construction. I reveal innovative approaches to memory in the communal interventions of a youth collective with displaced populations in the village of Jaqué, Panama. I discuss their articulation of memory with social and environmental justice activism and how this practice promotes personal and collective projects of civic engagement and a range of opportunities for their members and the communities with which they work, a process I refer to as network agency. This process reveals a great potential for the reestablishment of peace and reconciliation in marginal rural areas. It also reveals an understudied potential for bridging practices of memory with resilience and solidarity in communities that have been excluded from the dynamics of social and economic development. As Simich and Andermann argue, resilience is the outcome of not only individual and psychological dispositions but also of social processes "that reside in relationships among people, systems and institutions at the level of families, communities, and organizations, governments and transnational networks" (2014, vii).

Methodology

For this discussion, I rely on data and insights from the accumulated experience of institutional ethnographies I conducted between 2009 and 2012 with the former Commission of Historical Memory. During this period, I attended several public presentations such as the main yearly cultural event, the "Week for Memory," interviewing commissioners as well as communications and public outreach staff. Follow-up interviews quoted in this chapter were conducted in July 2016 at what is now the National Center of Historical Memory. I also rely on testimonial documentation and archival research conducted between May and August of 2013 for the production of *After the Crossfire: Memories of Violence and Displacement*, a film I produced in collaboration with a group of victims in Colombia's north Pacific coast region.[1] In addition, the discussion of the initiatives by the youth cultural collective Hacia el Litoral is based on ethnographic research conducted between 2016 and 2018 in Jaqué, Panama, a coastal town near the Colombian border, which has been the recipient of victims of the armed conflict forcibly displaced from neighboring Colombian villages. The empirical approach is intended to supersede what has been termed the "methodological nationalism" prevalent in memory studies

(Erll 2011; de Cesari and Rigney 2014). This methodology allows a focus on processes by which discourses and practices of memory are institutionalized as a national project, as well as on their circulation beyond the nation-state frame. It also allows an emphasis on border crossing processes that result from complex flows that include the movement and agency of specific state and civil society actors. As a result, new articulations of memory practices emerging from the tension between the local, the national, and the transnational are foregrounded. In what follows, I elaborate on the historical and political context that will situate my discussion of these practices.

Transitional Justice and the Emergence and Institutionalization of a Culture of Memory and Reconciliation in Colombia

The recent importance that memory has acquired in Colombia's public sphere can be located within a transnational context in which, by a particular conjunction of cultural, historical, and political factors, the victims of human rights violations and the problem of the reconstruction of the memory of atrocious events have become prominent moral concerns and state responsibilities. In countries that have undergone peace or democratization processes to overcome pasts marked by violence, systematic repression, and human rights violations, as is the case of Colombia, the preponderance and political relevance of memory can be linked to the institutionalization of transitional justice.

Transitional justice is defined as the set of judicial and extrajudicial institutional reforms initiated by a state to facilitate the transition from an authoritarian regime to a democracy, or from a belligerent condition to one of peace, through concrete political agreements (Rettberg 2005; Minow 2002). Even though there is no unique model to follow, the result of the agreements must incorporate measures for the prevention of impunity and guarantee the rights of the victims to *justice, truth, reparation, and guarantees of non-repetition*, the so-called Joinet Principles. Two elements are of fundamental importance within the operational dynamics of transitional justice with respect to these principles. First, the clarification of truth is not restricted to the juridical domain but conceived to encompass the search for a shared narrative about an abusive past (Maurino 2003). Second, the principle of reparation is not limited to material economic compensation and is understood as a broader category that includes different initiatives of symbolic character aimed to dignify the victims and to promote reconciliation. This symbolic realm is of key importance not only for the promotion of peaceful coexistence among communities affected by violence but also for the sustainability of this process.

In Colombia, it was only after the implementation of Law 975 "of Justice and Peace" in 2005 that the conditions for the emergence of public and official interest in the clarification of the events of the conflict were consolidated, and it is in this context that the discourse of memory emerged. After 2005, and during the subsequent stage of transitional justice that followed the implementation of Law 1448 "of Victims" in 2011, the consolidation of a memory of the conflict became a fundamental state responsibility. Classified as a mechanism of symbolic reparation, the preservation of the memory of events of violence was formulated by law as a duty of society and the state toward the victims for the reestablishment of their dignity and their rights. As such, the institutionalization of memory in Colombia is entangled in the transnational assemblage of discourses, trans-institutional and transgovernmental practices, actions, and modes of enunciation that define transitional justice according to the Joinet Principles' model (1997).

The normative framework that emerged as a state response to the atrocities of the armed conflict led to the creation of the National Commission for Reparation and Reconciliation (CNRR), and within it, the Subcommission of Historical Memory (MH), founded in February 2007. In 2011, with Law 1448, MH transitioned into the National Center of Historical Memory (CNMH). As one of its defining objectives and ethical imperatives, CNMH proposes to "elaborate an inclusive and conciliatory narrative in tune with the voices of the victims" about the origins and evolution of the armed conflict in Colombia (Memoria Histórica 2008, 2). According to Gonzalo Sánchez, CNMH's director from 2007 to 2018, the inclusion of victims' testimonies carries an ethical and political significance by being formulated as an act of symbolic reparation within the conceptual architecture of Laws 975 and 1448. In a statement delivered during the inauguration of the Second Week for Memory in Bogotá, Sánchez stated that CNMH hopes that "the victims do not feel simply that truth is being told to them, but that they are actually part of its construction."[2] This inclusive ethos has had a significant impact on the circulation of the experience of victims in the public sphere. It has also made possible the emergence of victims' organizations, or the strengthening of those already existing, as important sites for interlocution with state institutions.

The initiatives taken in order to achieve this ethical imperative include a range of cultural practices and activities of commemoration initially channeled through the annual celebration of "The Week for Memory." This space was designed to give visibility to the Center's official reports presented in the form of editorial and audiovisual cultural products. With these vehicles of dissemination, CNMH aims to make visible their cases of study to a wide audience and construct a space for the dignification and recognition of the victims. In this respect, documentaries and other media products fulfill a crucial function. According to Natalia Rey, former communications coordinator, this is because of the possibility that the audiovisual language offers to emphasize testimonial record and give visibility to the victims, and because of the versatility of digital media formats as vehicles for dissemination.[3] Exploiting this versatility has been a central strategy of CNMH to meet their challenge of reaching communities across a vast territory and to foster the necessary conditions for peace and reconciliation. However, media and digital communication initiatives have also important limitations, especially for rural communities within and beyond national borders because of their unequal access to these resources.

Current Outreach Initiatives by the National Center for Historical Memory

The implementation of Law 1448 in 2011 initiated a second stage in the transitional justice process with important institutional transformations that included MH's transition into CNMH. With a more robust institutional infrastructure and significant investments in the area of communications, the emphasis of the CNMH's public engagement campaigns has notoriously shifted from editorial production toward new communications strategies with the aim of bringing the results of the investigations to a wider audience and diverse sectors of the population, including diasporic victims. The production of official reports still is a fundamental aspect of the work of the Center. However, since their circulation is limited mostly to academic and specialists circles, audiovisual products and digital platforms for the dissemination of interactive content have come to the forefront of CNMH's cultural production. As Adriana Correa, coordinator of the Center's communications division, states:

> The reports about the cases are still central, but the issue is that those reports reach only a very limited audience. We asked ourselves: how do we translate a report into an audiovisual language or into info-graphics? Each of the reports has to have at least a com-

municative piece in a different format, for instance a digital edition, an audiovisual piece, or a radio program. Our goal is to bring the content of the report to an ever-larger audience, thinking how to tell the story in a different way [. . .] and our website, where we make everything available, is the launching platform for these new ideas and formats. (Personal interview, July 2016)

With an inclusive objective, the statement reveals that significant efforts are being taken to diversify the resources for dissemination and for making content accessible.[4] The transition of the initial MH commission into the CNMH was a pivotal moment. At the end of their mandate in 2011, MH presented their final report "Basta Ya!" (Stop Now), an overall analysis of the origins and evolution of the conflict with statistical data about displacements, disappearances, and estimated numbers of victims since 1962 (Memoria Histórica 2016). The report was accompanied by a documentary and a digital database entitled "Rutas del Conflicto" (Routes of the Conflict),[5] made available for downloading or viewing through the CNMH's website, Facebook, and YouTube pages. These digital resources have produced the conditions of possibility for reaching out to victims and actors beyond national borders, including networks of human rights and nongovernmental organizations, memory initiatives, and transitional justice institutions worldwide.

The main initiative developed with a transnational focus started in 2014 with the aim of including diasporic communities of victims in the process of memory construction and reconciliation. I refer to "Voces del Exilio" (Voices of Exile), a "virtual space" that, as stated on its web platform,[6] makes visible personal and collective experiences of exile and return and brings together "the plurality of the memories of all victims of forced displacement beyond national borders." The platform includes testimonies of victims, infographics, links, and resources with information of how CNMH supports victims and their organizations living in exile. It is also a space where victims can share information about their own initiatives. The resource is the first to include forcibly displaced and persecuted victims living outside the nation into the CNMH agenda. Yet, despite its communicative functions, several problems limit its possibilities for outreach and for the consolidation of inclusive conditions that can be favorable for civic engagement and participation in peacebuilding. Of these limitations, three require particular attention.

First, the complex sociocultural geography of Colombia's border areas, especially with Panama and Brazil, embed communities in a situation of isolation. These are remote jungle areas with the highest indicators of poverty and unsatisfied basic needs, and people who are marginalized from the dynamics of social and economic development. Without robust communications infrastructures, rural communities in these areas lack proper and efficient Internet connectivity. In many cases, they even lack cultural venues where audiovisual materials can be presented or circulated. Internet connectivity is mostly achieved through cellular service, an access that significantly varies by age, income, and technological literacy. As Internet access becomes central to active citizenship in today's social and political life (Brown et al. 2001), the severe gap in access to Internet technologies can significantly impact the participation of rural border communities in the process of reconciliation and in the cultural transformations that the transitional justice framework has initiated. This is particularly the case if the communications approach to the inclusion of these communities relies on online dissemination and media platforms. For instance, in Jaqué, Panama, where the population of displaced victims from Colombia's Pacific coast region exceeds three hundred people (by 2016, according to officials of the Colombian consulate), there is only one public facility with Internet access, and its five computers are mostly used by local elementary and middle school children. All the victims I interviewed use Internet services through cellular connection—which often interrupts—and almost exclusively for personal communication purposes through apps such as WhatsApp. All stated that they don't consult CNMH's resources and only few have taken part of initiatives developed during visits by Colombian institutions of transitional justice. Thus unequal Internet access in border regions and throughout rural Colombia constitutes one of the great challenges faced by transitional institutions in the implementation and development of their communication strategies, which constitute their foundation for building the conditions for inclusive memory construction and peaceful coexistence among displaced populations.

Second, a large number of forcibly displaced victims who have crossed the national borders belong to ethnic minorities. Their cultural categories, dynamics, and habits, including uses of technology, greatly differ from those of majoritarian urban groups, and particularly metropolitan, to which the commissioners and CNMH staff belong. While CNMH and other transitional institutions are driven by an inclusive ethos, their strategies and plans of action do not fully take into consideration the cultural gaps between urban groups and rural communities. This is the case not only as it relates to information consumption and circulation but also with respect to differing notions of inclusion, participation, and coexistence in civic life. There are additional limitations of illiteracy among sectors of this population, as in the case of many elders of indigenous groups. Tackling this problem would require different approaches designed specifically for the needs and limitations of this group. Finally, for indigenous communities, Spanish is a second language, and this makes communication and access to the resources available for consultation even more difficult. Translation or use of indigenous languages would need to become a priority as a tool for inclusion in the dissemination of information.

In "Exilio Colombiano," a report by CNMH dealing with the effects of the conflict beyond national borders, it is stated that the side of the history of exile that corresponds to Panama is "the least visible and understood of the memories of the Colombian armed conflict" (Memoria Histórica 2018, 151). The trajectories and experiences of thousands of Colombians who crossed the border along the Darien Jungle, according to the report, still remain largely unknown. In the last section, I will discuss how the work of uncovering these experiences has started not by technological developments but by the agency of civil society actors involved in border crossing, microscale cultural projects. Here it would suffice to suggest that digital initiatives attempting the task of bringing to light the experiences and trajectories of displaced populations who cross the Panamanian border into exile are unlikely to prosper under the conditions discussed. However, transnationally focused digital initiatives have been more successful with victims that have migrated to urban centers in Ecuador, Venezuela, Spain, and other Latin American nations, as evident in the online platform "Voices of Exile," where most of the narratives and testimonies presented belong to these groups.

A last limitation of current official initiatives is related to the centralization of institutional practices and resources. CNMH's initiatives still remain structured around metropolitan approaches to culture, such as the annual celebration of the Week for Memory. The event showcases the cultural production of the center in prestigious cultural venues such as the Museum of the Bank of the Republic and the National Museum of Colombia, among others. Strategic alliances with these venues generate the institutionalization of CNMH's cultural products in what Pierre Bourdieu (1993) terms "a restricted field of cultural production." Bourdieu argues that within a field of cultural production, restricted cultural circuits have the property of attributing to the cultural product that circulate within it the power and symbolic capital of those institutions that authorize and make them legitimate. But in contrast to the large-scale circuits of the cultural industries, the aim of which is the maximization of profit, within the field of restricted production institutions and actors "trade" with mainly symbolic values, such as prestige, authenticity, or legitimacy. By structuring its activities around this logic, CNMH makes an "investment" by which its cultural products capitalize in power and symbolic values of official character. Individual victims or their organizations further contribute to this centralized valorization of cultural capital with the legitimacy that their presence bestows upon the events, if we consider the central importance victims as social actors have within the transitional conjuncture.

The new communication and public outreach strategies aimed at disseminating CNMH's work to national and transnational audiences follow a similar pattern. They are launched in the main cultural venues of the capitals of other Colombian departments or of the countries where displaced victims live. Because of unequal access to circuits of cultural production, those able to participate or benefit from these initiatives tend to be near main urban centers. In sum, while all efforts are concentrated in diversifying memory initiatives by using versatile digital formats, and in constructing a robust platform where these products can be viewed or consulted, less attention is being put on the assessment of the unequal accessibility to cultural and digital resources for remote rural and border communities. This is also the case with the assessment of how the information is received and incorporated into actual practices. Under these conditions, the question remains whether sustainable peace and coexistence can be achieved if the design of the central initiatives and policies that structure and move this process forward reproduce historical structural inequalities in the access to resources.

Victims and human rights activists react to these realities. For instance, at the end of 2016 it was announced that a report made by the Center, entitled "Hasta Encontrarlos" (Until We Find Them), was going to be publicly presented at the National Museum of Colombia. The report deals with the vast and understudied problem of forced disappearances in the context of the armed conflict (Memoria Histórica 2016). When the event was posted on CNMH's Facebook page, a member of a victims' organization of Colombia's southeast region, near the border with Brazil, made a critical comment regarding the centralization problem that for him is characteristic of state institutions in general: "Too bad that for you the country is limited to Bogotá and Medellín. It will not do if you dress up as inclusive scholars, and at the end you reproduce and give strength to the centralist practices that have driven our country to be one that promotes exclusion toward the periphery."[7]

The commentary touches upon a sensibility that is deeply engrained in

Colombian society, derived from the reality of the government's highly centralized structures, and one of the reasons why most of the benefits of economic and social development do not reach rural areas. The commentary does not do justice to CNMH's efforts and its ethical imperative of inclusion, but it does point out the problem of an inclusive agenda that is difficult to achieve without close analysis of its condition of production, circulation, and reception in a centralized developing nation with most of its resources concentrated in the capital and a few other enclaves of economic development. After discussing the limitations and problems of this institutional model of memory initiatives and the construction of a culture of peace among rural and border communities, I will discuss two different approaches by actors from civil society in the remote north Pacific region and across the border with Panama.

Grassroots Civil Society Cultural Initiatives of Memory in the Border Region between Colombia and Panama

Audiovisual Testimony and Activist Research in Memory Construction and Documentary Practice

On December 12, 1999, the Revolutionary Armed Forces of Colombia (FARC) attacked the remote coastal village of Juradó. A platoon of approximately five hundred men besieged the small town assaulting naval and police bases. One noncombatant civilian and twenty-five members of the Colombian armed forces died in the attack. In addition, thirty-five marines were wounded, a group of seventy-five were taken hostage, and a large part of the population was forced to leave the town, their homes and all their possessions. On December 14, after a forty-eight-hour delay, television news brought to light the case—a single incident among thousands in six decades of internal conflict. Any news from this isolated village near the border with Panama was and still is rare. The northern Pacific coast region is a marginalized area of tropical rain forest with the highest indicators of poverty in the country. With a majoritarian Afro-Colombian and indigenous population, and peripheral to the imaginary of the nation, it is a region significantly abandoned by the institutions of the state and marginalized from the dynamics of social and economic development. Until the 1990s, the area had also remained largely isolated from the dynamics of the conflict. In fact, it was only during this period that cases of large-scale violence started to be reported.

Yet only this event gained visibility at a national scale. From a military perspective, the attack could be interpreted as a strategy to get control over what constitutes a key territory in the transnational arms and drugs trade in an isolated jungle area where the presence of the state and the rule of law is weak. In effect, that was the narrative that prevailed once meteorological conditions allowed reporters to arrive in the field on December 14. The preponderance of public narratives strongly emphasizing the military aspects of the event contributed to a process by which not only the dramatic effects of violence on the civilian population became invisible but also the complex array of vectors that had configured the conditions of possibility for the emergence of war in the region. This problem, which can be considered a common denominator in mainstream news coverage of the conflict throughout its recent history, became even more pronounced in cases affecting marginal rural communities inhabited by ethnic minorities. In fact, the only news that came after the initial reports on the attack were a few short newspaper articles documenting the closing of the police and military bases in Juradó. After this period, the case was forgotten.

With the aim of bringing this case to public light, in 2013 I started a collaboration with a group of victims for the production of the testimonial documentary *After the Crossfire: Memories of Violence and Displacement* (see note 1). The country was in the middle of a "memory boom" at the time. Yet the notion of memory did not have any currency in this region, as it became evident in my initial interactions with collaborators, and corroborated through archival research. As discussed above, the emergence of a preoccupation with memory had been introduced by the state through its classification as "symbolic reparation," and as part of the transitional justice mechanisms initiated in 2005. CNMH played an initial key role in this process through the elaboration of reports about what they categorize as "emblematic cases" because of their capacity to illustrate differential dynamics of the conflict throughout its history. Particularly revealing was the fact that by 2013 only one investigation had been undertaken with respect to the conflict in the Pacific coast, a region that had suffered from an unprecedented escalation of violence and which represents a large portion of the national territory. A regime of invisibility was evident in how both the media and the state had almost completely ignored the dynamics of the conflict and its effects on communities in this border region. Several historical and social factors were at play, including geographical isolation, historical marginalization, and weak governance, as well as issues of racialization that are beyond the scope of this chapter to examine.

Nancy Wood has proposed that the circulation of the silenced voices of the victims in the public space demonstrates an institutional and political intentionality "on the part of a social group or artifact of power, in order to select or organize representations of the past" (Wood 1999, 2). For Wood, the silenced memory of a particular event begins to penetrate the public domain at the moment when this memory incorporates a social, political, or institutional intentionality, which promotes or authorizes its consolidation as "official memory." Following Wood's argument, I conceptualize the forgetting surrounding the dynamics of the conflict in the Pacific coast as a form of structural amnesia. In other words, the state had failed the people of the region in its memory duty, the same way it has historically failed in promoting institutions of social and economic development. There was no political or institutional intentionality to bring this case into public light, and the structural conditions made the possibility of oblivion a concrete reality. The very notion of memory was absent from public and civic discourse in the area.

During the period of the attack, a peace process between the government and FARC was in the middle of a crisis. As the actors involved were trying to show their military capacities, violence escalated to unprecedented levels. The negotiations, which had started in May 1999, eventually broke off in February 2002. In this context, the media visibility of the attack to Juradó can be seen as serving an antisubversive propaganda purpose at a specific moment when the government wanted to make public FARC's contradictions regarding their intentions of peace, and use this as a leverage strategy in the table of negotiations. This helps explain the emphasis given in the news to the military aspects of the event, but only partially explains the invisibility of the victims. While doing audiovisual archival research at one of Colombia's main private media networks, I corroborated how news coverage gave voice to officers and wounded soldiers, but in contrast the only members of the community interviewed were the priest and the mayor of the town, who gave brief statements emphasizing mostly the material damage. For the reporters at the time, the only people who had a voice were those invested with institutional authority.

In response to the invisibility and structural amnesia that had prevailed in the case, in *After the Crossfire* I follow a testimonial rather than a historical-archival approach. Its main communicative function is to make the victims visible as well as their experiences of war, without putting forward a totalizing truth claim. Yet the documentary process is about the social and collaborative interactions by which the victims actively exert their agency in the construction of a resilient memory that speaks about a violent past but also about present claims around the conditions and actors that made this violence possible. I followed the conceptualization of witnessing as a necessary condition of agency as proposed by Dominick LaCapra, who argues that witnessing can constitute a creative or transformative act by which a victim of trauma "may overcome being overwhelmed by numbness and passivity, reengage in social practice, and acquire a voice that may in certain conditions have practical [political, juridical, or social] effects" (2001, 12). The film creates these conditions in a context not constrained by the dominant discursive frameworks of transitional justice. As in the case of the work by the CNMH, these frameworks situate testimony among other nonjuridical mechanisms of reparation and reconciliation, therefore encoding the enunciation and inscription of the narrative within specific state rationalities, or what Allen Feldman (2004) calls normative and moralizing regimes of truth.

During the interviews I conducted, shifts in intonation and in the position of enunciation contradicted established conceptions of testimony. In contrast to the notion of a personal narrative enunciated in the first singular person (Beverley 1987; Yúdice 1996), the majority of the witnesses interviewed moved freely from the first singular to the first plural person, a shift emphasizing collective over individual agency. Through a constant alternation between a narrative form of discourse in the past tense and an active present tense, they articulated their memories with claims about the abandonment of the state as the foundation for the emergence of armed groups in rural Colombia. They also insisted on including specific statements regarding the emergence of paramilitarism and felt an urge to denounce the complicity of the state in this process. The medium of documentary constituted a powerful tool to disseminate these claims. Even though they were affected more directly by the actions perpetrated by FARC, with the massive displacement that followed the 1999 attack, they asserted their agency by ensuring that the picture of violence in the region depicted was more complete and nuanced than that previously presented by the media, and that all involved actors were included.

The position taken by those giving testimony carried significant risks, and for this reason interviewees asked me to confirm that the film would not be disseminated through national TV and to avoid the use of naming labels. The fact that *After the Crossfire* was being produced in a US university became a motivation for wider dissemination in contexts that did not pose direct risks. The main avenues for dissemination discussed were human rights film festivals and academic conferences, because of receptivity to the topic and the possibilities for debate these spaces can open. The documentary process introduced the notion of memory as an arena for symbolic struggles and resilience, a possibility that has been neglected in the absence of related initiatives within a regime of invisibility. Memory construction emerged as a dialogical encounter to engage with the past beyond the constraints of human rights and transitional justice discourses, making possible claims of justice with relevance in the present. This approach follows what Hale (2006) has termed "activist research," a method through which the researcher: 1) affirms a political alignment with the struggles of the communities being studied, and 2) establishes a dialogue with these communities that informs and actively shapes each of the stages of research. Rather than the exclusive site of data collection, observation, and analysis, the field emerged as a space for the articulation of political praxis, and as such, a site where particular struggles, in this case memory struggles beyond official discursive constraints, could be mobilized.

Individual agency, collaboration, and dialogical negotiation of objectives shaped the tone, structure, and communicative function of *After the Crossfire*. This process made possible a strategic appropriation of the documentary medium by the victims interviewed. Within this creative dynamic, testimony emerged as an act of resilience to denounce impunity, state abandonment, and the structural amnesia surrounding cases of war in marginal areas of the country such as the northern Pacific coast region.[8] Between 2014, the year of its completion, and 2018, *After the Crossfire* has circulated in several international human rights film festivals and academic conferences. Channeled through these cultural and academic circuits, the audiovisual medium offers important possibilities for memory construction as a platform for mediation and dissemination of testimonial memory across national borders, and as a facilitator of debate to prevent historical closure in relation to forgotten cases of violence.

Border Crossing Memory, Cultural Activism, and Community Engagement

In Colombia's current transitional conjuncture, the practices of memorialization and the cultural activism promoted by grassroots organizations are emerging as fields of symbolic contestation in the reconfiguration of notions of citizenship through participation in post-conflict civic engagement. These practices reveal new articulations of agency for demanding and practicing inclusion and civic transformations in rural areas historically abandoned by the institutions of the state. Increasingly, these practices are also transgressing national and symbolic borders and engaging with displaced populations living in exile.

This is the case of the practices of Hacia el Litoral, a collective and platform for creative praxis based in the city of Cali. Between January 2015 and July 2017, this collective developed a small program of artistic residencies and cultural exchanges between the northern Pacific coast region and the town of Jaqué, Panama. Jaqué is the first municipality across the Colombian border and a receptor of victims of the armed conflict that fled the escalation of violence in the region between the early 1990s and the late 2000s, particularly after the 1999 attack by FARC discussed above. The members of the collective, including its leader Yolanda Chois, are young graduates from art and communication programs at public state universities, sharing an interest in social and environmental justice. A particular point of contact between their experiences has also been difficulties in finding stable jobs and sources of income in their early professional stage. However, their digital media literacies, and the wide range of opportunities taken up through their digital and cultural practices, have enabled them to connect with other cultural collectives interested in cultural activism and with a supporting network of grants provided by governmental and nongovernmental organizations.

By online opportunities taken up, I refer to the gradations of digital inclusion developed by Livingston and Helsper (2007), who discuss the digital divide in terms of a continuum in the quality of use of online resources, which maps the number and types of online opportunities taken up by users. These range from basic information seeking, through intermediate creative and entertainment uses, to more complex uses such as job and funding seeking, networking, and creation of websites to showcase creative work. In the case of the members of Hacia el Litoral, their practices also allow them to establish creative forms of collaboration among their peers, and with other organizations with which they share interests across national borders. As observed by Ito et al., new digital media can enable "active participation of a distributed social network in the production and circulation of culture and knowledge" (2010, 19). This in turn allows for the distribution and maintenance of social capital within particular cultural and creative circuits, and to the actual exertion of agency and citizenship through cultural practices, which in the case of Hacia el Litoral is shared and distributed with the local communities with which they work.

What started as a series of itinerant interventions in towns across Colombia's northern Pacific region—with actions that included mural painting, creative video and photography documentation, and radio performances—converge into a process of community engagement in the village of Jaqué after members of the collective crossed the border between Panama and Colombia by boat in early 2015. There were already seeds of cross-border environmental and cultural activism initiatives as well as an incipient infrastructure that made the site fertile for the project. In the early 2000s, a Colombian anthropologist and social activist fled the town of Juradó after the attack by FARC. In a few years after settling in Jaqué, she helped promote several community initiatives. These included the founding of a kindergarten she called "The Little School for Peace" (built with a grant from the US Agency for International Development or USAID); a program for the conservation of sea turtles; a yearly cultural and environmental event entitled "The Turtle and Mangrove Festival"; and a program of volunteers for conservation efforts, for which a house was built. These antecedents as well as a network of interpersonal connections made possible both the material and cultural conditions for the program of residencies proposed by Hacia el Litoral.

A series of flexible directives, which grew out of improvisation and dialogue with members of the village, were given to members of Hacia el Litoral to dwell in the community for periods of four to twelve weeks to work around a few selected topics during their residency. The main themes were the social, economic, cultural, and environmental conflicts along the Colombia-Panama border and how these affect displaced populations. The topics proposed to stimulate creative actions included violence, the weak presence of institutions, and issues of food sovereignty affecting displaced populations, among other problems. The approach developed by the collective to these problems through cultural practices of memory focused on promoting civic participation and activating agency and resilience within the community. The main project developed with local residents and a group of displaced Colombian victims was entitled "Jardines en Balsas" (or Gardens in Canoes; see fig. 9.1), codirected by botanist Michelle Szejner and founded by a small grant offered by a program of the office of United Nations in Panama.

The project tackled the loss of small-scale agricultural practices in the area, the lack of productive projects, and the severe problem of food autonomy and security faced by vulnerable families such as those belonging to displaced populations. In response to these issues, the project proposed to reactivate or bring back to life an ancestral family agricultural tradition among Afro-Colombian coastal communities to cultivate herbs, fruits, and vegetables in canoes no longer used or in small wooden structures that resemble canoes. For the cultural activists in residence, the conflicts at the border have contributed to the decline of this small-scale agri-

Fig. 9.1. Example of gardens in canoes, or "Jardines en Balsa," a cultural tradition of planting herbs and vegetables to promote food autonomy among rural coastal communities.

cultural practice, with material effects in the daily lives of hundreds of families. Reactivating and fostering "Jardines en Balsas" promoted the notion of memory as a practice of resilience, and as a process of engagement with past traditions to face concrete problems in the present. This vision stands in clear contrast to that promoted by state institutions. Aware of the digital divide between the collective members' urban context and that of the rural communities of this border region, they relied on the recovery of a traditional cultural practice for promoting agency and focalized action in response to local needs, understanding the possibilities of this practice for fostering resilience, solidarity, and peaceful coexistence.

By reactivating this specific form of cultural memory, "Jardines en Balsas" is bringing back to life a tradition of local food autonomy and sovereignty, and promoting resilience and the strengthening of social capital within a community in vulnerable conditions. Following Simich and Andermann (2014), I understand resilience not as the outcome of an inherent quality or capacity among individuals but rather as a dynamic process of social interactions among members of a community in response to external adverse circumstances. Memory as a practice of resilience and

engagement with productive traditions, in the way proposed by this project, allows not only new opportunities to engage with the past beyond
national frameworks and discourses. It also promotes a generative
approach through the reorganization of social relationships and the production of new ties among social groups that are not founded exclusively
by their belonging to a specific territory. Through their cultural practices,
the members of Hacia el Litoral are fostering links of solidarity and civic
engagement within the local populations, as well as promoting webs of
support for the displaced Colombian community. As a dynamic process of
social interactions around local empowerment and peaceful coexistence,
these practices were able to reactivate autonomous processes to counteract state abandonment and marginalization.

Other initiatives that emerged out of the program of artistic residencies included environment conservational efforts such as the reforestation
of the mangrove to prevent erosion and communal interventions for plastic waste management.[9] These efforts help in creating collective engage-
ments that encourage the inclusion and assimilation of the displaced
Colombian community within the local population, therefore fostering
links of solidarity and peaceful communal coexistence. The families of the
victims found in these activities ways to contribute to the host community
and environment, and to regain their social agency and adaptability in the
process. Another memory initiative was developed with indigenous young
girls with the collaboration of their local boarding school. Some of the
girls belonged to families that have been forcefully displaced from river
communities of the Darien Jungle, in the border region between Panama
and Colombia. In a workshop led by a member of the collective with a
background in narrative and communications, they were taught a series of
narrative tools and then asked to create a story of how they remembered
their communities, complementing these narratives with drawings and
other graphic activities (see fig. 9.2). Shapiro in this volume discusses a
similar approach to narrative for strengthening group belonging and cultural heritage. Her chapter illuminates the uses of memory narratives in
Cambodian dance-drama to contribute to peacebuilding in the aftermath
of genocide. Shapiro discusses how narrative and dance harness "the
moral potency of expressive culture" to strengthen the social cohesion and
cultural heritage weakened by the Khmer Rouge's terror regime. Similar in
its ethos, the goal of the narrative workshop proposed by the member of
Hacia el Litoral was to harness the potential of memory to strengthen ethnic identity among indigenous youth to promote a sense of pride in their
cultural heritage and ways of living. This form of empowerment is of great

Fig. 9.2. Narrative workshop with displaced indigenous youth in the village of Jaqué.

relevance within the context of vulnerability brought about by displacement and deterritorialization.

The cultural activities promoted by Hacia el Litoral in their work with displaced communities are documented with video and used for different communication purposes. This documentation made accessible through online social networks can allow other collectives to promote similar forms of cultural activism in other marginal communities across the country. Their work is promoted to other actors in their network, demonstrating their agency and contributions to the larger collaborative efforts of civic engagement with displaced populations in rural regions and across national borders. The flow of information and cultural capital is not restricted by the structure of cultural production, as in the institutional logic discussed, but is instead shared and promoted among participants in the network at large.

This logic of cultural production and dissemination is the result of what I term "network agency." I use this concept to refer to the process by which individual or collective action and civic participation are exerted in coordination with a complex transnational flow of actors, information, resources, dispositions, and particular articulations of cultural and social capital. It is through the workings of network agency that the members of Hacia el Litoral leverage their media and cultural literacies to contribute to reconciliation beyond national borders, and to promote peaceful coexistence founded on a principle of inclusion and solidarity. Their practices of memory help empower displaced communities to confront and overcome some of their immediate problems. Their activism, cultural practices, and media literacies become platforms by which the communities with which they work build or strengthen their social ties through what Robert Putnam (2000) calls "bridging social capital." For Putnam, this is a form of social capital that creates bridges across social cleavages, connecting people despite differences of class, ethnicity, race, or nationality. These cultural practices of Hacia el Litoral promote strong links of solidarity, resilience, and coexistence and motivate other youth creative collectives to contribute to society with their social interventions in marginalized communities at a crucial historical and political conjuncture for Colombia and for displaced communities living in exile.

Conclusion

In this chapter, I have described the border crossing cultural activities and memory practices promoted by state institutions and civil society actors working with forcefully displaced victims of the armed conflict across the Colombian-Panamanian border. Institutions such as CNMH develop initiatives to give visibility to the victims, as well as programs and platforms for the dissemination of resources and information about the process of national reconciliation across the national territory and beyond national borders. However, while this approach has brought the plight of the victims to the public sphere, creating awareness and a necessary cultural transformation of recognition and solidarity with the victims throughout the country, centralized institutional dynamics limit the possibilities for fostering autonomous organizational developments and civic participation among victims. This is particularly noticeable in rural and border areas historically marginalized by the institutions of the state. When digital technologies are used with a transnational focus, they are incorporated into a dissemination logic that reproduces centralized policies that restrict and control the distribution of resources, and of cultural, symbolic, and social capital. The conceptualization of digital communication strategies aiming at providing victims with vital information and resources fail to take into consideration the digital divide between urban and rural communities, as well as related issues of literacy and access. In these conditions the possibilities for reconciliation and sustainable peaceful coexistence are significantly limited.

Activist research in documentary practice can constitute a form of sharing agency in the construction of memory, allowing for inclusive participation in current symbolic reparation initiatives with transnational focus. As I showed with the example of the documentary *After the Crossfire*, a collaborative approach in the stage of testimonial recollection allows the strategic appropriation of the audiovisual medium by the victims. This appropriation takes place both from their positionality as victims, which carries significant ethical implications, and from their position of historical marginality, which opens an important political potential. Beyond its concrete possibilities for memory construction and symbolic reparation, the act of testimony in the practice I describe emerges as an act of agency and resilience to denounce impunity, state abandonment, and what I have termed the "structural amnesia" surrounding cases of war in marginalized areas at the limits of the nation.

Finally, the small-scale initiatives developed by the youth cultural collective Hacia el Litoral overcome some of the limitations of institutional models and technology-centered approaches for the inclusion of marginal rural communities in the process of national reconciliation. Their cultural practices have the potential to promote peaceful coexistence through community-based interventions developed around concrete problems and necessities. These practices also help in mending social ties broken by violence and displacement. Implemented in semistructured and contingent creative spaces, the practices of Hacia el Litoral foster solidarity and promote civic engagement through a network of interactions that I termed network agency. This network of interactions must be further examined for their potential in the activation of forms of resilience among displaced communities in marginal and remote rural areas. The complex interpersonal dynamics and forms of civic participation that result from network agency are of great relevance at a moment when the promotion of autonomous grassroots engagement in memory and reconciliation processes become critical for the sustainability of peace in transitional Colombia.

NOTES

1. This documentary constituted my Masters of Arts thesis in Social Documentation, completed in 2014 in the Department of Film and Digital Media at the University of California, Santa Cruz. It was produced with a grant from UC Berkeley's Human

Rights Center, where I was involved as Fellow from May to December 2013. Visit www.afterthecrossfire.com

2. Public statement during the inauguration of the "Second Week for Memory" at the National Museum of Colombia in Bogotá, September 21, 2009.

3. Personal interview conducted at the site of the former MH Commission in Bogotá, on September 8, 2010.

4. See http://www.centrodememoriahistorica.gov.co

5. See http://rutasdelconflicto.com

6. See http://www.centrodememoriahistorica.gov.co/vocesdelexilio

7. Retrieved from CNMH's Facebook page on November 22, 2016.

8. This act of resilience is similar to that described by Gordon in Somaliland (this vol.). The acts of resilience demonstrated there served to strengthen social cohesion and state-building in the face of external pressures.

9. Ethnographic audiovisual documentation of this and other initiatives discussed can be consulted at https://www.culturalecologiesofmemory.com/gardens-in-canoes, a section of the companion digital platform to my PhD dissertation.

REFERENCES

Beverley, John. 1987. "Anatomía del testimonio." *Revista de Crítica Literaria Latinoamericana* 13, no. 25: 7–16.

Bourdieu, Pierre. 1993. *The Field of Cultural Production: Essays on Art and Literature.* New York: Columbia University Press.

Brown, Kate, Scott Campbell, and Richard Ling. 2011. "Mobile Phones Bridging the Digital Divide for Teens in the US?" *Future Internet* 3, no. 2: 144–58.

De Cesari, Chiara, and Ann Rigney. 2014. "Introduction." In *Transnational Memory: Circulation, Articulation, Scales,* edited by Chiara De Cesari and Ann Rigney, 1–25. Berlin: De Gruyter.

Feldman, Allen. 2004. "Memory Theatres, Virtual Witnessing, and the Trauma Aesthetic." *Biography* 27, no. 1: 163–202.

Hale, Charles. 2006. "Activist Research v. Cultural Critique: Indigenous Land Rights and the Contradictions of Politically Engaged Anthropology." *Cultural Anthropology* 21, no. 1: 96–120.

Ito, M., et al. 2010. *Hanging out, Messing Around and Geeking Out: Kids Living and Learning with New Media.* Boston: MIT Press.

Joinet, Louis. 1997. *Informe final del Relator Especial sobre la impunidad y conjunto de principios para la protección y la promoción de los derechos humanos mediante la lucha contra la impunidad.* ONU, Comisión de Derechos Humanos. Subcomisión de Prevención de Discriminaciones y Protección de las Minorías Doc. E/CN.4/Sub.2/1997/20/Rev.1, anexo II.

LaCapra, Dominick. 1998. *History and Memory after Auschwitz.* Ithaca: Cornell University Press.

Livingstone, Sonia, and Ellen Helsper. 2007. "Gradations in Digital Inclusion: Children, Young People and the Digital Divide." *New Media & Society* 9, no. 4: 671–96.

Maurino, Mauricio. 2003. "A la búsqueda de un pasado en la democracia Argentina." *Revista del Instituto de Estudios Comparados en Ciencias Penales y Sociales.* Córdoba, Argentina, octubre 2003.

Memoria Histórica. 2008. *Narrativas y voces del conflicto: Programa de investigación.* Bogotá: Comisión Nacional de Reparación y Reconciliación.

Memoria Histórica. 2013. *Basta Yá! Colombia: Memorias de Guerra y Dignidad.* Bogotá: Imprenta Nacional.

Memoria Histórica. 2016. *Hasta Encontrarlos. El drama de la desaparición forzada en Colombia.* Bogotá: CNHM.

Memoria Histórica. 2018. *Exilio Colombiano. Huellas del Conflicto Armado Más Allá de las Fronteras.* Bogotá: CNMH.

Minow, Martha. 2002. *Breaking the Cycles of Hatred: Memory, Law and Repair.* Princeton: Princeton University Press.

Putnam, Robert. 2000. *Bowling Alone: The Collapse and Revival of American Community.* New York: Simon and Schuster.

Rettbergh, Angelika. 2005. "Reflexiones introductorias sobre la relación entre construcción de paz y justicia transicional." In *Entre el perdón y el paredón: preguntas y dilemas de la justicia transicional,* edited by Angelika Rettbergh, 1–15. Bogotá: Ediciones Uniandes.

Simich, Laura, and Lisa Andermann, eds. 2014. *Refuge and Resilience: Promoting Resilience and Mental Health among Resettled Refugees and Forced Migrants.* New York: Springer.

Wood, Nancy. 1999. *Vectors of Memory: Legacies of Trauma in Postwar Europe.* Oxford: Berg.

Yúdice, George. 1996. "Testimonio and postmodernism." In *The Real Thing: Testimonial Discourse and Latin America,* edited by George Gubelberger, 42–57. Durham: Duke University Press.

10 | The Politics of Resilience in Somaliland

The Contribution of Political Community and Autonomy to Post-Conflict Stabilization and Coexistence

Matthew Gordon

On May 18, 2018, the Republic of Somaliland celebrated its twenty-seventh year of existence, as well as two decades since its last experience with internal warfare. In that time, the country had established a viable and relatively stable hybrid governance system, which combines modern institutions of the bureaucratic state with formal and informal systems of traditional governance, as was institutionalized in a constitution ratified through a nationwide popular referendum in 2001. Six democratic elections have since followed, two for local councils, three for the presidency, and one for parliament, including a peaceful transfer of power—quite a feat in a Horn of Africa region where popular voting is either rendered meaningless by authoritarian governments (Ethiopia, Djibouti, and Sudan), ruled out due to fears of terrorism and instability (Somalia), or regularly marred by fears of intercommunal violence (Kenya). Somaliland continues to rank low on many economic and social indicators, yet it has proven itself capable of ensuring a secure and functional enough political environment to facilitate rapidly increasing foreign investment, expanding service delivery (including in education and health), and the relatively efficient and timely management of humanitarian aid, allowing the country to respond to drought more effectively than neighboring Somalia (World Bank 2014; Rossi 2014).

Such success has pleasantly surprised many observers, but the very survival of the polity and its institutions is remarkable enough in its own right. Since northern Somali communities gathered together to declare their sovereign independence in 1991, they have faced innumerable internal challenges and external pressures. Counterinsurgent warfare against the northern Somali people at the hands of the Somali military regime throughout the 1980s culminated in their mass victimization, including the indiscriminate killing of an estimated fifty thousand northern Somali people and the displacement of half a million more. These wounds and trauma were fresh when society went about constructing the state, and it would take several years of internal fighting and countervailing reconciliation efforts before calm would return. Much of the already meager infrastructure had been destroyed during the military campaign, and service delivery had grinded to a standstill, all of which left a daunting number of tasks for reconstruction (Somaliland Centre for Peace and Development, SCPD 1999). At the same time, poverty, youth unemployment, drought, and land disputes have posed endemic threats to social stability, as has the threat of piracy and terror (including a potentially destabilizing bombing attack in 2008) emanating from neighboring Somalia.

Internationally, the most significant challenge to Somaliland's existence has come from the refusal of the international community to formally recognize such existence, not only designating Somaliland a region within a larger failed Somali state instead of an independent nation, but even continuously maneuvering to coerce and incentivize Somaliland's political reintegration back into larger Somali state structures (albeit while dealing with Somaliland practically and providing it with international aid). Nevertheless, despite these obstacles, Somaliland persists as an autonomous de facto state, while many of its former compatriots in the rest of the (arguably former) Somali Republic have continued to languish in fragmentation, violence, and volatility since the collapse of the state in 1991.

What accounts for the resilience of the Somaliland state? Several authors have proposed answers to this question, largely by identifying certain societal traits that have made stability and peaceful coexistence more likely. This includes the latent potency of traditional authority structures (Richards 2014), the comparative homogeneity and cohesion of northern clans at that historical moment (compared to the more divided clans of the central and southern Somali territories) (Ridout 2012), the absence of foreign interference (Ahmed and Green 1999), and the innovative and hybrid nature of the country's evolving governing institutions (Renders and Terlinden 2010). However, this paper will step back from the immediate and conspicuous factors underpinning societal resilience to identify the political conditions that enabled such manifest characteristics to emerge in the first place. The emphasis on the political stems from an oft-criticized deficiency of mainstream resilience thought, in which adaptation seems to come about through automatic, natural, individualized, or technocratic response, without any accounting for the political dynamics of social change (Scott-Smith 2018; Welsh 2014). To address this deficiency through concrete examples, this chapter then goes on to highlight two main political enabling factors for Somaliland's resilient collective trajectory: first, the emergence of a *political community* that bound (and continues to bind) society together in the face of such numerous shocks, and, second, the absence of external constraints on Somaliland society's *political freedom to act* to adapt to a volatile environment (autonomy).

Not coincidentally, these two enabling factors correspond to the three main pillars of resilience—durability, adaptation, and fortification—with the implication being that Somaliland society itself became politically geared toward and programmed with the overriding logic of societal resilience. As will be described in the following sections, this political inflection consumed core peacebuilding and state-building processes such as traditional governance, justice, reconciliation, and identity formation, shaping them to act in a way that promoted coherence and adaptation of society as a whole, rather than destabilizing fragmentation or stagnation in the service of competing particularist interests. As a result, the various Somaliland factions and actors were granted the space, direction, and incentives to cooperate, confront difficult issues, endure setbacks and the slow pace of change, withstand shocks, and develop creative responses toward the creation of a system of governance that is itself resilient and inclusive.

The Resilience Paradigm: Peacebuilding, State-building, and Societal Survival

The resilience framework, which interrogates the ways in which individuals, communities, and societies resourcefully respond and adapt to shock and trauma, has recently begun to make its mark within peacebuilding theory and practice (Menkhaus 2013; Pouligny 2014; Van Metre and Calder 2016). By homing in on the embedded resources, capacities, and strategies of societies to remain steadfast and even positively transform themselves in the face of external stressors, resilience offers a potentially paradigm-shifting means for rescuing notions of local agency, flexibility, informality, and multidirectionality in how we think about ideas of post-conflict social change, which have often been lost in the largely prototypic and stage-based models of liberal peacebuilding (de Coning 2016). Seen from the bottom-up—or from the perspective of *what is* rather than *what could be*—collective responses to violence are no longer necessarily judged to the extent to which they meet or fall short of what a state or peaceful society is expected to look like institutionally or social-relationally, by instead recognizing that social interventions and self-organization by communities can proceed along diverse pathways to greater cohesion and stability (Menkhaus 2013; Pouligny 2014; Van Metre and Calder 2016). Such a perspective implicitly incorporates the insights developed by proponents of hybridity theory, subaltern studies, and postcolonial studies, in as much as it deconstructs binaries such as war and peace, reactivity (survival) and progress (development), stability and change, and state failure and state effectiveness, instead recognizing that most states operate at liminality and flux within and between these various oppositions.

However, the promising theoretical potential of resilience has yet to fundamentally alter how peacebuilding is conceived or implemented in practice, in large part because the paradigm remains vague and full of conceptual variations (Menkhaus 2013). One area of conceptual vagueness relates to notions of how and why change occurs within social systems, which is largely unexplored within the existing literature (Menkhaus 2013; Pouligny 2014; Van Metre and Calder 2016). While this literature has generally done well to highlight many of the characteristics required of a society to remain resilient in the face of violence and volatility, it has much less to say on how societies come to develop those characteristics. Theoretical models borrowed from psychology, engineering, ecology, and even community resilience do not offer much guidance, as within these approaches change seems to come about automatically (as in ecological systems) or through rational, consensus-based and resourceful calculation (in the case of communities) (Ungar 2012; Norris et al. 2008). Such depoliticized, technocratic, and teleological notions of change cannot account for the wide variety of interests, complexities, internal conflicts, and inequalities that shape societies and how they act (and which make them much more complex than the conception of a unitary system these theories offer), and therefore cannot account sufficiently for why and how a social system will act to protect the interests of the entire system rather than working for the particular interests of the few or in a way that divides the system from within (Fabinyi et al. 2014; Smith and Stirling 2010). As the answer to these issues involves an understanding of power and collective decision-making, it necessarily revolves around politics, something absent in most studies of peacebuilding and resilience. In the sections below, I will further explore certain theories of the politics of resilience, and then demonstrate how such politics operates in the case of Somaliland.

The Political Community

Conventional resilience theory has received criticism for taking the concept of the "whole" for granted, be it the system, the community, or the society (Vale 2014; Davoudi 2012). When it comes to the notion of society (or other collectives for that matter), resilience theory offers little conceptual guidance for setting out the boundaries of that system—i.e., between what is inside and what is outside—and thus no clear idea of what it would mean to keep the "identity" and "function" of such an entity intact, as the definition of resilience requires. As with standard state-building practice, the nation-state would seem to form the foremost limit of the object of analysis, but given the general transnational and subnational dimension of conflict in the current era of globalization, state "failure," civil war, and intercommunal violence, this seems increasingly arbitrary. How, for example, would we describe the resilience dynamics of a conflict between two neighboring countries, if such a conflagration undermines peace between them but nevertheless creates cohesion and stability within each country by increasing nationalist sentiment and social bonds? And what does it mean for notions of societal resilience when two subnational ethnic groups engage in conflict but over time such conflict brings about settlement toward a higher shared national unity between the two parties? Failure to interrogate assumptions over the limits of the collective in such a manner echoes a similar failure among both liberal peacebuilding and its postmodern critics. While the former treats the nation-state as the natural (or at least unavoidable) expression of the social whole, the latter, although challenging this postulate, often offers an equally essentialist notion of "authentic" communities, which, based on the amorphous nature of what an authentic society looks like, generally becomes codeterminate with the nation-state in practice (Chandler 2013, 18–22; Randazzo 2016, 1359–62).

If we follow resilience theory's clarion call to take things as they exist without imposing external significations onto the social field, we can treat Somaliland society not as something that is or is not a nation-state or society but instead as a collective entity that emerges and fluctuates through a process of becoming. Such an approach places our ontological perspective of Somaliland society in the company of emerging theoretical developments within social theory, in which the nebulous and politically constructed nature of society is unearthed (Owens 2015). Thus, by avoiding taking as our object of analysis the society as a fixed entity (such as the nation-state) and instead treating it as a concept with flexible dimensions and characteristics—what, for heuristic reasons of clarity, I will call a "political community"—we can better understand the political dimensions involved in creating the resilient system (or society) itself. With these considerations in mind, we can now turn to the specific political community that is Somaliland.

The "idea" of Somaliland traces its origins to the colonial era, when the British Empire established and delineated the territory of the British Somaliland Protectorate, as part of a diplomatic agreement to parcel up the Horn of Africa between Ethiopia, Italy, and France. On June 26, 1960, the protectorate attained independence, which it enjoyed for five days before uniting with the neighboring population of former Italian Somaliland, with the eventual goal of joining all Somali peoples under a single "Greater Somalia" state. This vision was never realized, and the inhabitants of the former British protectorate in the north (who make up present-day Somaliland) found themselves subjected to nearly three decades of economic exclusion, political repression, mass surveillance, social control, unequal national representation, and mass displacement, while throughout the country economic stagnation, corruption, and warfare against neighbors was endemic. In 1981, community leaders and diaspora predominately from the north's Isaaq clan formed the Somali National Movement (SNM), an armed guerilla movement aimed at resisting such oppressive conditions, setting in motion a decade-long campaign for liberation that would eventually contribute to the toppling of the military regime. This shared experience of struggle and victory, as well as the harsh collective punishment experienced by the Isaaq people in retaliation for this opposition—involving killings, physical destruction, and torture on a massive scale—also helped to instill a "first, albeit incomplete, 'national identity' founded on militant solidarity, shared suffering, and the abhorrence of the idea of Greater Somalia" (Renders and Terlinden 2010, 729–30; Spears 2003). This experience is typified in the words of a former SNM officer interviewed by political analyst Matt Bryden, who proclaimed that "the aerial bombings, the bombardment, strafing of refugees as they fled to the border, all helped to solidify our sentiment of separateness . . . [and the realization that] we had nothing in common with these people from the south" (Bradbury 2008).[1]

The unifying power of past trauma and collective struggle among the Isaaq was soon combined with an emerging shared vision of the future. On the one hand, this involved an increased awareness that the postregime order in Somalia not only would offer no new promise but would instead likely constitute an existential threat to their survival (Academy for Peace and Development, APD 2008; Ridout 2012). This was because, in the vacuum left by the authoritarian state, rival factions of military strongmen had crowded out room for cooperation and peaceful dialogue, instead violently jockeying for exclusive power over Mogadishu and its surroundings (Bradbury 2008). While no one could predict such conflict would persist for a quarter century, as it has, it was clear at the time that continued reliance on the Somalia project would lead to bloodshed, while only self-governance offered to protect against such an eventuality (Richards 2014).

At the same time, a credible alternative way of coexisting hovered in the back of people's minds: the ambitions, hopes, and political demands conjured up by the SNM during the liberation struggle. These were based on both the movement's political program, which called for greater local autonomy, decentralization, and the incorporation of traditional authorities into modern state structures, and its actions, with the SNM developing an organizational culture built around internal democracy, including inclusive decision-making, dialogue-based dispute resolution, customary moral economies of reciprocation, and communal solidarity, and a large degree of consensual collaboration with sympathetic communities (Compagnon 1992; Bobe 2017, 72; Spears 2003; Bakonyi 2009, 43–45). Galvanized by this combination of fear of deadly social contamination and hope for long-awaited decentralized coexistence and freedom, popular support for independence quickly grew, and by the time local leaders met in Burao in the spring of 1991 to conduct one of the first major peace conferences, they were left with little choice but to bend to the collective will and endorse the creation of the Republic of Somaliland.

The potentiality of "Somaliland" (as both a nascent identity and political project) formed the seed from which the political community grew. The shape and character that the political community assumed was determined by both internal and external factors. Internally, reconciliation efforts centered on healing divisions and reinstating cooperative and peaceful relations between clans, at first to ensure continued survival through resumed livelihood activities and later to establish a structure of governance to manage and transform social affairs. The banner of the Somaliland state served as common political framework (a "symbolic reference point") that offered a means to both manage and potentially transcend clan divisions, helping to anchor efforts at staving off social disintegration while providing impetus and a centripetal force to ever greater integration between a wider expanse of communities (Phillips 2013; Balthasar 2013).

As state-building progressed from the Peace Charter of 1993 to the Interim Constitution of 1997 to the eventual ratified version of the national constitution in 2001, what began as the forging of a loose confederation of clan territories—which were responsible for their own peace and security, but cooperated in matters of wartime compensation, intercommunal dispute resolution, and resource sharing—evolved into a formalized, structured political order. Drawing from a variety of sources of inspiration, including historic interclan mediation and representation practices, modern bureaucratic forms of rule (including a parliament, presidential executive, and independent judiciary), and religious forms of authority (where constitutional adherence to Islamic principles offers legitimacy and value guidance to the political community), this hybrid political order has established a presence and influence across much of the country (Renders 2012). By delivering security and political redress to communal grievances, as well as instilling a sense of shared meaning through the dissemination of common national currency, the propagation of national symbols (flags and memorials), and the fostering of a common ground for national political dialogue via the media, the Somaliland government has contributed greatly to the sustenance and expansion of the political community over time (Bradbury 2008).

Here it is worth mentioning the role that the arts, and in particular poetry and oral storytelling, played as a source of this common ground in Somaliland's peacebuilding context. As with Llanos's exploration of the role of media testimony in building empathy and resilience in this edited volume, so too in Somaliland did poetry and storytelling allow for grievances to be aired, authoritative voices and narratives to be legitimized, historical solutions to be resurrected for contemporary dispute resolution purposes, and messages of peace to be delivered across parties to the conflict (Kaariye 2016; Farah and Lewis 1997). Through the use of poetry and lecture, activists within society pressured clan negotiators to reach compromises and convinced young militiamen to lay down arms, with the performative sphere serving as one of the few areas where women were granted space to play a prominent role (Ingiriis and Hoehne 2013, 321; Dini 2009, 31–36; Kaariye 2016). Through the existence of this historically unifying and respected medium of communication and dialogue, mediated through authorized traditional structures and forms of sociality, common bonds and relations were able to be translated into forms of political community.

The development of the political community had an international dimension as well. From the inception of the Somaliland project, its leaders campaigned for international recognition, both as a means to secure domestic legitimacy for the state and to secure the benefits of statehood (such as increased development aid, foreign investment, and diplomatic voice). The basis for its claim to legitimate statehood was in part legal (the legality of disunion) and moral (justice for the atrocity suffered), but it also rested on the viability of the state, including its ability to embody the norms of the international community. This required Somaliland to "act like a state," and, as several authors have pointed out, this need compelled Somaliland's leaders to construct a society in the image of what the international community conceives as a credible and well-functioning nation-state (Richards and Smith 2016). This "mimesis"—in which internal developments were undertaken with one eye fixated on how it would be received by the international community, while also serving the purpose of giving the unprepared and directionless leaders a blueprint to follow in building the state—entailed the creation of ministries, a civil service high court, a central bank, and other commonplace government architecture, because it was seen that "their establishment was necessary in order to demonstrate that a state was being created" (Hoehne 2009, 258–61; Gilkes 2003, 180). In this way, electoral democracy was introduced as much a means of signaling to the world that Somaliland was a committed player within the liberal order (especially relevant in the post-9/11 period when Islamic populations were increasingly demonized as a threat to that order) as it was a means of managing the politics of representation and power (Richards 2014; Phillips 2013).

While the aesthetic and symbolic value of these national institutions may have preceded their effectiveness, with many ministries providing little more than window-dressing for more informal management of society and resources, over time they served as a "self-fulfilling prophecy" for state-building efforts, helping to solidify an "imagined community" of Somaliland citizenship among large segments of the population, thereby strengthening the legitimacy and authority of state institutions domestically (Hoehne 2009, 258–76). This constellation of imaginative reference points, which seeped deep into the collective imagination through everyday practices such as the exchange of a shared currency or the exposure to the same national media publications, has, in other words, helped to create a broad public sphere where disparate groups conceive of issues of justice, morality, and political equality in relational terms to others falling under the Somaliland "national" umbrella. Here we find echoes of Zucker's exploration in this volume of the role that stories and rituals have played in Cambodian rural life in creating a shared moral imaginary with which to negotiate social transformation in the present. And, as with the Cambodian case, so too in Somaliland does a shared past serve as glue holding this imaginary together, with Somaliland's historical memory of genocide and then rebirth creating fellow travelers out of geographically and familially divided communities.

It should be noted, in passing, that this "imagined community" came into being through a process very different than those explored by Benedict Anderson (2006) in his famous exploration of the rise of nationalism— either in its Western or (post)colonial setting. Whereas Anderson described a largely centralizing and homogenizing process, in which unitary identities are conditioned (to varying degrees of success) into a people, for Somaliland this imagined community emerged as a contingent and circumstantial coming together of various groups (clans) who retained their separateness but agreed to live together in peace. In other words, what was "imagined" was not a single, distinct people but a community of relative equals who had all bought into a historically specific agreement to work together to preserve the security and stability of the whole. As such, the construction of a "Somaliland" identity speaks more to continued adherence to a political program—based on shared norms, sources of legitimacy, and preexisting practices—than it does the building of an organic social subjectivity, as traditional ideas of nationalism conceive it.

This international-local dialectic—in which the Somaliland state molds its character to fit international perceptions, thus altering those perceptions and being again motivated to transform on the basis of such altered perceptions—helped further cultivate the durability of the political community. For example, international acknowledgment and celebration of Somaliland's peace and democracy would over time be internalized among the Somaliland population, serving as a source of pride and dignity, as well as being treated as constitutive elements of the narrative of Somaliland-ness (Richards 2014; Phillips 2013). In other words, by being recognized by the international community as peaceful and democratic, Somalilanders began to self-identify with and embody these traits, and this self-recognition would have material effects—by taking pride in their peaceful and democratic nation, communities have taken extra strides to protect against any threats that might undermine this image, including by remaining vigilant against terror and extremism, and maintaining a commitment to popular elections. Similarly, the need to be legitimized as a fully-fledged nation rather than a clan enclave has compelled the Isaaq-led government to reach out and include smaller clans to a larger degree than it might otherwise. As former President Egal noted in a 1999 public address: "we could only be accepted as a member by the world community if we move to a new stage of nationhood. . . . The international community does not recognize congregations of clans, each remaining separately independent" (as quoted in Richards 2014, 117). In practice, this has meant that, instead of using their immediate postwar military advantage to either exact revenge on former foes or establish an Isaaq-dominated clan enclave, the SNM leadership and traditional elders prioritized reconciliation efforts in order to build the legitimacy and functionality of a state based on preexisting borders.

One final contributing factor to Somaliland's political community is that of leadership. Without the shrewd, strong political maneuverings of power brokers like Somaliland's second president, Mohamed H. I. Egal, who used political bargaining, war, and the strategic mobilization of traditional leadership to build a state structure atop the various pockets of clan authority, the political community might never have remained intact (Balthasar 2013; Ridout 2012; Renders 2012). However, while the specific personalities of politicians like Egal serve as contingent factors propelling the state-building project forward, it is arguably more appropriate to treat them as conduits and focal points through which the phenomenon of political community was embodied. As argued by Balthasar (2013), Egal's decision-making agenda and success were not the result of personal ambitions, a self-designed ideological project, or any other particularist factors, but were instead the amalgamation and coalescence of a variety of stakeholder interests within a singular political project, in which his own power, the economic welfare of the business class, the desire of ordinary people for peaceful livelihoods, and the need for political accommodation by each clan were all addressed under the single umbrella of the Somaliland state. In other words, the atmosphere and groundwork for such political change from above was afforded by the political community from below.

Autonomy

As shown above, the resilience paradigm is founded on notions of self-organization, internal transformation, and embedded capacities—all integrated and solidified into durable and fortified forms of collective coexistence—creating intrinsic parallels between societal resilience and collective autonomy. However, as many critics have argued, the link between resilience and autonomy is not so straightforward, as resilience theory also contains within it the theoretical and practical potentiality to be exploited in ways that allow for greater entrenchment of biopolitical control (Evans and Reid 2013). In this view, the promotion of indigenous ingenuity and self-sufficiency become bywords for neoliberal self-regulation and market forces, while also providing ideological cover for governments and the international community to abdicate development, humanitarian, and welfare responsibilities for vulnerable communities (Davoudi et al. 2012; Grove 2013). Additionally, by reducing "local agency" to positive adaptation to shocks and confining political activity to reaction and preparation against worst-case scenarios, the resilience paradigm shrinks the horizon of political possibility to the point that autonomy loses much of its meaning, as it rules out the viability (and even desirability) of intentional, profound social transformation toward a desired end state (Shaw 2012). Nevertheless, this potential use of resilience is neither inevitable nor unchallengeable, and, as this paper argued above, a transformative potential simultaneously exists within resilience theory, in which the promotion of inclusive and autonomous responses to shocks and threats can catalyze creative and innovative change in social relations and governance structures toward a more socially desirable new order (Biermann et al. 2016).

The parameters under which social systems respond to stressors and change is thus not only determined by inherent capacities, external resources, and other environmental factors but also by the wider possibilities afforded by the political climate. This includes the political horizon of possibility for societal change offered by the external world, the incentives and restrictions imposed on social actors, and the way in which those outside the society themselves respond to the society's adaptations. In this section, we will look at the types of freedoms and constraints faced by Somaliland in its engagement (or lack thereof) with the outside world to demonstrate the nature of autonomy and freedom to act that existed for its people when attempting to establish peace and build a governance system. This will hopefully shed some light on what substantive autonomy could look like in other societies attempting to resiliently and meaningfully respond to violence and its aftermath.

In many ways, Somaliland's autonomy, its freedom to act, simply derived from an absence of external interference—both from the international community and Somalia (Richards 2015, 18). With the collapse of Siyad Barre's regime and the descent of the south and central of the country into protracted infighting, Somaliland was freed from the yoke of central state control emanating from Mogadishu (Gilkes 2003, 178). While Somalia's power vacuum would eventually provide fertile ground for other nonstate threats, including terrorist and piracy networks, and while the establishment of the neighboring Puntland regional government would threaten the territorial integrity and security of Somaliland's eastern border, these external pressures would not emerge until nearly a decade after Somaliland's founding, by which time Somaliland had proven itself stable enough to protect itself. Regardless, for the first ten or so years, Somaliland was largely isolated from the violence, political infighting, and clan polarization that plagued other Somali territories,[2] affording it the space to concentrate on constructing its own political community and peaceful relations.

At the same time, Somaliland was able to resist being drawn into the international community's designs for rebuilding the old Somali state, as well as its military and political interventions into the region. While US troops entered Mogadishu in late 1992 as part of the new UN mission in Somalia (UNOSOM), the Somaliland government rejected a similar proposal a year later, denying any deployment of American troops into its territory "on the ground that its claim to autonomy would thereby be jeopardized," following widespread protest from among the public (Banks and Muller 1998, 839; Lansford 2019). In the same vein, in 1994, civilian representatives of UNOSOM were expelled from Somaliland's capital of Hargeisa for allegedly attempting to manipulate internal Somaliland politics in order to steer the country toward reintegration with Somalia (Prunier 1996). Somaliland has also managed to resist UN pressure to send delegates or endorse any of the numerous internationally sponsored reconciliation conferences held for Somalia since 1991, and in the early years held several mass demonstrations against Somalia's unwelcomed attempts to assert sovereignty over Somaliland's territory (Huliaras 2002, 168; Kibble 2001, 13). These conferences—highly publicized, costly, and top-down affairs—were generally held outside the country and attended by unaccountable elites, offering "quick fix" solutions to the major challenges of peacebuilding and state reconstruction (Ahmed and Green 1999, 124). Lacking both the legitimacy of local communities and an understanding of circumstances on the ground, it was not surprising these conferences failed to both make a positive impact or to inspire Somaliland stakeholders to participate. By refusing to take part in any of these ill-fated initiatives, Somaliland extricated itself from the deleterious effects of a Somali-wide elite power struggle and instead was free to concentrate its energies on building a viable state from the bottom up.

The practical advantages of avoiding outside intervention have been noted by several authors. In the absence of significant international revenue streams, development assistance, or political legitimacy, Somaliland leaders were forced to rely on local funds and buy-in to bolster their authority and peacebuilding efforts (Eubank 2012). As such, political elites were accountable to the business and communal interests that supported them, and what these interests sought above all was substantive peace, so that business activity and nomadic grazing practices could resume, unhindered by illegal roadblocks, roaming armed gangs, and conflict over rangeland (De Waal 2007; Bradbury 2008). This is in contrast to Somalia, where substantial international intervention created perverse incentives and divorced politics from the situation on the ground. Foreign military intervention mostly served to empower the hardliners and well-armed militias strong enough to thrive in the militarized setting, while lavish UN-sponsored reconciliation conferences held in foreign capitals entrenched a new and unaccountable governing elite (Lewis 2002). Furthermore, in Somalia the injection of humanitarian aid not only provided competing militias with additional spoils to fight over but also made Somali leaders beholden to the priorities of donors instead of those of their people (Menkhaus 2009; Menkhaus 2003).

Furthermore, in the absence of externally imposed timelines or parameters weighing down the political process, Somalilanders had no choice but to experiment in coping with issues of power-sharing, rights, accountability, and reconciliation using the indigenous tools at their disposal—although applied to circumstances of vastly more widespread and systematic injustice than previously encountered (Baadiyow 2014). Given the predominance of locally legitimized representatives within this process (rather than technical experts or legal actors deemed suitable by external standards), Somaliland's stakeholders were afforded the power and institutional control to ensure that the incentives for peace (which were spread evenly across vast majority of the country) won out over the incentives for conflict (which existed for very few) (Farah and Lewis 1997). As the SNM's military might threatened to lead it to self-destruction, it would be traditional authorities, diaspora business leaders and intellectuals, women, and savvy politicians, unencumbered by external constraints, who would help ease the transition toward civilian rule, with the traditional leaders filling the local governance void and the politicians helping to rein in potential spoilers through demobilization, elite pacts, and the centralization of key institutional functions (Balthasar 2013).

With such institutional coherence taking shape, an enabling environment appeared in which the bases for justice—trust, cooperation, goodwill, forgiveness, social equivalence, and the overcoming of hatred and fear—were built into the larger politics of the state-building process. For example, the SNM, cognizant of the popular demand for peace, felt compelled to institute a "policy of non-retribution" against clans formerly allied to Siyad Barre (Walls 2009, 387). At the same time, national leaders were able to transform power struggles between elites into an ideological struggle to "strengthen people's resolve for independence," thus building common cause between former adversaries (Bradbury 1997, 31; Balthasar 2013). Additionally, because the emerging state was able to open up political space for grievances to be addressed, potential spoilers were incorporated into power-sharing arrangements rather than allowing their sense of injustice to fester and reignite conflict (Desai and Ursing 2015, 19–20). Bradbury, Abokor, and Yusuf (2003) summarize the positive dynamics at work powerfully:

> The lack of recognition and support for reconstruction, while detrimental in many ways, has given people a certain freedom to craft an indigenous model of modern African government that fuses indigenous forms of social and political organisations within a democratic framework . . . the notion of a Somaliland state appears to be rooted in the popular consciousness, rather than imposed from above. The incorporation of non-state social institutions into Somaliland's political institutions means that politics has been more representative than in the past and it has given the Somaliland administration a popular legitimacy that Somalia's previous governments lacked. (475)

The Explanatory Potential of Political Community and Autonomy Examined

As the above two sections have argued, the resilience of the society, its ability to survive and even thrive under conditions of international marginalization and intercommunal and environmental volatility, depended upon the emergence of a political community and the freedom of that community to act collectively to innovatively address challenges. The conduit for the continued peaceful coexistence of this political community is the "hybrid state"—one characterized by a blend of indigenous and imported political institutions—which is itself defined by these three pillars of resilience: adaptation (flexibility), durability, and fortification. From its inception to the present, the hybrid state has constantly changed to incorporate new factions, continuously developed new political "rules of the game," regularly expanded to new areas, and relentlessly adapted to changing external circumstances (such as increasing climate change and the emergence of a recognized government in Mogadishu), while retaining its overall shape—that outlined by the original social compact establishing the state (Renders, 2007). Additionally, the society fortified itself by crafting a robust and sturdy governance structure (the Somaliland Republic, as both institutions and an idea) that could withstand outside pressures to return to a governance arrangement (as part of a united Somali state) that would again leave them vulnerable to oppression and mass violence. As was shown, such institutions do not emerge on their own, either as a rational communal response to shock and trauma or naturally through the inherent capacities of the people, but are instead conjured into being under the right political circumstances, through the agency of various actors.

This political perspective on societal resilience can serve as a much-needed corrective to the overly technocratic or essentializing approaches of resilience criticized in preceding sections. Discussions of resilience in Somaliland are not immune to this trend. Policy experts and practitioners often dispense with the richness and complexity found in the field's most thoughtful historical and anthropological analyses,[3] and instead treat Somaliland's societal resilience as a product of the innate capacities and drives of communities and individuals—thus mimicking the most limiting methodologies of conventional communal and social resilience theory. The following subsections will look at two of the primary lenses through which conventional explanations for Somaliland's resilience often view the situation, and, while not questioning their partial or relative validity, instead seek to add depth and historicity to these explanations by demonstrating the political dimensions that underpin them. These two explanations are as follows: (1) the influence and cultural efficacy of traditional authorities and their customary governance practices, and (2) the existence of a shared clan identity among the majority of Somaliland people.

Traditional Authority

As is clear from the analysis above, traditional governance systems derived from clan loyalties and customary social relations undoubtedly played a fundamental part in constituting Somaliland's resilience. Because of their embeddedness within the community, their kin-based loyalties to the clan, their proximity to the people (which makes them both accountable and accessible), their vast historical experience in dispute resolution, and their resilient nature (requiring only respected elders and a congregation point to operate), traditional governance structures maintain great authority within Somaliland society (Mohamed 2007; Abdile 2012; Zuin 2008). This authority has enabled them to play a key role mediating between clans in basic matters of intergroup justice and local governance, such as the management of resources and social relations. This mediation process is based around decentralized and informal negotiations that flexibly juggle both legal and political considerations to further the cause of peaceful coexistence as the ultimate goal (Mohamed 2007; Abdile 2012). Yet, as will be touched upon below, these institutions are not without their internal tensions and exclusions, with the voices of women in particular generally being excluded from political forums, instead being relegated primarily to indirect and surreptitious means for influencing political life (Dini 2009).

While ever-present within Somali society, customary institutions have seen their political significance ebb and flow with the political possibilities of the time. Traditional leadership was partially co-opted during the colonial era and suppressed during the period of authoritarian rule, leaving it generally weakened and fragmented. It would take the SNM rebellion to shake up the political system, mobilizing clan elders to mediate between the movement and local communities (Richards 2010; Bradbury 2008). During the period of reconciliation, newly reinvigorated traditional leaders expanded their role (especially in the more peripheral areas such as Erigavo), but it was not until clan-based political fragmentation within the SNM military wing threatened to rip Somaliland society apart that civilian politicians truly ceded ground over the state reformation process to clan leadership (Academy for Peace and Development 2008). And as Somaliland transitioned from the period of peacebuilding to that of state consolidation, it would take the decisive leadership of President Egal to tame and channel traditional leadership into a more integrated and durable governance structure, one capable of dealing with the responsibilities of national sovereign rule (Mohamed 2017). This interrelation between clan and the political community is well summed up by Richards (2010): "Because of the utilisation of and dependence upon the clan in the 'making' of Somaliland, the state and clan are inextricably entwined. The clan is invested in the state, and because of the nature of the Somaliland government and state-building project, the state is rooted and invested in the clan. There is a centralised and permanent amalgamation of state and clan" (12).

Therefore, contrary to theories in which communal capacities exist as a latent and a priori cultural force within society, emerging rationally to address challenges (as in the technocratic assumptions of certain resilience theorists and Somalia experts), traditional leaders in Somaliland in reality returned to prominence only once their legitimacy and influence was negotiated and substantiated within larger processes of political community formation and social empowerment.

Such a misreading of the mechanisms through which traditional leadership capacities are harnessed can be witnessed in the international community's latest state-building interventions in Somalia. While being more sensitive to the importance of customary clan-based institutions than in past top-down state-building efforts, UN-led state-building has continued to channel the inclusion of customary institutions through highly structured and procedural institutions and processes, such as through an Upper House of clan elders, formal reconciliation dialogue forums, and a commitment to the 4.5 clan representation system (which requires proportional representation between the country's four overarching clans and various minority elements [the .5]). As Balthasar (2014) argues in critical assessment of this international effort, such focus on procedures and institutions without consideration of the (political) process through which they emerged has stifled the energies of traditional authorities and even turned them against each other, instead of offering them the freedom and political self-organization that Somaliland was afforded through which to innovate and experiment. In other words, trapped in a technocratic process with imposed parameters, traditional authorities in Somalia have had neither a political community to mobilize and harness their potential nor the autonomy with which to undertake the nonlinear, creative work required to build resilient institutions.

Shared Identity

Several commentators have looked to the fact that the core of the Somaliland state is numerically dominated by a single clan, the Isaaq, in order to explain Somaliland's resilient and successful governance, the suggestion being that relative clan homogeneity provides a more stable foundation to construct a cohesive society than a clan-diverse society, as is the case in southern Somalia. For example, the Atlantic Council's Bronwyn Brown offers the following line of reasoning for the different trajectories between Somaliland and Somalia: "Somaliland gets a ton of good press for being stable and kind of a peaceful island in a sea of violence that is Somalia. . . . The reality is that unlike southern Somalia, where you have a lot of violence, Somaliland is essentially a single clan territory" (Beaubien 2017). This view generally takes into account the fact that momentum for the Somaliland project evolved from the political trajectory taken by the SNM, which derived much its cohesion from its Isaaq-majority identity (although even the extent of this has been called into question), as well as the fact that Somaliland's most steadfast supporters continue to be the Isaaq, whereas other clans exhibit a more volatile allegiance to the state (Ridout 2012; Hoehne 2015). Neighboring Puntland, the only other Somali society to emerge out of the civil war and establish a relatively coherent political order and governance system, defines its constituency and legitimacy on exclusively single clan terms—i.e., Darood unity—giving further credence to the idea that clan is the prime mover of politics in Somali society, and that, just as this shared identity can unite groups, its fragmentation can divide society and lead to conflict (World Bank 2005).

However, this rather reductive rendering of clan politics fails to take into account the ways in which certain clan identities become salient at different times, as well as the way they interact with other political affinities, such as national belonging or indeed religion. Clan affiliations, which are derived from patrilineal familial lineages, are highly fluid and can coalesce at many different points within a lineage chain depending upon the circumstances (Lewis 1961, 158–60). Clans divide into subclans, which can divide further until they reach the most basic community unit, the *diya*-paying group (in which members are responsible for handling the affairs of each other when dispute occurs). As such, while Somalilanders hailing from the Isaaq clan have indeed actively defined themselves through the Isaaq umbrella in struggles against external foes (and particularly Somalia, past and present), not only has divisions *within* the Isaaq been some of the most heated and destabilizing within Somaliland's history, but the nation-state that has been created to contain Isaaq ambitions for freedom cannot be mapped easily along clan lines (Renders and Terlinden 2010, 729–30; Spears 2003; Ridout 2012, 150–51).

To the former point, the early days of Somaliland's post-conflict statebuilding were characterized by armed struggle for power, land, and resources between subsections of the Isaaq, while subsequent electoral contests, which have on occasion been highly polarizing, also took the form primarily of intra-Isaaq competition (World Bank 2005, 16; Bradbury 2008; Academy for Peace and Development 2012). In fact, what in these cases fortified and safeguarded the political community from disintegration was the mediation of non-Isaaq clans, who capitalized on their standpoint outside the conflict to act as credible mediators (Bradbury

2008). This leads to the second point, for the fact remains that Somaliland as a bordered and self-conceived political entity is one grounded on shared territorial delineations and histories (those forged under British colonialism), not clan lines, and what animates its politics is not ethnic homogeneity as such but the dynamic interplay of mutual and conflicting interests between groups along a number of lines—which includes clan but also takes the form of gender, generational, religious, and class politics. As the above sections have shown, it is only when identities, affinities, and cultural legacies are employed and directed in certain ways—i.e., in the service of reconciliation, cohesion, and cohabitation by empowered authorities (such as traditional leaders and shrewd politicians)—that they become sources of resilience and durability, rather than of disintegration and maladaptation.

Conclusion

This exploration of Somaliland's state-building through the lens of resilience has sought to bring to light several insights. First, it has argued that resilience can indeed be seen as a productive lens to view state-building, as it offers a nonteleological understanding of the dynamics underpinning certain forms of successful postcolonial societal reconstruction efforts—ones based less on the abstract end-goal of establishing highly developed institutional architecture and more on the ambition of establishing peaceful, protected, and livelihood-enabling forms of cohabitation as a durable and flexible collective. However, it has also argued that, for "resilience" to contain serious analytical purchase, it must avoid being diluted or engineered into just another catchall technocratic paradigm such as "state-building," which comes to stand in for a set of programmatic assumptions and designs of the aid industry (Menkhaus 2013) and instead takes on a political character, one that recognizes the ways in which the durability, fortitude, and productive adaptability of social structures relies on political efforts and processes promoting inclusivity, fairness, representativeness, and interdependence.

In other words, resilience cannot be guaranteed by developing the correct capacities or enabling the right institutional feedback loops, but is made substantive through becoming embedded in society through politically forging the social bonds that promote resilient mutuality. This lesson also resonates in Velasco's account in this collection of how grassroots movements in Colombia have secured more resilient ways of reckoning with past violence. Here, under circumstances in which dominant state historical narratives had drowned out the voices of populations still reeling from the aftereffects of conflict, collective political struggle served as a means to open up avenues for more durable, fortifying, and inclusive post-conflict social relations. Absent such political momentum, resilience comes to stand for nothing more than coping and survival, a condition of running in place while remaining vulnerable to global and external forces outside one's control.

However, while this chapter has sought to highlight certain underappreciated positive forms of resilience, it is also worth commenting on the large price that Somaliland has paid in maintaining a resilient society. First, in placing peace and security above all else, Somaliland has been forced to dedicate much of its budget, programmatic efforts, capacities, and political attentions to efforts to control and ease tensions, with the serious pursuit of developmental change or service delivery expansion often subordinated as a result. Second, and in a similar vein, many within and outside Somaliland society see the reliance on vesting power and authority in clan representatives—who have great knowledge of peace-building but not of governance and management—as leaving Somaliland in a holding pattern, able to stave off conflict but without the leadership or institutional direction and capacity to translate peace and stability into drastic socioeconomic improvement (Hoehne 2013; The New Humanitarian 2013; Renders 2007, 449). This not only risks prioritizing present stasis over the development of a future socioeconomic system more resistant to shocks like climate change, drought, and unemployment but also serves to institutionalize these formerly dynamic and experimental traditional institutions in ways that make them more sclerotic, complacent, and politically compromised (Hoehne 2013; Renders 2007, 449). Last, while Somaliland's political community, in both its cultural and national forms, have provided a platform for a wide range of actors to participate, integrate, and have their voice heard, it has also entrenched certain historical forms of inequality and injustice, particularly when it comes to women, youth, and minority groups, a status quo that many have argued can only be overcome through abandoning certain retrograde elements of the present social arrangement (Yusuf 2012, 95–96).

Additionally, the context-specific nature of Somaliland's post-conflict transition must be appreciated. The various communities' focus on reconciliation and recovery as principal and foremost goals once the large-scale fighting had ended reflected a particular set of circumstances, in which the desire for revenge, retribution, justice, and accountability, while certainly all present, were constrained by both an exhaustion with war (and a realization that the likely rifts exacerbated by such alternatives would likely unsettle a precarious opportunity to end the fighting) and the lack of a dominant enough power (whether as militant group, political organization, or clan alliance) to push forward such an agenda. In this case, "peace" and "security" became near sacred ends in themselves, requiring certain outstanding grievances to be displaced to the future, and certain marginalized voices to sacrifice for the good of the whole. Whether other contexts of post-conflict and postgenocidal violence could or should reproduce such sequences and prioritizations is beyond the scope of this research, but, as this account hopes to show, under certain conditions the dichotomies of peace or justice, stability or positive change, can be at least partially transcended by embedding these goals within a politics oriented toward autonomy and the creation of an inclusive community with promise of a brighter future.

In sum, while resilience should not be underestimated as a political goal to the extent that it involves innovative and durable forms of social reproduction, and thus forms the foundation on which any further political headway is to be made, it can neither be fetishized nor overly relied on. As Somalilanders repeat regularly, peace and stability should be cherished, as without these blessings their country would be too mired in conflict and trauma to move forward, but such a prerogative becomes problematic when all positive change is held hostage to the status quo. As such, just as resilience entails enabling a social system to emerge that is adaptive and flexible, so too does it involve taking an adaptive and flexible stance to social systems as such, experimenting with ways to combine existing arrangements with new institutions, authorities, and political demands that satisfy changing collective ambitions.

NOTES

1. This typical reaction to events echoed by renowned Somali human rights activist Rakiya Omaar, who wrote "the scale and ferocity of the war in the north had nurtured a visceral hatred not only of the regime but of everything it represented, including the union" (Omaar 1992, 234).

2. While Somali politicians in the south did on many occasions attempt to intervene to disrupt Somaliland's state-building efforts, including by buying certain politicians over to the side of Somali unity in exchange for posts in any number of transitional government arrangements in Mogadishu, these had relatively little impact over Somaliland's political trajectory.

3. A nonexhaustive list would include Lewis (2002), Hoehne (2009), Moe (2011), Bradbury (2008), Walls (2009), Phillips (2013), Renders (2012), and Richards (2014).

REFERENCES

Abdile, Mahdi. 2012. "Customary Dispute Resolution in Somalia." *African Conflict and Peacebuilding Review* 2, no. 1: 87–110.

Academy for Peace and Development. 2008. "Peace in Somaliland: An Indigenous Approach to State-Building." Interpeace: The Search for Peace. Nairobi.

Academy for Peace and Development. 2012. "A Vote for Peace II: A Report on the 2010 Somaliland Presidential Election Process." Interpeace: The Pillars of Peace. Nairobi.

Ahmed, Ismail I., and Reginald Herbold Green. 1999. "The Heritage of War and State Collapse in Somalia and Somaliland: Local-level Effects, External Interventions and Reconstruction." *Third World Quarterly* 20, no. 1: 113–27.

Anderson, Benedict. 2006. *Imagined Communities: Reflections on the Origin and Spread of Nationalism*, rev. ed. London and New York: Verso.

Baadiyow, Abdurahman M. Abdullahi. 2014. "Conceptions of Transitional Justice in Somalia: Findings of Field Research in Mogadishu." *Northeast African Studies* 14, no. 2: 7–43.

Bakonyi, Jutta. 2009. "Moral Economies of Mass Violence: Somalia 1988–1991." *Civil Wars* 11, no. 4: 434–54.

Balthasar, Dominik. 2013. "Somaliland's Best Kept Secret: Shrewd Politics and War Projects as a Means of State-making." *Journal of Eastern African Studies* 7, no. 2: 218–38.

Balthasar, Dominik. 2014. "Thinking Beyond Roadmaps in Somalia: Expanding Policy Options for State Building." *Center for Strategic & International Studies (CSIS) Report*, November.

Banks, Arthur S., and Thomas C. Muller. 1998. *Political Handbook of the World: 1998*. Binghamton: CSA Publications.

Beaubien, Jason. 2017. "Somaliland Wants to Make One Thing Clear: It Is NOT Somalia." *NPR*, May 30. http://www.npr.org/sections/goatsandsoda/2017/05/30/530703639/somaliland-wants-to-make-one-thing-clear-it-is-not-somalia

Biermann, Maureen, Kevin Hillmer-Pegram, Corrine Noel Knapp, and Richard E. Hum. 2016. "Approaching a Critical Turn? A Content Analysis of the Politics of Resilience in Key Bodies of Resilience Literature." *Resilience* 4, no. 2: 59–78.

Bobe, Abdirahman Yusuf Duale. 2017. "Reconciliation and Peacemaking: The Somali National Movement and the Somaliland Experience of State Building." In *State Building and National Identity Reconstruction in the Horn of Africa*, edited by Redie Bereketeab. Cham: Palgrave Macmillan.

Bradbury, Mark. 2008. *Becoming Somaliland*. Bloomington: Indiana University Press.

Bradbury, Mark, Adan Yusuf Abokor, and Haroon Ahmed Yusuf. 2003. "Somaliland: Choosing Politics over Violence." *Review of African Political Economy* 30 no. 97: 455–78.

Chandler, David. 2013. "Peacebuilding and the Politics of Non-linearity: Rethinking 'Hidden' Agency and 'Resistance.'" *Peacebuilding* 1, no. 1: 17–32.

Compagnon, Daniel. 1992. "Political Decay in Somalia: From Personal Rule to Warlordism." *Refuge* 12, no. 5: 8–13.

Davoudi, Simin, Keith Shaw, L. Jamila Haider, Allyson E. Quinlan, Garry D. Peterson, Cathy Wilkinson, Hartmut Fünfgeld, Darryn McEvoy, and Libby Porter. 2012. "Resilience: A Bridging Concept or a Dead End?" *Planning Theory & Practice* 13, no. 2: 299–307.

De Coning, Cedric. 2016. "From Peacebuilding to Sustaining Peace: Implications of Complexity for Resilience and Sustainability." *Resilience* 4, no. 3: 166–81.

Desai, Misha, and Carl Ursing. 2015. "Understanding Somaliland's Regional Stability: Comparative Analysis on the Prevalence and Effects of Spoilers on the Contrasting Situations Observed in Somalia and Somaliland." Lund University.

De Waal, Alex. 2007. "Class and Power in a Stateless Somalia." *Social Science Research Council.* https://items.ssrc.org/crisis-in-the-horn-of-africa/class-and-power-in-a-stateless-somalia/

Dini, Shukria. 2009. "Women Building Peace: Somali Women in Puntland and Somaliland." *Conflict Trends* 2: 31–37.

Eubank, Nicholas. 2012. "Taxation, Political Accountability and Foreign Aid: Lessons from Somaliland." *Journal of Development Studies* 48, no. 4: 465–80.

Evans, Brad, and Julian Reid. 2013. "Dangerously Exposed: The Life and Death of the Resilient Subject." *Resilience: International Policies, Practices and Discourses* 1: 83–98.

Fabinyi, Michael, Louisa Evans, and Simon J. Foale. 2014. "Socio-ecological Systems, Social Diversity, and Power: Insights from Anthropology and Political Ecology." *Ecology and Society* 19, no. 4.

Farah, Ahmed Y., and Ioan M. Lewis. 1997. "Making Peace in Somaliland." *Cahiers d'Etudes africaines* 37, no. 146: 349–77.

Gilkes, Patrick. 2003. "National Identity and Historical Mythology in Eritrea and Somaliland." *Northeast African Studies* 10, no. 3: 163–87.

Grove, Kevin. 2013. "On Resilience Politics: From Transformation to Subversion." *Resilience: International Policies, Practices and Discourses* 1, no. 2: 146–53.

Hoehne, Markus V. 2009. "Mimesis and Mimicry in Dynamics of State and Identity Formation in Northern Somalia." *Journal of the International African Institute* 79, no. 2: 252–81.

Hoehne, Markus V. 2013. "Limits of Hybrid Political Orders: The Case of Somaliland." *Journal of Eastern African Studies* 7, no. 2: 199–217.

Hoehne, Markus V. 2015. *Between Somaliland and Puntland: Marginalization, Militarization and Conflicting Political Visions.* Nairobi: Rift Valley Institute.

Huliaras, Asteris. 2002. "The Viability of Somaliland: Internal Constraints and Regional Geopolitics." *Journal of Contemporary African Studies* 20, no. 2: 157–82.

Ingiriis, Mohamed H., and Markus V. Hoehne. 2013. "The Impact of Civil War and State Collapse on the Roles of Somali Women: A Blessing in Disguise." *Journal of East African Studies* 7, no. 3: 314–33.

Kaariye, Barkhad M. 2016. "The Role of Somali Poetry for Somaliland Disarmament." High-quality Research Support Programme (HQRS), Hargeysa.

Kibble, Steve. 2001. "Somaliland: Surviving Without Recognition; Somalia: Recognised but Failing?" *International Relations* 15, no. 5: 5–25.

Lansford, Tom, ed. 2019. *Political Handbook of the World 2018–2019.* London: CQ Press.

Lewis, I. M. 1961. *A Pastoral Democracy: A Study of Pastoralism and the Politics among the Northern Somali of the Horn of Africa.* Suffollk: James Currey.

Lewis, I. M. 2002. *A Modern History of the Somali: Nation and State in the Horn of Africa.* Oxford: James Currey.

Menkhaus, Ken. 2003. "State Collapse in Somalia: Second Thoughts." *Review of African Political Economy* 30, no. 97: 405–22.

Menkhaus, Ken. 2009. "Somalia: 'They Created a Desert and Called it Peace(building).'" *Review of African Political Economy* 36, no. 120: 223–33.

Menkhaus, Ken. 2013. "Making Sense of Resilience in Peacebuilding Contexts: Approaches, Applications, Implications." *Geneva Peacebuilding Forum Paper no. 6.* Geneva: The Graduate Institute.

Moe, Louise W. 2011. "Hybrid and 'Everyday' Political Ordering: Constructing and Contesting Legitimacy in Somaliland." *Journal of Legal Pluralism and Unofficial Law* 43, no. 63: 143–77.

Mohamed, Ali Noor. 2017. "Crisis of Identity in a Hybrid Polity: The Case of Somaliland." In *State Building and National Identity Reconstruction in the Horn of Africa,* edited by Redie Bereketeab. Cham: Palgrave Macmillan.

Mohamed, Jama. 2007. "Kinship and Contract in Somali Politics." *Africa: The Journal of the International African Institute* 77, no. 2: 226–49.

New Humanitarian. 2013. "Debating Reform of Somaliland's House of Elders." July 18. http://www.thenewhumanitarian.org/news/2013/07/18/debating-reform-somalil and-s-house-elders

Norris, Frank H., Susan P. Stevens, Betty Pfefferbaum, Karen F. Wyche, and Rose L. Pfefferbaum. 2008. "Community Resilience as a Metaphor, Theory, Set of Capacities, and Strategy for Disaster Readiness." *American Journal for Community Psychology* 1–2: 127–50.

Omaar, Rakiya. 1992. "Somalia: At War with Itself." *Current History* 91: 233–39.

Owens, Patricia. 2015. *Economy of Force: Counterinsurgency and the Historical Rise of the Social.* Cambridge: Cambridge University Press.

Phillips, Sarah. 2013. "Political Settlements and State Formation: The Case of Somaliland." Development Leadership Program Research Paper 23. University of Sydney.

Pouligny, Beatrice. 2014. "The Resilience Approach to Peacebuilding: A New Conceptual Framework." *Insights Newsletter* (Summer). Washington, DC: United States Institute of Peace. https://www.usip.org/sites/default/files/page/pdf/Insights_Summer_2014.pdf

Prunier, Gerard. 1996. "Somalia: Civil War, Intervention and Withdrawal (1990–1995)." *Refugee Survey Quarterly* 15, no. 1: 35–85.

Randazzo, Elisa. 2016. "The Paradoxes of the 'Everyday': Scrutinising the Local Turn in Peace Building." *Third World Quarterly* 37, no. 8: 1351–70.

Renders, Marleen. 2007. "Appropriate 'Governance-Technology?': Somali Clan Elders and Institutions in the Making of the 'Republic of Somaliland.'" *African Spectrum* 42: 439–59.

Renders, Marleen. 2012. *Consider Somaliland: State-Building with Traditional Leaders and Institutions.* Leiden: Brill.

Renders, Marleen, and Ulf Terlinden. 2010. "Negotiating Statehood in a Hybrid Political Order: The Case of Somaliland." *Development and Change* 41, no. 4: 723–46.

Richards, Rebecca. 2010. "The State, the Clan and Resilience in Somaliland." *Community Resilience in Fragile Societies.* DSTL-funded project (Gordon and Manyena).

Richards, Rebecca. 2014. *Understanding Statebuilding: Traditional Governance and the Modern State in Somaliland.* Farnham, Surrey: Ashgate Press.

Richards, Rebecca. 2015. "Bringing the Outside In: Somaliland, Statebuilding and Dual Hybridity." *Journal of Intervention and Statebuilding* 9, no. 1: 4–25.

Richards, Rebecca, and Robert Smith. 2016. "Playing in the Sandbox: State Building in the Space of Non-recognition." *Third World Quarterly* 36, no. 9: 1717–36.

Ridout, Timothy A. 2012. "Building Peace and the State in Somaliland: The Factors of Success." *Journal of the Middle East and Africa* 3, no. 2: 136–56.

Rossi, Emilia. 2014. "Participation and Effective Governance in Somaliland: Assessment Report." September. Hargeisa: Progressio. http://www.progressio.org.uk/sites/progressio.org.uk/files/peg_cs_assessment_final_5_sept.pdf

Scott-Smith, Tom. 2018. "Paradoxes of Resilience: A Review of the World Disasters Report 2016." *Development and Change* 49, no. 2: 662–77.

Shaw, Keith. 2012. "'Reframing' Resilience: Challenges for Planning Theory and Practice." *Planning Theory & Practice* 13, no. 2: 308–12.

Smith, Adrian, and Andy Stirling. 2010. "The Politics of Social-ecological Resilience and Sustainable Socio-technical Transitions." *Ecology and Society* 15, no. 1.

Somaliland Centre for Peace and Development. 1999. "A Self-Portrait of Somaliland: Rebuilding from the Ruins." Hargeysa: War-Torn Societies Project.

Spears, Ian S. 2003. "Reflections on Somaliland and Africa's Territorial Order." *Review of African Political Economy* 30, no. 95: 89–98.

Ungar, Michael. 2012. "Social Ecologies and Their Contribution to Resilience." In *The Social Ecology of Resilience*, edited by Michael Ungar. New York: Springer.

Vale, Lawrence J. 2014. "The Politics of Resilient Cities: Whose Resilience and Whose City?" *Building Research & Information* 42, no. 2: 191–201.

Van Metre, Lauren, and Jason Calder. 2016. "Peacebuilding and Resilience: How Society Responds to Violence." *Peaceworks.* Washington, DC: United States Institute of Peace.

Walls, Michael. 2009. "The Emergence of a Somali State: Building Peace from Civil War in Somaliland." *African Affairs* 108, no. 432: 371–89.

Welsh, Marc. 2014. "Resilience and Responsibility: Governing Uncertainty in a Complex World." *The Geographical Journal* 180, no. 1: 15–26.

World Bank. 2005. "Conflict in Somalia: Drivers and Dynamics." Washington, DC: World Bank. https://openknowledge.worldbank.org/handle/10986/8476

World Bank. 2014. "New World Bank GDP and Poverty Estimates for Somaliland." January 29. World Bank Press Release. http://www.worldbank.org/en/news/press-release/2014/01/29/new-world-bank-gdp-and-poverty-estimates-for-somaliland

Yusuf, Haroon. 2012. "The Saga of the Pursuit of Women's Quota in Somaliland." In *Reflections and Lessons of Somaliland's Two Decades of Sustained Peace, Statebuilding and Democratization.* Hargeisa: SORADI (Development Series No. 2).

Zuin, Margherita. 2008. "A Model of Transitional Justice for Somalia." *PRAXIS: The Fletcher Journal of Human Security* 23: 89–108.

11 | Conclusion

Laura McGrew and Eve Monique Zucker

When lives and communities are torn asunder by the ravages of war, genocide, and extreme and pervasive violence it is no simple task to gather the fortitude, will, imagination, and empathy to rebuild a cohesive and functioning society where people can live fulfilling lives and plan a future on the assumption that peace will prevail. The processes for repairing relationships in order to achieve peaceful coexistence are myriad and each individual and each society has its own cultural, historical, political, and economic circumstances and requirements making no one set of policies or processes absolute or appropriate in every case. Nonetheless, the contributors of this volume have found that empathy, imagination, and resilience, either on their own or in combination, have surfaced across a variety of cases and settings as a valuable conceptual framework for working through the difficulties of learning to live together again, building relationships and a foundation for sustainable peace. While we have presented a number of ways in the introduction and within the chapters of how this multifaceted framework might work, here in the conclusion we would like to focus on some of the areas where policy approaches may be of help to those working as scholars or practitioners in understanding the processes taking place within societies and working to support those processes or provide supportive interventions—and where more research is needed.

This volume includes a variety of case studies of societies and communities that were impacted by mass violence and are now in the process of moving toward peaceful coexistence or even reconciliation. While our cases occurred over different time periods, geographic locations, and sociopolitical contexts, they nonetheless share many of the challenges of overcoming the violence of the past to build relatively cohesive communities and societies capable of long-lasting peaceful coexistence or even reconciliation. How can the cultural values that promote compassion and camaraderie be supported? What does a future of peace and fellowship look like and how can it be established? While many pathways to achieving these goals exist, in these chapters we focused on three that we found to be crucial elements in this peacebuilding process; these are imagination, empathy, and resilience. In many cases the themes complement or are premised on one another.

Resilience appears in three different forms across the cases. First, there is the resilience in the form of durability. This is found in the continued presence or reemergence of traditional and moral values, beliefs, and culture that may include supernatural entities, ancestral pasts, myths, folktales, and stories (see chapters by Burnet, Kahn, Gordon, Shapiro-Phim, and Zucker). This form of resilience is dependent on the imagination and may also include models for empathy (Burnet, Kahn, McGrew). Second, as all of our cases show, there is the resilience of individuals, communities, and societies to recover in the aftermath of violence. Here resilience implies adaptability. This form of resilience may be due in part to an ability to imagine other worlds and futures, to exercise empathy and tolerance, and to utilize and adjust to new ideologies, tools, and resources available. Third is the resilience of societies to maintain peace through stressful periods and/or the resilience of individuals to maintain their humanity (such as the rescuers) in periods of conflict. This type implies fortitude. A more empathetic society is likely to be more resilient to stress allowing for the development and continuation of peaceful coexistence. Moreover, such resilience may also be fortified through the employment of the imagination in positive ways.

The imagination—all that is beyond the objective reality, including visions of the future (Gordon, Llanos, Mieth, Shapiro-Phim, Velasco, Zucker); imaginings of other worlds (Shapiro-Phim, Zucker); and imagining different possibilities for relationships or outcomes, other identities, or circumstances (Burnet, Kahn, Llanos, McGrew, Shapiro-Phim, Velasco, Zucker)—has a central role in creating and sustaining peaceful coexistence. We see that imagination is integral to both empathy and, in particular, to the first type of resilience having to do with morals and values. Moreover, it allows for the second form of resilience by enabling individuals and communities to look forward to the future rather than just back at the violence.

Finally, empathy, which relies on the imagination, may also draw on the first form of resilience adhering to a durable moral code (Burnet,

Kahn) or recognizing the humanity of others (Llanos, McGrew). Those who have practiced empathy in the context of violence may also prove to be more resilient in the second sense of the term (the resilience of individuals, community, and society to move past trauma and its wake) in the recovery period following mass violence. A more empathetic society is likely a more peaceful society and therefore links to the third type of resilience, that is, the resilience of societies to maintain peace, and individuals to preserve their humanity.

A key component of social repair and one that connects to all the three themes is the sociocultural and traditional moral frameworks that individuals and communities draw from to remake their worlds and build relationships with one another. If these remain resilient to the rupture then they can inspire rescuer behavior (Burnet and Kahn), provide a resource for rebuilding social moral framework for relations (Gordon, Kahn, Shapiro-Phim, Velasco, Zucker), and encourage empathy (Burnet, Kahn, Llanos, McGrew). We saw that in Gordon's chapter local elders and their communities drew from their cultural heritage and its strengths to create a stable state despite pressure from the international community and the presence of conflict in the region. Shapiro-Phim's traditional stories and art forms are a template for considering new political models that facilitate peaceful coexistence rather than cycles of revenge. Kahn and Burnet demonstrate how the strength and durability of moral values led some individuals to act heroically and rescue others from harm. In McGrew's chapter empathy is facilitated through understanding of traditional concepts of ignorance and virtue. Zucker showed how Cambodian moral tales, traditions, and beliefs provided a foundation for social repair and allowed for envisioning ways of living harmoniously together. While subtler in Llanos's chapter, women prisoners retained their moral belief systems expressed through their public narratives resulting in them empathizing with one another. The value of tradition and heritage in recovery is also stressed in Velasco's chapter. The one notable exception to this pattern is Mieth's chapter, where Sierra Leonians chose to live peacefully with one another with the primary purpose of achieving development goals and prosperity rather than drawing from traditional cultural values to support coexistence. It will be interesting to see over time whether traditional values are brought into the process or whether their aspirations for development are sufficient.

This volume has advocated for a grassroots approach to the study and support of social repair processes that encourages and supports peaceful coexistence. One dimension of this approach is the study of ways in which interventions have included local actors in peacebuilding processes. Another dimension is to examine the ways in which communities have drawn from traditional cultural sources or their own ideas and resiliencies; borrowed and incorporated ideas and practices from global activist groups and development and human rights agencies; or some combination of these varied sources. A question that arises out of such locally instigated projects is whether and to what extent differing social, economic, and cultural factors inform or impact the forms of social repair available? That is, how, when, and why are communities and societies limited in the choices that are available to them? For example, a community that is educationally, economically, or politically constrained might not have the same means to embark on a program of human rights activism as another in different circumstances would. In the age of increasingly authoritarian governments worldwide and an ever-widening economic gap, local communities with limited access to outside ideas may or may not benefit from lessons learned in other settings.

Moreover, local cultural sources may be limited where there has been a concerted effort by a regime to destroy a group's cultural knowledge and heritage, and family and societal ties may have been destroyed, such as was attempted in Cambodia, the Holocaust, and against the Yazidi. Sexual and gender-based violence is also used in conflict as a potent tool to destroy self, identity, and futures, while inflicting great trauma. While the trauma suffered by the victims is without a doubt an enormous obstacle to returning to what could be called a functional life ahead, the bystanders and perpetrators must transition to a different social and moral context and find some way of understanding their pasts and building a life in the present. The relative degrees of trauma experienced and the individual's and community's capacity to manage the trauma—that is, the degree of resiliency—impact the pathways available for recovery and the establishment of peaceful coexistence.

It is clear from our case studies that additional analysis of local, customary, traditional—that is, *preexisting* forms of social repair—should serve as the basis for the design of peacebuilding initiatives, if indeed outside intervention is even needed. We come down on the side of the recent research by Autesserre, which questions assumptions of international, top-down, "outsider" peacebuilding initiatives: two of those "widespread and misleading" assumptions are that, first, "outsiders" must bring new innovative initiatives to the local level, and second, this must be done because the local people are lacking or missing something (2017, 124). Our volume gives ballast against these assumptions as our contributors show

how individuals and communities recovering from mass violence have been using imagination, empathy, and resilience based on their local situations and cultures to build their own futures. Well-meaning outsiders must use local capacities as a starting point and must also give more credence to sociocultural and anthropological approaches that are based on long-term study, rather than on quick impact initiatives that may not have the depth or time needed to interpret the situation at the local level. Additionally, it is crucial that outsiders allow adequate time and resources for local consultations and joint planning. Indeed, in some cases, outside intervention may actually be harmful (Autesserre 2014; Monk and Mundy 2014) or create unnecessary obstacles as in Somaliland (Gordon, this volume). However, when interventions are already underway, examination through our proposed innovative lenses may provide creative solutions and ensure that local perspectives are considered. The combination of scholar and practitioner approaches provides additional richness to the analysis. In spite of lip service to the contrary, and somewhat greater emphasis on the local in recent peacebuilding and transitional justice initiatives, huge gaps between local perspectives and top-down interventions persist and must be addressed at all levels. Recent advances in communication technologies and wider access to these tools and resources offer great promise to both prevent violence and to promote peace, both locally and globally (keeping in mind the risk of great negative consequences of uncontrolled rumor mongering and violence dissemination through social media, especially Facebook).

This volume further suggests that intervenors should consider when and how individuals and communities build empathy between themselves during the recovery process, use their imaginations to focus on peace in the future, and rely on their self-identified resiliencies to forge a path together. Interventions can thus be built on actual local realities. Another way of incorporating local ideas about the ways in which people ought to live and what peaceful coexistence looks like is to bring local communities into civic engagement where they actively participate in policymaking. This is especially important for marginalized communities such as the Rohingya or Yazidi, for example, who are often excluded from participation in the political processes impacting them.

The arts, including theater, music, drawing, storytelling, or other forms of artistic expression, are an essential component of the social repair process. As a template where new ideas can be explored and old ones reexamined, the arts can be a powerful tool that is both a product of the imagination and a source of imagination. Shapiro-Phim's chapter most directly demonstrates the power of art to address past trauma and speak to current issues through metaphor and poetics. The arts were also recognized in other chapters such as the storytelling in Zucker's chapter and the efforts to support the arts in Velasco's. Art provides a pathway to social repair through the invocation of the imagination, the ability to generate empathy, and by drawing on resilient traditional and cultural values and beliefs while at the same time creating a fuller and resilient society.

Addressing the ways in which gender impacts experiences of trauma during mass violence episodes and through the recovery period in its aftermath is also a central concern for us. These experiences are addressed directly in Burnet's and Llanos's chapters, drawing attention to the gendered experiences and responses to the violence. Llanos, for example, describes female survivors of dictatorial repression in the Southern Cone who were able to show empathy and resilience as expressions of affective bonds and resistance. These qualities allowed not only their survival in clandestine detention centers but also the possibility of memory narratives that provide meaning to individual and collective traumatic experiences. These examples show the strength and resilience of women to play important roles in social recovery, as these roles have often been unexamined and unrecognized by both insiders and outsiders. As women continue to be the target of sexual violence in conflict, and as more women than men usually survive after war, gender analyses are crucial in determining directions of social rebuilding. The examination of men's, women's, and other gendered persons' experiences and roles in the conflict, as well as in the recovery, should by now be mandatory in order to ensure equal participation in governance and policy-setting. Moreover, sexual violence should be considered as such regardless of which gender is the recipient, and the cone of silence of sexual violence committed against men and other gendered persons needs to be lifted.

Courage and morality are two additional themes that arose in many of our chapters. Courage is highlighted specifically in the two chapters about rescuers (Burnet, Kahn); however, it is also evident in Llanos's chapter where women found the will to prevail despite the violence and degradations they were subjected to. Subtler is the quiet courage of the Cambodians willing to empathize with former perpetrators (McGrew) and the people of Somaliland who, despite a lack of international support, continue to fight for recognition (Gordon). Similarly, in Velasco's essay marginal communities in Colombia find the courage to speak out, and the Cambodian villagers in Zucker's chapter summon the courage to work together to create a communal event despite the erosion of trust due to internal betrayals. In several of these cases, courage was displayed through the compiling and publicizing of narratives about experience as rescuers or victims of mass violence (Burnet, Kahn, Llanos, Velasco). Airing such narratives publicly may, as these authors suggest, work to prevent further atrocities in the future.

Morality is shown to be connected to courage in the chapters on rescuers who say they acted because it was the right thing to do. The heroism of their acts was thus downplayed in the rescuer's straightforward and moralistic testimonies, which collectively conveyed the idea that their behavior was grounded in the assumption of common humanity rather than heroics. This idea of basic moral tenets by which people should live also emerged in Zucker's chapter. These moral tenets, cultural practices, and beliefs that existed before the violence have proved durable in many cases despite the strain on them in the context of mass violence. Likewise, in Shapiro-Phim's chapter morals are drawn from traditional stories, and in McGrew's essay cultural ideas around virtue and ignorance influence the practice of empathy. Finally, Kahn and Burnet both find that rescue had a positive impact on rescuers and served as a model for others to emulate. In other words, they became transmitters of traditional moral values. An examination of the ways in which courage and morality influence behavior and impact recovery may yield additional implications to guide interventions.

The role of narratives in social repair processes is connected to this volume's three conceptual themes in establishing coexistence. The use of "narrative" was mentioned by almost all of our chapters and is indeed another aspect emphasizing the importance of including local voices in peacebuilding processes. Narrative (in its many forms) is just one of many vehicles in which the concepts of imagination, empathy, and resilience can be seen, heard, and described. In Burnet's and Khan's chapters, sharing of rescuers' narratives was found to be profoundly impactful in many cases. Hopefully, the narratives not only tell what happened from each party's perspective but inspire future generations to learn from the past and work toward prevention of future violence. Burnet, drawing on Gordon, suggests however that the equal distribution of narratives is also important in processes that lead to coexistence, to ensure that all voices are heard, including victims, perpetrators, and bystanders (for example, in Rwanda the narratives were one-sided in the past and needed to be redistributed). McGrew's and Mieth's respondents spoke to the importance of narratives of shared suffering (though not equivalent suffering) in the development of empathy, and thus of coexistence. In a similar vein, Kahn speaks to the collective memories on which narratives are based—some of the rescuers she highlights refused to dwell on memories of past violence, instead focusing on positive memories of communal harmony or "willed memory." Velasco describes a process through his documentary filmmaking where testimony (a form of narrative) emerged as "an act of resilience to denounce impunity, state abandonment, and the structural amnesia surrounding cases of war in marginal areas of the country." This act of resilience is similar to that described by Gordon in Somaliland, whereby a new narrative of a self-reliant and independent state was created that has served to strengthen social cohesion in the face of external pressures.

While hope for the future was mentioned by respondents in all of the case studies, this hope was exhibited in different ways—such as women gaining agency and voice in the Southern Cone through narratives of their shared suffering in the past (Llanos) and Somalilanders standing steadfast to their hope through reliance on traditional conflict resolution methods in refutation of conflict in states all around them (Gordon). Shapiro-Phim finds great hope in the social commentary portrayed in the innovative dance performances in Cambodia, and Zucker locates hope in imagining of what relationships might look like in an ideal Cambodian society. McGrew illustrates how Cambodian victims show remarkable grace in their ability to empathize with their former torturers, as both, especially victims, try to understand the difficult circumstances at that time and to focus on the future. Velasco shows how Colombian villagers in extremely isolated locations and difficult circumstances are showing hope and resiliency through their environmental projects, while the rescuers depicted in Burnet's and Kahn's studies in Rwanda and elsewhere are exhibiting remarkable courage that gives others hope for their own futures.

While our most basic underlying premise is clear and definitive—that peacebuilding should be based upon, and rely upon, local views, practices, and traditions, we have some additional preliminary questions to consider: whether or not there should be state or outsider intervention, whether local processes (occurring without outside intervention) should be left to develop on their own, and whether interventions should follow a set of guidelines (and if so, which ones)? While some of the following suggestions may seem self-evident, they are not in fact always adhered to, so we include them here. First, there should be an assessment of local processes that may already be occurring without any form of intervention. These processes may take familiar forms such as local judicial processes; religious practices such as blessings, rituals, and other rites; educational programs; local memorial practices; traditional healers' practices; the use of stories and myths; adoption of new ideologies; and so forth. However, two caveats are important. One mistake that has often been made by outsiders is misreading local forms of recovery. This misreading may be addressed in part if the international community were to more frequently engage with various locally grounded experts including anthropologists, peacebuilders, and local representatives of the communities. And second, it should also be understood that there may be other processes that help mend the ruptures that look different than those outlined in traditional peacebuilding initiatives. While there may be no reason to intervene when positive change through local practices and initiatives is already happening in communities, local processes nonetheless should be considered when deciding whether or not to intervene, and if so, what types of interventions states and/or peacebuilding and transitional justice institutions should pursue. In the past, local processes have often been overlooked due to ignorance of their existence or seen with a short-sighted view that only regards measures sanctioned by international frameworks as effective. A second step then should be to assess whether additional methods or support would be helpful, and if so, when and how. Then a third step would be to initiate collaboration with the relevant local communities using careful methods to ensure inclusion and "Do No Harm" principles (Anderson 2010).

A focus of this volume is on how individuals and communities in the aftermath of mass violence bring their visions of the future into their rebuilding efforts. In doing so, they hold or develop visions of how the world ought to be. What language do they use to describe it? What are the sources they draw from for inspiration? These are questions that can and should be asked in post-conflict studies within academia and other institutions and when planning and carrying out interventions in societies recovering from the past. What visions do people have of a more peaceful future and how can they get there? What grammars, discourses, metaphors, and ideologies do they use to articulate these ideals and ideas? By understanding the sources of inspiration, the language used to describe them, and the forms of transmission, practitioners will ideally be able to work in conjunction with these visions and apply more nuanced support reflective of this understanding. Incorporating locally derived visions of peace into a peacebuilding process increases the likelihood of its adoption and success in creating a foundation for coexistence, reconciliation, and a shared and peaceful future.

Timing and duration are two other factors that should be considered more deeply both from a research and policy standpoint. This applies to all three of the conceptual themes. How do people's perceptions of each other, themselves, the world around them, the past, and the future change over time? Is empathy more likely as individuals, societies, and communities move further away from the violence that occurred? What might resilience look like in five years, ten years, or more? How many years must pass before we can judge if recovery is successful? Also how do our imagined worlds and futures change over time? Longitudinal studies that inform interventions and policy are very necessary here. While there has been increasing attention to the effects of mass trauma from war and genocide on survivors at different points in their lives and of second and perhaps even third generations, the research on this is still limited. Furthermore, in spite of repeated cries from the peacebuilding community, funding opportunities to work on building peace and assisting with recovery from mass violence remain limited and are often short-term. This must be changed!

While these chapters have provided a detailed illustration of how these concepts work in Cambodia, Africa, South America, and other places, there is still much work to be done. What forms will empathy take when the violence in Syria eventually recedes? What traditions and cultural resources might the Yemenis draw from to imagine a future when the bombs stop falling? Where is resilience found among the Yazidi and how can it be sustained? And while these three cases are in places where conflicts continue, there are also questions remaining for the places now at peace such as those covered in this volume. While over the years there has been an increase in research on rescuers, the ways in which rescuers are imagined, imagine themselves, and enact and promote empathy is still underdeveloped. More questions remain than are answered. Do survivors empathize more with groups that persecuted them if they are able to identify rescuers among them? Do perpetrators empathize more with victims knowing that some of their group do not see the victims as "others" but instead as fellow human beings? How are the ways in which rescuers are imagined allow for individual and social recovery?

The suggestions noted throughout this volume, and in this conclusion, point to directions in which to deepen our understandings of recovery in the aftermath of mass violence; provide pathways to better alternatives for individuals, local communities, external actors, and agencies faced with the task of repairing social relations; and help in promoting a sustainable coexistence between former adversaries. The case studies all show the remarkable recovery of the individuals and societies and the flexibility, perseverance, and durability of the human spirit. We hope that this volume has provided some new lenses and perspectives based on imagination, empathy, and resilience, increasing refinement of understanding of peacebuilding in the process of social repair. From a starting point of the local, we focused on the strengths of the individual, village, and community to heal themselves—with a little help from their friends from outside if and only if needed and wanted, and if and only if local inputs are the baseline for interventions.

REFERENCES

Anderson, Mary B. 2010. *Do No Harm: How Aid Can Support Peace—Or War*. Boulder: Lynne Rienner.

Autesserre, Severine. 2014. *Peaceland: Conflict Resolution and the Everyday Politics of International Intervention*. New York: Cambridge University Press.

Autesserre, Severine. 2017. "International Peacebuilding and Local Success: Assumptions and Effectiveness." *International Studies Review* 19: 114–32.

Monk, Daniel B., and Jacob Mundy. 2014. "Introduction." In *The Post-Conflict Environment: Investigation and Critique*, edited by Daniel B. Monk and Jacob Mundy. Ann Arbor: University of Michigan Press.

Contributors

Jennie E. Burnet is Associate Professor of Anthropology at Georgia State University in the United States. Her research explores the social, cultural, and psychological aspects of war, genocide, and mass violence and the microlevel impact of large-scale social change in the context of conflict. Her award-winning book, *Genocide Lives in Us: Women, Memory and Silence in Rwanda*, was published in 2012 by the University of Wisconsin Press.

Matthew Gordon is currently a PhD candidate in the Department of Politics and International Studies at the School of Oriental and African Studies (SOAS), where he is researching indigenous approaches to social reconstruction and their intersection with notions and practices of statehood in Somaliland. Mr. Gordon previously worked for more than five years as a professional in the fields of diplomacy, development, and policymaking in the Horn of Africa.

Leora Kahn is the founder and president of PROOF International and a Lecturer in Human Rights at the University of Dayton, where she founded the Moral Courage Project. She is a former fellow at the Genocide Studies Program at Yale University, where she continues to conduct research on rescuers and rescuing behavior. Leora has interviewed and researched rescuers in Rwanda, Cambodia, Bosnia, Sri Lanka, and Iraq and works on projects concerning the ethics of representation pertaining to refugees and forced migrants.

Bernardita Llanos is Professor of Spanish at Brooklyn College, CUNY specializing in the works of Latin American women writers and documentarians. Her book *Passionate Subjects/Split Subjects in Twentieth Century Narrative in Chile. Brunet, Bombal and Eltit* was published in 2009.

Other publications include numerous articles on Latin American culture and women writers that have appeared in well-known American, Latin American, and European journals; several coedited and authored books, the most recent being *Poner el cuerpo: visibilizar y rescatar las marcas sexuales y de género de los archivos dictatoriales del Cono Sur* (2017); and *Chile de Memoria: A 40 años del golpe* (2017).

Laura McGrew is an independent researcher and peacebuilding consultant with a PhD in Peace Studies from Coventry University and a Master's in Public Policy from Johns Hopkins School of Advanced International Studies. She is the author of several articles and book chapters on transitional justice, coexistence, governance, peacebuilding, and civil society networks, primarily related to Cambodia. Her current research focuses on post-mass violence recovery including relationships between victims, perpetrators, bystanders, and rescuers. She has been a consultant for various organizations for more than twenty-five years working with the United Nations and NGOs in many countries in Southeast, South, and Central Asia; Africa; and the United States, in the fields of development, gender, human rights, rule of law, conflict analysis, peacebuilding, and coexistence. Laura is an affiliate of the Center for Khmer Studies, and cofounder with Dr. Eve Zucker of the Reflections in the Aftermath of War and Violence project and consortium.

Friederike Mieth is a researcher and consultant working on human rights and conflict transformation. Her previous research has explored local practices of dealing with the past, individual and collective resilience in the aftermath of mass violence, and the impact and acceptance of transitional justice institutions. She has consulted for various organizations in the fields of human rights education, transitional justice, reparations programs, international criminal justice, and active citizenship. Friederike is a coeditor of *Transitional Justice Theories* (Routledge, 2014) and *The German Compensation Program for Forced Labor: Practice and Experiences* (EVZ Foundation, 2017). She holds a PhD in Social and Cultural Anthropology and Peace and Conflict Studies from the Philipps University Marburg, Germany.

Toni Shapiro-Phim, Associate Professor of Creativity, the Arts, and Social Transformation and Assistant Director of Peacebuilding and the Arts, at Brandeis University, received a PhD in Cultural Anthropology from Cornell University. Her research, writing, teaching and applied work focus on migration and displacement, war, genocide and gender violence, and the relationship between the arts and social justice concerns, with publications on, among other things, dance and human rights, dance and transitional justice in Cambodia, and Liberian artists, community building, and anti-violence activism.

Ricardo A. Velasco is a Postdoctoral Fellow of the Mellon Engaged Scholar Initiative in the College of Liberal Arts at the University of Texas at Austin. His research focuses on memory and cultural production in contexts of transitional justice. In his work, he combines creative documentary practices with digital humanities methods for exploring the intersections between historical memory, human rights, cultural activism, and peacebuilding, particularly in Colombia.

Eve Zucker is a Lecturer in the Departments of Anthropology at Columbia University and Yale University. Her research focuses on the aftermath of mass violence through the lenses of social memory, morality, the imagination, trust, and everyday practices. Her most recent work is about digital technologies and memorialization, social transformation, and political violence in Southeast Asia. Her books include *Forest of Struggle: Moralities of Remembrance in Upland Cambodia* (University of Hawai'i Press, 2013), and the coedited volumes *Mass Violence and Memory in the Digital Age: Memorialization Unmoored* (Palgrave-MacMillan, 2020) and *Political Violence in Southeast Asia Since 1945* (Routledge, in press). She is a research affiliate at the Council for Southeast Asian Studies at Yale University and serves on the boards of the Yale Genocide Studies Program, the Center for Khmer Studies, and the New York Southeast Asia Network. Together with Laura McGrew, she cofounded the Reflections in the Aftermath of War and Genocide project and consortium. Eve holds a PhD in Anthropology from the London School of Economics.

Index

Abramowitz, Sharon, 12, 14

Abuelas of Plaza de Mayo, 173, 176, 183

activism, 8, 15, 16, 20, 171, 182–89, 195–96, 208–10, 213–14, 247

activist(s), 78; feminist, 189; global, 247; groups, 176; human rights, 239n1; identity, 178; research, 196, 204, 208, 215; social, 210

acts of rescue, 126, 127, 131, 134–36, 138

Adekunle, Julius, 158

Aegis Trust, 133, 156

Afghanistan, 2

Africa, 55, 253; Central, 2; Horn of, 218; 223; West, 55

Afro-Colombian(s), 171–72, 204, 210

After the Crossfire: Memories of Violence and Displacement (film), 171, 196, 205–8, 215

agency: collective, 194; local, 220, 229

Agenda for Peace, 10

aid, 76, 237; development, 226; humanitarian, 218, 231; international, 219

altruism, 104, 115, 129, 149

amnesty (-ies), 12; laws, 180

Amrita Performing Arts (Cambodian NGO), 87

ancestors, 31, 36, 38–48. *See also* ancestral spirits; spirits

ancestral spirits, 29, 33, 38, 39, 64. *See also* guardian spirits; tutelary spirits

Andermann, Lisa, 196, 211

Anderson, Benedict, 6, 8, 35, 227

anger, 17, 74, 102, 103, 109, 112–13, 118–19, 125

Angkar (Khmer Rouge leadership organization), 76, 114

Angkor (Wat), 71, 97

anthropology, 5, 6, 12, 14

apology, 5, 108, 113, 117, 119

Argentina, 19, 171–90

art, 71, 75, 77–78, 82–90, 92n21, 209, 246, 248, 249; the arts, 14, 15, 16, 20, 72, 73, 76, 77, 81–85, 90n7, 91n12

attitudes, 7, 104, 129

Austro-Hungarian Empire, 154

Autesserre, Severine, 11, 247, 248

autonomy: food, 210, 211; national, 19, 20, 218–39

Balkans, 10, 156

Bangura, Zainab, presidential candidate (Sierra Leone), 10, 156

Barre, Siyad, 232

Basso, Keith, 50n28

Becker, Nubia, 184

Belgium, 161

Bernstein, Leonard, 86

Bilewicz, Michal, 157

Blaustein, David, 173

Bloch, Maurice, 6, 31, 32, 46

Bloomfield, David, 21n5, 189

Bon Dalien (ritual harvest festival), 35–40, 45, 46, 50n24, 91n12

Bordaberry, Juan, 175, 191n5

border crossing, 135, 194, 195, 197, 202, 208–14

Bosnia (Bosnia-Herzegovina), 8, 15, 17, 18, 120, 138, 150, 152–56; Bosniaks, 152, 153; Bosnian genocide, 150 (*see also* genocide); Bosnian Serbs, 152, 153 bottom-up approach, 11–13 135, 194, 195, 197, 202, 208–14. *See also* local turn

Bradbury, Mark, 223, 224, 225, 231, 232, 234, 236, 240n3

Brahmanism, 73

Brazil, 177, 200, 203

Brown, Brené, 103, 120n2, 121n8, 123

Brown, Bronwyn, 235–36

Bryden, Matt, 223

Buddha, 32, 38; Buddhism, 30, 33, 73; Buddhist(s), 150

Buruma, Ian, 21n3

bystanders, 1, 2, 17, 98, 100, 101, 131, 134, 140–43, 149, 162, 247, 250

Cambodia, 10, 14, 16, 17, 20, 29–48, 64, 71–92, 97–120, 137, 142, 150, 185, 247, 251, 253

Campaign Against Genocide Museum, 133

Camus, Albert, 164

Carter, Alexandra, 72

Catholic(s), 138, 139, 154; base groups, 177; parish, 143; Croats, 152

Čehajić-Clancy, Sabina, 156–57

Chandler, David, 30, 42, 49n6, 50n29, 222

Charbonneau, Bruno, 11, 14

Chatterjea, Ananya, 91n16

Chayes, Antonia, 8, 14

Chey, Chankethya, 89, 92n23

Chhang, Youk, 88, 99

Chhim, Sotheara, 102, 121

Chhit, Choeun (*aka* Ta Mok), 79

children, 36, 44, 76, 77, 112, 118, 134, 135, 139, 157–59, 165, 171, 173, 175, 176, 179, 201. *See also* youth

Chile, 19, 171–81, 184–90

China, 14

Christianity, 33, 138; Christians, 65, 135, 150, 160, 161; churches, 138; civilization, 174; Orthodox, 145; values, 174

Christianson, Paul, 49n15

civic engagement, 13, 19, 195, 196, 200, 208–15, 248

civil society, 68n5, 74, 82, 127, 140, 149, 194, 195, 197, 202, 204–14

civilization, 9, 174

cohabitation, 127, 237

Cohen, Cynthia, 83, 91n14, 129

cohesion, 212, 216n8, 219, 221, 222, 236, 237, 251

Cold War, 173, 174, 180

collaborator(s), 1, 182, 187, 188, 205

Collins, Cath, 186, 187

Colombia, 11, 13, 19, 92n21, 140, 171–72, 194–215, 216n2, 237

colonial era, 144n3, 233, 234; history, 62; colonialism, 136, 144n3, 165, 237

commemoration, 14, 131, 132, 140, 150, 198

Commission of Historical Memory (MH), 196, 198

communal: harmony, 154, 250; relationship, 46. *See also* social relationships

communitas, 39

community, political, 19, 220, 222–28, 230, 232–38

compassion, 17, 47, 79, 80, 81, 85, 88, 89, 98, 104, 109, 116–18, 121n12, 137, 163, 185, 245

conflict resolution, 13, 132, 251

Congo, 11, 91n7, 133, 151, 158, 159

coping, 64, 66, 68n7, 231, 238

Correa, Adriana, 199–200

corruption, 3, 56, 79, 100, 223

courage, 126, 137–39, 147, 150, 156, 158, 160–62, 165, 184, 249–50, 251, 255; courageous acts, 133, 134, 140, 155, 162; courageous people, 7, 19, 130, 149, 150; courageous rescuers, 13, 104, 105, 130

creativity, 6, 64, 73, 84; creative template, 43

crime(s), 3, 17, 79, 84, 86, 98, 110–14, 118, 137, 141, 157, 178–80, 186; against humanity, 79, 91n10, 179, 190, 191n5; genocide, 18, 79, 125, 131–33, 141, 143; intimate, 100; sexual, 92, 182, 185, 188, 190, 191n10; war, 12, 55, 179

Croat(s), 150, 152, 154, 155; forces, 152; Croatia, 120, 156; Croatians, 155

culture, 2, 8, 9, 12, 15, 74, 83, 129, 144n3, 162, 194, 195, 202, 209, 245, 248; Cambodian, 16, 31, 40, 49n3, 72, 82, 108; expressive, 75, 82, 212; norms, 72, 152, 158; organizational, 224; Rwandan, 158; traditions, 7, 127

culture of; inclusion and participation, 194; empathy, 120n2, 162; memory, 197–99; peace, 2, 194, 204; tolerance, 162
curiosity, 103, 104, 120, 129
customs, 3, 154, 158, 161, 165

De Cesari, Chiara, 195–97
de Greiff, Pablo, 54, 74, 82–83
democracy, 82, 171, 176, 189, 197, 224, 226, 227; informed, 83
Democratic Kampuchea, 35, 76, 122
Des Forges, Allison, 161
development agencies, 3, 47. See also aid; development
di Tella, Andrés, 173
Diagne, Captain Mbaye, 150
dialogue, 2, 11, 13, 15, 17, 20, 98, 99, 107, 110, 113, 115, 116, 119, 120, 133, 161, 162, 208, 210, 224, 225, 235; community, 13, 133, 161, 208, 210; facilitation, 98; interventions, programs, and projects, 2, 99, 107, 113, 115–16, 119, 120; process, 110
diaspora, 131, 223, 231
Diaz, Gladys, 185–86
digital divide, 209, 211, 214; media and communication, 199, 200, 202, 209, 214; digital resources, 200, 203
disease, 3, 57, 63, 76, 97, 101. See also illness, global viruses, HIV/AIDS
displacement, 65, 74, 171, 200, 207, 213, 215, 219, 223; forced, 34, 195, 200
the disappeared, 173, 175, 176, 183, 184, 191n6
distrust, 3, 16, 30, 35, 74, 76, 78, 90, 142. See also mistrust; trust
Documentation Center of Cambodia, 88
Duch, 79, 177. See also Kaing, Guek Eav
durability (resilience), 8, 30, 40, 220, 227, 232, 237, 245–46, 253
Dusabimana, Josephine, 151
Duthie, Roger, 82

education, 6, 14, 34, 56, 62, 88, 99, 100, 104, 105, 113, 149, 161, 177, 218, 247, 251
Egal, Mohammed H. I., President (Somaliland), 227–28, 234
empathic: involvement, 127; listening, 7, 104, 106, 107, 129, 130

employment, 32, 56, 58, 62, 100; unemployment, 56, 219, 238
empowerment, 178, 189, 212, 235
enchantment, 29–52; enchanted realm (world), 29, 35, 42, 43, 44, 47
enemy (-ies), 6, 29, 34, 49n6, 76, 79, 97, 105, 161, 163, 172, 174, 175, 181
Erbil, 162
Esta boca es mía (film), 178
ethnicity, 54; 129, 130, 144n1, 214
excombatants, 53. See also former combatants
Extraordinary Chambers in the Courts of Cambodia (ECCC), 79, 88, 91n10, 92n21, 101, 117. See also Khmer Rouge Tribunal
Eyal, Gil, 155

Facebook, 200, 204, 248
fear, 19, 30, 32, 83, 97, 102–3, 111, 113, 117–19, 131, 138, 155, 173, 175, 182, 184, 188, 218, 224, 232
Feitlowitz, Marguerite, 174–75. See also Lexicon of Terror
Feldman, Allen, 207
Fernandez, James, 10
Flacks, Richard, 91n15
folktales, 42, 245. See also storytelling and moral tales
forgetting, 58, 154, 176, 188, 206
forgiveness, 4, 5, 98, 109, 118, 187, 231
former combatants, 1, 58, 59–60, 63, 67, 68. See also excombatants
fortification (resilience), 8, 220, 232
Frankl, Viktor, 47, 67
Freetown, 53, 54, 56, 57, 61, 62, 64
friction, 12

Galtung, Johan, 5, 10
Geertz, Clifford, 37, 49n21
genocide: Bosnian, 150, 152–57; Cambodian, 29–52, 71–94, 97–124; crimes, 18, 125, 131, 132, 141, 143; Rwandan, 125–48, 157–62; studies, 5
Genocide Studies Program (Yale University), 150, 162
George, Terry, 132, 145n11

Germany, 21n3
Ghali, Boutros-Boutros, 10
Gisenyi, 132, 133, 135–36, 139, 140
Gisozi Memorial Museum, 161
global viruses, 3, 55. *See also* disease
good deeds, 113–14, 118–19, 140
Graeber, David, 45
guarantees of non-repetition, 197
The Guardian, 163
guardian spirits, 36, 40. *See also* ancestral
    spirits; tutelary spirits
Guzmán, Patricio, 173, 191n4

Habineza, Joseph, 159–61
Hacia el Litoral, 196, 209–10, 212–15
Hakizimana, Celestin (Father), 133
Halpern, Jodi, 6, 103, 104, 105, 115, 120,
    125, 128, 129, 137
Hansen, Anne, 30, 50n30
hatred, 86, 102, 103, 120, 125, 231, 239n1
health care, 6, 56, 97, 99
heart(s), 15, 45, 104, 106, 109, 116, 117–18,
    119, 120, 121n9, 121n11, 140, 142; change
    of, 113–14; disease, 101; good, 127, 129,
    135–38
Helsper, Ellen, 209
Hijos por la Identidad y la justicia Contra
    el Olvidio y el Silencio (HIJOS), 176
Hillary Clinton, US Secretary of State,
    151
Him, Sophy, 87
Hindu(s), 29, 32; deities, 29, 32, 38; tem-
    ples, 71; Hinduism, 73
Hinton, Alex, 11, 12, 111, 127, 49n6
Hoellen, Burkhard, 66
Holocaust, 20, 129, 134, 138, 247. *See also*
    US Holocaust Memorial Museum
honesty, 40–44, 46, 188
Hotel Rwanda (film), 132
Human Rights Watch, 161
humanization, 108, 120; dehumanization,
    105, 137, 162; rehumanization, 103–5,
    108, 114, 117, 118. *See also* inhumanity
humiliation, 178, 184
Hutu, 18, 126, 128, 131–35, 140, 142–43,
    144n1, 144n3, 151, 157–62
Huyse, Luc, 6–7, 103, 125, 189

ideal(s) (noun), 33, 37, 40, 46, 47, 81,
    91n12, 98, 181
identity, 20, 37, 55, 58, 74, 91n12, 142, 162,
    175–78, 180, 181, 186, 187, 212, 220, 222,
    224, 247; shared/group, 36, 46, 105, 142,
    154, 165, 223, 227, 233, 235–37
ignorance, 63, 86, 109, 111, 112–13, 246,
    250, 252
illness, 36, 45. *See also* disease; global
    viruses
imaginary (noun), 17, 30, 31, 47, 194;
    Argentine, 181; Cambodian, 32, 35, 40,
    42–44, 47, 74, 91n12, 226; Colombian,
    204; Somaliland, 227; transcendental,
    44
imagined community, 35, 226, 227
immortality, 42, 50n31
impunity, 12, 88, 127, 150, 174, 177, 197, 208,
    215, 251
indakemwa, 133, 135, 142
inhumanity, 77–78
Interahamwe, 134, 135, 136, 138, 140–41
Internet, 201
interpretive labor, 45–46
intervention(s), 2, 11, 18, 20, 42, 47, 48, 53,
    74, 100, 103, 119, 120, 134, 157, 189, 209,
    231, 235, 244–54; communal, 196, 212,
    215; outside, 2, 12, 127, 230, 251; political,
    176, 230; social, 214, 221
Iraq, 15, 17, 18, 150, 162–64, 183
Isaaq (clan), 223, 227–28, 235–36
Isabel, Maria, 181–82
Islam, 136, 138
Islamic State of Iraq and Syria (ISIS), 150,
    163, 164

Jackson, Michael, 56
Jail Without Walls (play), 77
Japan, 21n3
Jaqué, Panama, 195–96, 201, 209
Jardines en Balsa, 210–11
Jews, 129, 155
Joinet Principles, 197, 198
Juradó, Colombia, 196, 204–6, 210

Kabbah, Ahmad Tejan, President (Sierra
    Leone), 63

Kabuga, 159
Kagame, Paul, President (Rwanda), 132, 133
Kagmaore, Augustin, 157–59
Kaing, Guek Eav (*aka* Duch), 91n10
Kang, Rithisal, 87, 88
karma, 59, 81
karuna, 109, 121n12
Karuna Center for Peacebuilding (NGO), 161
Kdei Karuna (Cambodian NGO), 92, 116
Khmer Rouge, 4, 13, 16, 17, 20, 29–52, 71–94, 97–124, 150, 212
Khmer Rouge Tribunal, 79, 88. *See also* Extraordinary Chambers in the Courts of Cambodia
Kiernan, Ben, 91n8
Kigali, 133
Kigali Genocide Memorial, 133
kin, 44, 126, 133, 137, 139, 233
Kornbluh, Peter, 174
Kraybill, Ron, 104, 137
Kurdistan, 163
Kwon, Heonik, 49n7

La Venda (film), 184–86
LaCapra, Dominick, 207
Lake Kivu, 135, 151, 157, 159
Lambek, Michael, 42
land, 1, 33, 34, 38, 45, 75, 100, 219, 236; spirits of, 73
Laos, 42, 77
Law 1448 of Victims, 198–99
Law 975 of Justice and Peace, 198
Lederach, John Paul, 5, 6, 41, 49n3, 73, 83
legitimacy, 190, 203, 225–28, 230–32, 235–36
Lelek, Borivoje, 152–55
Lelek, Ljubinka, 152–55
Levi, Primo, 21n1, 30
Lewin, Miriam, 182–84, 186
Lexicon of Terror, 175. *See also* Feitlowitz, Marguerite
Liberia, 55, 90
The Lives of Giants (Cambodian dance drama), 72–75, 79–81, 86, 90n5
Livingston, Sonia, 209

local practices, 20, 31, 47, 48, 252
local turn, 11–13. *See also* bottom-up approach
Lon Nol, Prime Minister (Cambodia), 34, 76
Luco, Fabienne, 102, 123
lustration, 11

Macedonia, 156
macho men, 176–77
Madina (Sierra Leone), 34, 57, 59, 60–61, 68n1, 68n2
Madres and Abuelas of Plaza de Mayo, 173, 176
market economy, 34, 45
Massero, Emilio, 175
McKinnon, Catherine, 189
memorialization, 2, 14, 54, 92n21, 208. *See also* memory
memory, 2, 10, 13, 14, 19, 32, 35, 37, 43, 53, 58, 89, 106, 131, 154–55, 165–66, 194–217, 227; construction, 140, 194–96, 200, 201, 204–8, 215; historical, 106, 165, 173, 196, 198, 199–204, 227; narrative(s), 18, 171–93, 195, 212, 249; collective, 10, 154, 155, 251 (*see also* historical memory; social memory). *See also* memorialization
Merino, Marcia Alejandra, 187
methodological nationalism, 196
migration, forced, 195
mimesis, 226
Ministry of Culture (Cambodia), 71, 90, 90n1
Minow, Martha, 8, 14, 154, 197
mistrust, 20, 89, 102, 120. *See also* distrust; trust
modernity (modern), 33, 38, 39, 46–47, 57, 172, 218, 224, 225, 232
Monk, Daniel, 11, 248
moral: compass, 136, 152; guidance, 7, 47, 48; tales and stories, 30, 31, 40–44, 47, 50n28, 246 (*see also* storytelling)
morality, 10, 14, 41–43, 84, 137, 138, 149, 152, 166, 226, 249, 250. *See also* immorality
Mosul, 163

MRND political party, 136
Mugandamure, 136
Mundy, Jacob, 11
Muslim(s), 135–36, 138–40, 145n22, 150, 152–55

National Center for Historical Memory (CNMH) (Colombia), 198–204, 205, 207, 214
National Commission for Reparation and Reconciliation (CNRR) (Colombia), 198
Nazis, 21n1, 155
network agency, 196, 213–15
neuroscience, 6, 98, 102, 129
Nigeria, 2
1951 Convention Related to the Status of Refugees, 150
Niyitegeka, Félicité, Sister (Rwanda), 133, 140, 145n9
Niyitegeka, Sosthene, Reverend (Rwanda), 133–34
Nordstrom, Carolyn, 64
Norodom, Buppha Devi, Princess (Cambodia), 58
Norodom, Sihanouk, King (Cambodia), 99
Nuremberg norms, 12

O'Lemmon, Mathew, 49n15
Oliner, Samuel, 129–30
Omaar, Rakiya, 239n1
Operation Condor, 177
Orthodox Christians, 154
Othello (play), 78, 84
Ottoman Turkish occupation, 154
Owen, Taylor, 91n8

Panama, 194, 195, 196, 200, 201, 202, 204, 209, 210, 212
participant-observation, 12, 15, 54
Path, Kosal, 4, 98, 101, 105, 117
Peace Charter of 1993 (Somaliland), 225
peace studies, 5, 6, 14, 73, 127
Pentecostal church, 64, 160
People's Republic of Kampuchea (PRK), 76, 99

perception(s), 50n34, 58, 60, 98, 104, 106, 108, 109, 115, 227, 252; of self, 185
Peru, 14, 181
Phka Sla (Cambodian dance-drama), 86–87, 92n21
Phnom Penh, Cambodia, 37, 46, 75, 101
Pholsena, Vattana, 9
Picturing Moral Courage (conference and exhibition), 156
Pinker, Steven, 8, 21n7
Pinochet, Augusto, President (Chile), 175
The Plague, 164
Pol Pot, Khmer Rouge leader (Cambodia), 17, 35, 37, 113, 150
political community. See community, political
political freedom to act, 20, 220
politics, 6, 34, 62, 172, 173, 175, 182, 183, 218, 221, 226, 230–32, 236, 237, 239; butterfly, 189
post-traumatic stress disorder (PTSD), 101, 102, 121n7
potency: aesthetic and moral, 75; moral, 212; political, 90; of traditional authority, 219; sexual, 181; of spirits and enchanted world, 43; transformative, 83
potentiality, 30, 32, 44, 46, 64, 224, 228
poverty, 3, 36, 37, 56, 58, 63, 73, 101, 109, 111, 112, 201, 204, 219
power (dynamics), 71
power-sharing, 20, 231, 232
predictability, 44
prejudice(s), 129, 162, 165
PROOF: Media for Social Justice (NGO), 133, 149, 150, 155
psychology, 5, 129, 221; individual, 129
Puntland, 230, 236
Putnam, Robert, 214

Ramayana, 79. See also Reamker
Reamker (Cambodia), 79, 81, 84, 91n15
refugee(s), 4, 61, 84, 100, 132, 135, 150, 152, 159, 223; camps, 83
reliability, 44, 157
religion(s), 3, 9, 14, 42, 129, 130, 138, 139, 144n3, 154, 236. See also particular religions

religious faith, 138. *See also* religion; *and particular religions*
religious institutions, 2, 10
renewal (social and moral), 44, 165
reparations, 92n21, 195, 197, 198, 205, 207, 215
Republika Srpska, 153, 154. *See also* Serb
rescuer(s), 1, 7, 9, 13, 15, 18, 85, 104, 125–48, 149–67, 183–84, 245, 249, 250, 251, 253
respect, 1, 15, 21n5, 42, 43, 87, 107, 108, 109, 113–15, 118, 158, 177, 195, 234
responsibility, 63, 67, 78–79, 81, 84, 88, 90, 91n10, 118; state, 198; Responsibility to Protect, 10
revenge, 79, 81, 97, 111, 118, 165, 228, 238; cycle(s) of, 3, 73, 79, 81, 86, 90, 246
Revolutionary Armed Forces of Colombia (FARC), 204. *See also* FARC
Rey, Natalia, 199
Richards, Rebecca, 234
Rigney, Ann, 195, 197
risk, 6, 18, 86, 130, 137, 143, 162, 207, 238, 248; imagination of, 74; of life, 7, 126, 131, 133, 137, 139, 150, 154, 155, 161, 163, 164
ritual(s), 13, 16, 30, 31, 33, 35–40, 43, 46–48, 73, 75, 84, 87, 89, 226
Rivers, Chérie, 90n7
Rogatica, 153
Rohingya, 2, 248
role models, 142, 149, 150, 152, 155, 161, 165–66
Rosenblum, Nancy L., 154
Rosenthal, Rob, 91n16
Rwanda, 8, 10, 13, 14, 15, 17, 18, 104, 121n11, 125–45, 150, 151, 157–62, 165, 183, 185, 250, 251; genocide, 18, 125, 126, 130, 143, 144n1, 150 (*see also* genocide)
Rwandan Army, 133, 138
Rwandan Patriotic Front (RPF), 125, 133

Saint Pierre Pastoral Center-Gisenyi, 133
Salih, Aliya Khalaf, 163–64
Samritechak (dance-drama, Cambodia), 78, 79, 82, 84, 90n1, 91n9
Sánchez, Gonzalo, 198
Sarajevo, 152, 155; School of Design and

Technology, 157
School of Fine Arts (Cambodia), 77, 89, 90n1
second generation effects, 101
Second Indochina War, 42
security, 35, 43, 101, 134, 139, 210, 225, 227, 230, 238, 239
Serb(s), 150, 152–56. *See also* Bosnia
sexual torture, 175
sexual violence. *See* violence, gender-based
shame (feel ashamed), 83, 87, 118, 179, 182
Shapiro, Sophiline Cheam, 17, 71–94
Shaw, Rosalind, 11–12, 14, 64–65
Sheffield, Carole, 188
Shiites, 150, 163–64
Sierra Leone, 13, 16, 53–68, 74, 183
silence / act of silencing, 90–91n7, 92n21, 126, 130–34, 176, 178, 182, 186, 205–6, 249
Simich, Laura, 196, 211
smartphone, 57
sobels (Sierra Leone), 63
social: change, 10, 30, 44, 64, 83, 91n16, 183, 190, 220; justice, 13, 14, 15, 16, 20, 89, 92n23, 133, 149, 177, 183; media, 248; memory, 14, 165 (*see also* memory, collective; memory, historical); relationships, 4, 16, 30, 31, 32, 43, 44, 136, 188, 212 (*see also* webs of relationships)
sociality, 32, 49n5, 225
solidarity, 8, 19, 36, 39, 46, 130, 178, 180, 184, 185, 189, 190, 196, 212, 214, 215, 223, 224
Solnit, Rebecca, 78
Somali National Movement (SNM), 223, 224, 228, 231–32, 234, 236
Somalia, 13, 19, 218–19, 223–24, 229–32, 235–36
Somaliland, 11, 13, 15, 18, 19, 20, 142, 216n8, 218–39, 248, 249, 251
Sophiline Arts Ensemble, Cambodian (NGO), 80, 90n5, 92n22
Special Court for Sierra Leone, 55
spirits (ancestral, guardian, imaginary, tutelary), 30, 31, 35, 38, 39, 40, 43, 65, 72, 73, 75, 83; spirit world, 32, 35, 40–43

Srebrenica, 153
Sri Lanka, 138, 150
State Crime (film), 65
state-building, 20, 127, 141, 216n8, 220,
222, 225, 226, 228, 232, 234–37, 239n2
Staub, Erwin, 104, 108, 109, 112, 115, 134,
165
stereotypes, 7, 83, 104
storytelling, 15, 19, 31, 72, 92n23, 107, 149,
185, 225, 247–48; performative, 72;
storyteller(s), 43, 85, 171
structural: amnesia, 195, 206, 208, 215,
251; conditions, 2, 8, 206; inequalities,
19, 82, 203
suffering (shared), 19, 59, 114–17, 223, 250,
251
Sunni(s), 150, 163–64
Supreme Court (Argentina), 176
Sutton, Barbara, 189

testimony (-ies), 13, 16, 18–19, 92n21, 125–
48, 149–67, 171–93, 196, 198, 199–200,
202, 204–8, 215, 225, 250, 251
Thailand, 46, 76
Theidon, Kimberly, 12, 14, 105, 181
transactional social, 31, 32, 40
transcendence, 5, 6, 40; imaginary 44,
social, 31, 32, 35, 48
Transcultural Psychosocial Organization
(NGO, Cambodia), 92n22
TRIAL International (NGO), 150
trust, 5, 21n5, 30, 34, 37, 44, 73, 83, 90n6,
101–2, 103, 117, 140, 142, 231, 249. *See
also* distrust; mistrust
truth, 4, 44, 48, 88, 90, 140, 171, 173, 176,
190, 195, 197, 198, 206, 207; truth (and
reconciliation) commission(s), 19, 55,
171, 179, 181, 185, 190n1; truth-telling, 11
Tsing, Anna, 12
Tuol Sleng Prison, 21n1, 79, 101, 117
Turino, Thomas, 91n12
Turner, Victor, 39
tutelary spirits, 32, 38. *See also* ancestral
spirits; guardian spirits
Tutsi, 18, 125–48, 151, 157–62
Twa, 18, 126, 133, 134, 140, 143, 144n1,
144n3

uncertainty, 3, 4, 10, 30, 78, 182
understanding, mutual, 98, 115, 118–19
Ungerer, Tomi, 66
United Nations (UN), 78, 127, 150, 210
United Nations Secretary General, 10,
21n9
United Nations Special Rapporteur on
Transitional Justice, 74
United Nations Transitional Authority in
Cambodia (UNTAC), 100
United States Government, 76, 173
upstander(s), 152, 165
Uruguay, 19, 171–73, 175, 177–80, 190
US Agency for International Develop-
ment (USAID), 210
US Embassy (in Bosnia and Herzegov-
ina), 155
US Holocaust Memorial Museum, 153
US State Department, 150, 152
utopian state, 4; vision, 33, 35

Varea, Roberto Gutierrez, 85
Videla, Jorge Rafael, 174, 175, 191n5
Vietnam, 35, 49n7, 76, 77, 99; Vietnamese,
29, 76, 77, 99
violence: cycles of, 73, 78, 86; domestic, 3,
90, 180; gender-based, 175–91, 191n10,
249; intercommunal, 218, 222; structural, 11, 67, 101, 102. *See also* crimes;
sexual torture
virtue, 17, 40, 42–44, 246, 250
visions, 6, 10, 39, 47, 245, 252
Vollhardt, Johanna, 104, 108, 109, 112, 115

Waterloo, Sierra Leone, 61
webs of relationships, 5, 6, 48
Week for Memory (Colombia), 196, 198,
199, 202, 216n2
Weinstein, Harvey, 6, 103, 104, 105, 115,
120, 125, 128, 129, 137
White Khmer, 29, 48n1
will to memory, 155
Winichakul, Thongchai, 46
Wiseman, Theresa, 103
witnessing, 207
women's rights, 7, 13, 177–81, 186, 188, 190,
191n10, 195

Wood, Nancy, 205–6
World Bank, 127, 218, 236
World Health Organization, 57
World War II, 10, 21n3, 91n8, 155
Wornat, Olga, 182–84
Wright, Robert, 9

Yazidi, 2, 247, 248, 253
Yemen, 2; Yemenies, 253

youth, 18, 21n1, 39, 54, 56–58, 60, 65, 88,
    100, 111, 140, 156, 158, 165, 176, 196, 212,
    214, 215, 219, 238. *See also* children
Youth Speak Out (NGO), 156
Yugoslavia, 109, 115, 152

Zaire, 135
Zani, Leah, 42, 46, 50n31
Zolli, Andrew, 7, 178